UNIVERSITY OF NORTH CAROLINA
STUDIES IN THE ROMANCE LANGUAGES AND LITERATURES
Number 92

ESSAYS IN HONOR OF
LOUIS FRANCIS SOLANO

LOUIS FRANCIS SOLANO

ESSAYS IN HONOR OF
LOUIS FRANCIS SOLANO

EDITED BY

RAYMOND J. CORMIER and URBAN T. HOLMES

CHAPEL HILL

THE UNIVERSITY OF NORTH CAROLINA PRESS

DEPÓSITO LEGAL: V. 809-1970

ARTES GRÁFICAS SOLER, S. A. — JÁVEA, 28 — VALENCIA (8) — 1970

ACKNOWLEDGEMENTS

The editors cannot deny themselves the pleasure of thanking publicly the following for their help:

Professor Seymour O. Simches, Tufts University, and Professor Douglas W. Alden, University of Virginia for their generosity in offering franking privileges in the preparation of this volume;

Professors Peter R. Grillo and David Pauling who gave unstintingly of their assistance and advice;

Professors Marcel Françon, Joan B. Williamson, Normand Cartier, Gail Meadows, Charles W. Dunn, James B. Wadsworth, and Nicolae Iliescu for their continued encouragement and support;

Professors Judith S. Merrill and Steven Hess; Mrs. Marcia Kaufman, Mrs. Willa Folch-Pi, Miss Diana Mériz, and Miss Marie-Dolores Solano for help with the details in the Biography.

TABLE OF CONTENTS

  Page

BIOGRAPHY
    Raymond J. Cormier   11

CELESTIAL PORTENTS AND MEDIAEVAL CHRONICLERS
    Normand R. Cartier   15

RAIMON DE LAS SALAS
    Frank M. Chambers   29

BREVI PROSE IN VOLGARE PIEMONTESE DEL QUATTROCENTO: I *TESTI CARMAGNOLESI*
    Gianrenzo P. Clivio   53

MONTAIGNE HUMANISTE ET FOLKLORISTE
    Marcel Françon   65

PRELIMINARIES TO A STUDY OF GALLICISMS IN OLD SPANISH
    Steven Hess   77

THE MONKEY IN MEDIAEVAL LITERATURE
    Urban Tigner Holmes   93

***INFERNO XV*: SE TU SEGUI TUA STELLA?**
    Nicolae Iliescu   101

LE SENS DES *TROIS CONTES*
    René Jasinski   117

LATIN *POSSUM*
    Allan R. Keiler   129

O. F. IMP. + *ET / OU* + IMP.: TWO PROBLEMS
    Diana T. Mériz   141

	Page
NARCISSE ET PYGMALION DANS LE *ROMAN DE LA ROSE* DANIEL POIRION	153
LOVE AND THE OTHERWORLD IN MARIE DE FRANCE'S *ELIDUC* HOWARD S. ROBERTSON	167
TWO TRANSLATIONS FROM RAIMBAUT DE VAQUEIRAS NATHANIEL B. SMITH	177
CHRISTINE DE PISAN'S TREATISE ON THE ART OF WARFARE CHARITY C. WILLARD	179
ELYAS AS A WILD MAN IN *LI ESTOIRE DEL CHEVALIER AU CISNE* JOAN B. WILLIAMSON	193
TABULA GRATULATORIA	203

BIOGRAPHY

"The Solano Legend": still felt is its immeasurable impact on the rise and development of Medieval Studies in the United States —spread by word of mouth across the country— through the intermediary of countless former students who deem it a privilege to have taken Old French, Old Provençal, Old Italian, Vulgar Latin, or Romance Linguistics, among others, under Louis F. Solano's uncompromising standards which always demanded a great deal of work and self-discipline. His "read and translate" method, used no doubt by his mentor Charles H. Grandgent and others before him, offered no chance of oversight. His formidable reading list of texts and criticism in Old French became a latter-day proverbial *corvée* for undisciplined first-year graduate students, but they survived, as we all did, and became perhaps better persons for it. Indeed, one former student remarks on Solano's masterful teaching ability: "In one term —meeting only twice a week— we covered Rumanian grammar, the history of Rumanian literature, the development of the language from Vulgar Latin to the present, and as the *pièce de résistance* we learned to read Cyrillic script with a fair amount of ease... Although somewhat dazed and numbed by the amount of work... it was a memorable experience — one of the highlights of my studies at Harvard." Solano has become something of a legendary figure over the years.

Born in Naples in 1904, Solano attended schools in Somerville and later at the Boston English High School. In 1924, with a distinguished and honor-filled undergraduate record, he completed the A. B. (summa cum laude), in 1925, the A. M., and in 1931 a Ph. D. in Romance Languages, all at Harvard. In fact, in 1949 he noted and often repeated that he was not in a position to compare any other university "system" with Harvard's since he had "never really been weaned from his alma mater." Still, while preparing his doctoral dissertation on the Neapolitan dialects, Solano received a Sheldon Travelling Fellowship, and he spent 1928-1929 in Paris studying palaeography with Mario Roques at the Sorbonne, Ecole des Hautes Etudes, and Rumanian and Albanian with J. Vendryes, at the Ecole Nationale des Langues Orientales Vivantes. He also found time to escape, as he wrote in 1930, "the damp and uncomfortable weather of Paris" to make three sojourns: a memorable one to fascist Italy for two months, one to Cologne, and a brief visit to northern Spain. And, on leave of absence from Harvard in 1966-1967, he served as Chairman and Professor of Modern Languages at Loyola University, Illinois.

Over the years, one special source of continual joy and lasting pride for Solano has been his seven children: Louis E., Francesca E. (first marriage), Teresa, Louisa, Karina, Marie-Dolores, and Cecilia —from a second marriage with Clelia Capelli in 1939. And, with the birth of Jessica, he recently became a grand-father....

Among his diverse interests, Solano's main occupation has been language in all its forms and manifestations. His lifetime pursuit can be perhaps best summarized by the Platonic apothegm: "All is one." While man is faced with a never-ending and astonishing diversity of linguistic phenomena, Solano insists that the essential similarity between various aspects of one language, when compared to another, seems to demonstrate an underlying unity and universality in human behavior. Always ready to borrow a lesson or a gloss from what he had learned of other languages, he would often overwhelm his students with thoughtful comparisons between the syntax of Swedish and Vulgar Latin, the phonology of Nahuatl and Portuguese, or just idiomatic usage in English and Old French. His preparation in these sundry languages began early: besides teaching courses in nearly all the principal and minor Romance tongues at Harvard, he spent his summers (1925-1928) studying modern Irish Gaelic at the South Boston Gaelic School; attended courses ("as the only foreigner") in Basque at the Eusko-Ikaskuntza in San Sebastián, Spain (1929); studying Nahuatl and Maya at the National University of Mexico (1936); and teaching at Middlebury College (1932-1939), where he co-founded, with Gabriella Bosano of Wellesley, the "very successful" (as he foresaw it in 1934) Italian Summer School and where he once taught, in Spanish, a History of the Spanish Language course!

Since his official special interest is the history of the Latin influence in non-Romance languages, he has directed his efforts increasingly during the past few years toward the East European branch of Indo-European, namely, Bulgarian, Albanian, and Russian. During the summer of 1966, Solano was in Leningrad to transcribe a manuscript of the *Roman de la Rose* in the Library there, and in 1968, after teaching Mediaeval Italian Literature at the University of Toronto Summer School, he again voyaged (the third trip) to the Soviet Union, this time to visit the Caucasus and Tbilisi in the Republic of Georgia. It was his intention to pursue scholarly research on the subject of the twelfth-century Georgian epic, *Vepxistqoasani*, [alternate form: *Vephkhistgoasani*] "The Knight in the Tiger's Skin" by the poet Sota Rustaveli. But he was in for a pleasant surprise....

Upon his arrival in Tbilisi, he found himself in the midst of an International Congress of Soviet Writers — to which he was immediately issued a formal invitation. At this Congress then, he was the only representative from the non-Communist western world.

One evening during his stay, presented with a volume of the poems of a famous Georgian Romantic poet by one of his Georgian hosts, Solano was asked to say a few words to the Congress the following day. The next afternoon, on September 11, 1968, Solano addressed, in Georgian, the International Congress of Soviet Writers and the Supreme Soviet of the Georgian Republic on the poetry of their own Romantic poet, Nikoloz Baratasvili (1817-1845) and related his work to that of other Romantic poets, in particular to Leopardi. "Until yesterday," began Solano, "I thought I knew poetry. Until yesterday, when I first read some poems by your great poet Nikoloz Baratasvili, I thought I knew all about poetic impulse and creativity. But I knew nothing...". At the end of his communication, a silence, then from the august body of dignitaries, writers, and artists, Solano received a standing ovation. The text of his triumph, together with his photograph, appeared the next day on the front page of the Georgian newspaper, *Komunisti*. On September 13, Solano was interviewed on National Russian Television (an appearance for which he is proud to say he obtained an honorarium of fifty rubles). The text of his address to the Congress subsequently appeared in the December issue of the only scholarly journal in Georgia, called, in English, "The Literary Gazette."

Since, at the time of his arrival in Tbilisi, Solano had been studying the Georgian language for less than a year —on his own— this entire occasion can only be taken as an example of his extraordinary linguistic ability and of the universality of his profound erudition.

Dubbed a "brilliant student" by his teachers and colleagues, it is understandably not surprising that Solano spent the greater part of his academic life as a teacher first, and also, in his typically open-minded way, as a student. Besides contributing articles and reviews to *Italica, Slavic Review, Speculum, French Review,* and to *Harvard Notes in Philology and Literature,* his important study "The History of Diphthongization and Metaphony in Rumanian," appeared in *Mediaeval Studies in Honor of J. D. M. Ford,* ed. Urban T. Holmes, Jr. and Alex. J. Denomy, C. S. B. (Cambridge: Harvard University Press, 1948).

In the Harvard tradition and in a manner mindful of the achievements of Socrates and Ferdinand de Saussure, Solano is probably one of the last great scholars to place more value on the *joys* of learning and to prefer the rewards of sharing it with his students. Whether it be in a graduate reading course in Albanian, in Mediaeval Latin Literature, in Mediaeval Philosophy, or in the Chansons de Geste, whether it be at a Departmental get-together, or as he walks across the Yard, Solano —rarely alone— is still to be found in the middle of a circle of students who block his exit, either deeply involved in some linguistic discussion or deploring, with Dantean, Yankee irony, the sad state of Massachusetts politics. With a sense of humor that is often arcane, with a spirit of justice that has often been criticized, Solano has always been, for us all, a PERSONA DELICTISSIMA... professor, mentor, amicus.

CELESTIAL PORTENTS AND MEDIAEVAL CHRONICLERS

By N. B. Cartier
Boston College

In our times, when the skies are furrowed by "dirty birds", vibrating with "choppers" or shattered by supersonic booms, it is natural to long for the good old days, when the silence of the azure was unbroken, except by the harmony of the heavenly bodies. Yet, there is evidence that all was not serene overhead in the pre-mechanized era, — even in the Middle Ages. The people of the fourteenth century, for instance, without the help of Mount Palomars or Jodrell Banks, saw and heard strange happenings in the skies that were sufficiently impressive to be registered for posterity in the chronicles.

Although fewer people were interested in astrology during the Middle Ages than today,[1] everyone knows how disturbing to our ancestors was the appearance of a comet, or such foreboding conjunctions as that of 1345, which featured Saturn, Jupiter and Mars in the same firmament, and inspired pessimistic prophecies by the likes of Jean de Murs and Jean de la Rochetaillade. The nefarious influences of these phenomena were catalogued in learned treatises by specialists on conjunctions such as John of Eschenden,[2] or by those on comets such as John of Legnano and the anonymous author

---

[1] According to Linda Gutstein, "Astrology boom: the sky's the limit," *Parade*, Feb. 9, 1969, Americans spent $100,000,000 on astrology during 1968; 1200 newspapers print daily horoscopes, and the Dell Publishing Company sold 8,000,000 horoscope pocket books.

[2] Lynn Thorndike, *A History of Magic and Experimental Science*, Columbia University Press, New York, 1934. Cf. Vol. III, Chap. XX, XXI, XXII, for Jean de Murs, John of Eschenden and Jean de la Rochetaillade.

of the 13th century Spanish *Liber de Significatione Cometarum*.[3] Geoffroy de Meaux, who focused his attention on the comets of 1315 and 1337, and analyzed *a posteriori* the astrological causes of the great plague, even prescribed palliatives against celestial influence. For him, *la machine infernale* imposed no determinism upon man. Against cold, Saturnine infirmities, for instance, he advised his contemporaries "not to ge cold, to eat and drink lightly, to sweat twice or thrice a week, to take two ounces of linseed and three of camomilla, cook them in wine, dip a sponge therein and rub the patient between the breasts, put him in a warm bed well covered with bed clothing and give him a sweat and administer spiced brandy. In spring and autumn, purge him of phlegm and melancholy.[4]

But these scientific treatises, which deal with relatively banal occurrences, are not the subject of this brief discussion.[5] I should like to focus upon a few of the more unusual phenomena "seen" or "heard" by the non-experts, to analyze the varied reactions of the chroniclers —who were also laymen in these celestial matters— and finally, to compare the mystifying problem of the ubiquitous U. F. O. —or Unidentified Flying Object— in mediaeval and modern times.

Strange Signes from Heaven —if we may borrow the title of a seventeenth century account of *happenings* in Cambridge, Suffolk and Norfolk on May 21, 1646— were recorded by almost every chronicler of the Middle Ages. It is reported that during a terrible storm on St. Luke's day in 1224, "fyry dragons and wykkes spirytes grete noumbre were seyn openly fleyng in the eyre." The same source informs us that in June, 1362, "fell a blody reyne in Burgoyn, and a blody crosse apered in the eire fro the morwe unto myd day at Boloyne, the whiche afterward moved hym and fel down into the

---

[3] Cf. Thorndike, *Latin Treatises on Comets,* between 1238 and 1368 A. D., University of Chicago Press, 1950.

[4] Thorndike, *A History of Magic,* III, p. 291. Geoffrey's prescription is not unlike those of modern medicine men against common colds, grippe, etc... and probably just as effective.

[5] According to Thorndike, they draw heavily from Aristotle's *Meteorology* and Seneca's *Natural Questions,* with assists from Albumasar *inter alia.* Cf. also Albertus Magnus, *Liber I Meteorum,* Tractatus III, Chap. XI on the significance of comets.

sea." [6] Readers of Charles Fort know that red rains, often recorded during the Middle Ages, have not lost their fascination for the twentieth century observer with imagination. [7] The bloody or fiery crosses are seen less frequently in our generation, except in the South; but in the fourteenth century, they were mentioned by none other than Dante [8] and Dino Campagni. The chronicler apparently saw with his own eyes the phenomenon which occurred on November 6, 1301:

> La sera apparì in cielo un segno maraviglioso; il qual fu una croce vermiglia, sopra il palagio de' priori. Fu la sua lista ampia più che palmi uno e mezo; e l'una linea era di lungheza braccia xx in apparenza, quella attraverso un poco menore; la qual durò per tanto spazio quanto penasse un cavallo a correre due aringhi. Onde la gente che la vide, e io che chiaramente la vidi, potemo comprendere che Iddio era fortemente contro alla nostra città crucciato. [9]

According to the *Chronicon Mutinense* of Johannis de Bezano, several such crosses, vermilion, red or snow white, appeared on August 3, 1345. [10] Ranulf Higden reported a similar phenomenon, as well as a rain "almost lyke to blood" over Burgundy in the spring of 1360. [11]

Less religious in inspiration perhaps, but no less ominous were the aerial battles waged in mediaeval skies — long before the Russians invented the airplane. The same Higden describes a typical happening of this nature, which is recorded with variants in several chronicles of the fourteenth century:

---

[6] *A Chronicle of London*, from 1089 to 1483, written in the fifteenth century, edit. by Edward Tyrrell, London, 1827, pp. 10; 65.

[7] *The Book of the Damned*, New York, 1941. Cf. pp. 31 ff.

[8] *Il Convivio*, ed. crit. a cura di Maria Simonelli, Bologna, 1966, II, xiii, 22, p. 62.

[9] *Cronica delle cose occorrenti ne' tempi suoi*, Muratori T. IX, P. II, edit. Del Lungo, Città di Castello, 1913, p. 124.

[10] Muratori, T. X, P. IV, Bologna, 1917, p. 129.

[11] *Polychronicon* (*Rerum Brit. Medii Aevi Scriptores* no. 41) Vol. VIII, p. 524. Roger de Wendover, *Flores Historiarum*, London 1887, Vol. II, p. 207, asserted that in May 1217, the province of Cologne was in a state of agitation because three crosses were seen in the air, the middle one bearing a human form which was nailed to it.

> Also in the same tyme was seen in Fraunce, in England, and in many other places appyre two castels, oute of whiche yssued oute two hoostes of armed men; that one was clothed in whyte, that other in black. And whan the bataylle was bygonne bytwene them the whyte overcome the black. And soone after the black overcome the whyte. And thenne they retourned in to theyr castels and soo vanyshed away.[12]

Other versions feature more easily imaginable but equally symbolic standards contending in the sky.[13] These too were considered prefigurations of impending struggles for the people below, and viewed with no less anxiety than that caused by intercontinental ballistic missiles in more civilized times.

Another category of phenomena was more baffling to mediaeval witnesses as a symbol; but it left unbounded play to the imagination. The following account is typical:

> Die jovis supradicta (16 jan. 1382) circa solis occasum, in itinere quod ducit ad nemus Vicenarum, et in eodem nemore, mirabilis casus accidit; consimilem in Francia accidisse nulla recolit etas, nulla refert historia. Nam ibidem ignis vehemens de celo repente descendit super terram, ita ut totum ardere videretur spatio sexte partis unius hore; unde multi in maximam multitudinem versi sunt, pluresque dicebant hoc multa mala pro futuro significare.[14]

---

[12] *Polychronicon*, VIII, p. 524. Latin versions of the same incident appear in John of Reading, *Chronicon*, edit. James Tait, Manchester, 1914, p. 149, and Adam Murimouth, *Chronica sui temporis* (Continuatio), London 1846, p. 196. It is found in Thomas Walsingham, *Historia Anglicana*, London, 1863-4, 2 vols. Vol. I, p. 295, together with red cross and bloody rain. *The Chronicon Angliae*, edit. Giles, London, 1845, p. 162, informs us that a similar omen, but less widespread and particularly sinister for the castle of Lancaster, over which it unfolded in 1321, provided advance warning of the bloodshed that followed.

[13] V.g. in Henry Knighton's *Chronicon* (*Rerum Brit. Medii Aevi Scriptores*), 2 vols. London 1889-1895, I, p. 80. Robert of Reading, *Flores Historiarum*, London 1890, Vol. III, pp. 210-211, speaks of a "rogus igneus ad magnitudinem et formam unius naviculae," pale in color, that fought in the air against a red one of superior dimensions, in November 1322. The fracas of the battle could be heard outside of London, at Ruystebrugge (Uxbridge?).

[14] *Chronographia Regum Francorum*, edit. H. Moranvillé (Soc. Hist. Fr.) 3 vols., Paris 1891-3, III, p. 8.

While the *ignis vehemens* may probably be classified as an unusually durable meteor, the following incidents present problems of interpretation. The cronicle of Agnolo di Tura del Grosso refers to a "grandissimo fluoco" which lit up the skies over Italy, reuning from north to south, on May 10, 1309. It was considered an extraordinary event, and was followed by another, seventy years later, described by Donato di Neri as a "fiama di fuoco", which went from east to west. [15] A similar occurrence observed in Spain over a century later was accompanied by sound effects, much to the amazement of the king and his entourage: "e caminando vieron todos una gran llama que iba corriendo por el cielo. é duró gran rato, á dende poco dió un tronido tan grande, que se oyó a siete ó ocho lenguas dende." [16]

Clearly, there was much to worry about overhead, in the Middle Ages; and while modern scientists describe those happenings as extraordinary but natural phenomena distorted by popular imagination and interpreted under emotional tension, the process was no different than that which, in the Age of Enlightenment, dictated an account of the *Epouvantable Apparition vue a Saint Petersbourg, le 8 avril 1788,* [17] or produced the rash of U. F. O. experiences in our time. But then as now, an interesting body of psychic reality was created by the occurrences, and we shall see how the chroniclers of the fourteenth century reacted to the happenings reported by the people or witnessed by themselves.

It may seem odd that Jean Froissart, that "most naif of men" as Kittredge calls him, [18] paid practically no attention to the omens that foreshadowed important events of his time, in the opinion of his contemporaries. He did describe a storm or two, such as Black Monday, in which God tried to get a message through to Edward III; but he was much too fascinated by the extraordinary men who molded their own destinies by deeds of chivalry, to turn his eyes upward for signs of events to come. True, the extrasensory perception of Gaston de Foix, in connection with the battle of Aljubarrota

---

[15] *Cronache Senesi* (Muratori T. XV, P. VI), 2 vol. Bologna 1931-34, I, p. 305; 677.
[16] *Cronica de Don Juan II* (B.A.E. no. 68), Cron. de los Reyes de Castilla, T. II, 1953, p. 512.
[17] Imprimerie de l'Oracle (no date).
[18] *Chaucer and his Poetry*, Harvard Univ. Press, 1915, p. 55.

in 1385, led him to record strange stories about the medium for the supranatural transmission of news; but that is not the subject of our discussion.

Under the threat of sinister omens from above, chroniclers of the Middle Ages revealed a whole gamut of reactions, from wary skepticism, to affected objectivity and detachment, and to psychological involvement strong enough to determine an historical vocation. Gilles le Muisit expressed more explicitly than any of his contemporaries the attitude of methodical doubt concerning hearsay and unfounded theory:

> Populus universis facile credit et facilius audita refert et publicat, unde modo falsa, modo vera dicunt; et ego non approbo dicta talium nec fidem adhibeo et maxime si talia registrarem de quibus certitudinem non haberem, totum opus meum esset reprobandum, et in aliis mihi non crederetur.

And in accordance with this affirmation, after relating details of a storm that accompanied the birth of Philippe VI's son Philippe, during which demons were reported to have been hovering about, he adds: "Super hoc fuit communis relatio, sed quia presens non fui, sic fuisse non affirmo." [19]

The author of the *Chronicle of London* considered comets important enough to be mentioned; but he abstained from comment. A significant relationship is implied, however, when he informs us that "in this yere (1326) were seyn in the firmament too mones, and in this yere were too popes. [20] A few sly observers of celestial happenings reported the appearance of comets without venturing to interpret their significance, but they carefully indicated the position of the tails. Up or down, the tails contained a message, like a finger of the Divinity pointed at some people marked for destruction. A bon entendeur, salut! [21] The Religieux de Saint Denis hid behind higher authority when it came to interpreting the strange occurrences that he recorded:

---

[19] *Chronique et Annales,* Paris, 1906, Introd. p. XV; 109.
[20] Cf. pp. 51, 56, 67.
[21] *Chronographia,* II, 373; III, 39. *Chronique du Religieux de Saint Deni*s, edit. Bellaguet, Paris 1839-52, 6 vols., II, 697-8; III 18-19.

> Pour moi, je laisse le secret de tous ces événements surnaturels à celui qui sait tout, qui commande au ciel, à la terre et à la mer. J'avoue pourtant que si l'on consulte l'histoire du passé, on ne peut nier que de pareils prodiges n'aient été presque toujours les avant-coureurs de quelque grand événement. [22]

In effect, whenever he related such incidents, he included the interpretation of contemporary astrologers, "les sages astronomiens" as they are called in the *Grandes Chroniques de France*, "i savi astrologi," as Agnolo di Tura del Grosso called his authorities.

Some chroniclers asserted boldly and on their own authority a direct relationship between celestial portents and the affairs of men — or women. In 1363, according to Jean de Venette, "a very small star was seen at Paris before noon, about the third hour, in the part of the sky where the sun commonly is at noon. The astronomers of Paris said that it signified peril to women in childbirth. This was clearly so in some cases, but in truth we believe that by God's will many more astonishing events than this followed upon the portent." Then he describes the ravages of the plague in and about Paris. [23] Conrad von Megenburg relates in his *Buch der Natur* that he saw a comet in Paris in 1337, and that subsequently he observed its ill effects in Germany upon his return. He considered it a cause or sign of the Hundred Years War and the death of king John of Bohemia. [24] The monk of Malmsbury pinpointed one harbinger of bad news with uncanny accuracy: "Super caput Henrici Percy apparuit stella comata, malum significans eventum." It is true that the portent was described after the grim fact that the designated victim had been killed in battle by Henry the future leper, and after his head had been displayed on the gate of York. [25] Giovanni Villani considered the September comet of 1301 to be a heavenly herald for the arrival of Charles de Valois. [26] Elsewhere, he devoted

---

[22] *Op. cit.* II, 483.

[23] *The Chronicle of Jean de Venette*, transl. by J. Birdsall, edit. by R. A. Newhall, New York, Columbia Univ. Press, 1955, p. 111. Cf. also Holinshed, *Chronicles*, London, 1807, vol. II, p. 554.

[24] Thorndike, *Latin Treatises*, p. 220.

[25] *Eulogium (Historiarum sive Temporis)*. Chronicon ab orbe condito usque ad annum Domini MCCCLXVI. Edit. Haydon, London 1863, 3 vols., I, 397-8.

[28] *Cronica (Storici e Cronisti Italiani I-III)*, Firenze, 1844, vol. II, p. 50.

an entire chapter to the conjunction of Saturn, Jupiter and Mars in 1345.[27]

Finally, there were chroniclers who found their historical vocations in the contemplation of celestial portents. In 1372, Galeazzo Gatari, having witnessed "moltissimi segni dai' cieli," decided that God, through the possible action of "corpi superiori," was trying to make men and particularly the rulers of Padua where he dwelled, understand that they should mend their wicked ways. He added: "per i quali segni a me hanno dato materia e casione de iscrivere tute quel cose che seguirano de tempo in tempo che siano notabile da notare, aciò che sempre quegli, che le legierano, possiano merittamente redire a salvacione di me, Galiazo oltra ditto, e di l'anima mia una laude a Dio e a nostra Donna."[28]

A similar motivation is apparent in the chronicle of Jean de Venette. "Should we attempt to determine some leading purpose behind the writing of this chronicle," says Newhall, "it would seem to lie in Jean de Venette's interest in the validity and interpretation of astrological portents and of prophecies." The beginning of his chronicle is focused upon a comet, and the end ushers in another, with a promise to relate subsequent fulfillment of prophecies which it inspired. His opening message to the reader reveals the essential guideline for the presentation and interpretation of his material. "Let anyone who wishes to be reminded of most of the noteworthy events which happened in the kingdom of France from 1340 on read this present work in which I, a friar at Paris, have written them down briefly, in great measure as I have seen and heard them. I shall begin with some hitherto unknown prognostications or prophecies which have come to hand. What they mean is not altogether known. Whether they speak truth or not I do not say but leave to the decision of the reader..."[29] It should not surprise us, therefore, that the learned treatises on comets, written by the "sages astronomiens" of the times, were also inspired by the appearance of a particular comet seen by them or at least adopted as a basis for

---

[27] *Istorie Fiorentine di Giovanni Villani cittadino fiorentino*, Milan, 1803, vol. 8, lib. XII, cap. 41.
[28] *Cronica Carrarese* (Muratori T. XVII, P. I.) Città di Castello, 1909, p. 9.
[29] *Chronicle*, pp. 9-10; 30.

their prognostications.³⁰ What may be more surprising is that, on August 4, 1946, the sighting of a supposedly authentic U.F.O. launched the prophetic career of Orfeo M. Angelucci. Carl Jung calls the account of this experience, in *The Secret of the Saucers*, a "pelerinage de l'âme," a "mystic experience associated with a U.F.O. vision." ³¹

It is a well-known fact that what we call U.F.O.'s today have been observed down through the centuries since antiquity, and that defenders and opponents of their material existence have used the historical prototypes to prove diametrically opposed views. Many sightings of phenomena which would probably be classified as U.F.O.'s, or are suggestive of occurrences reported in the twentieth century, are described in chronicles of the fourteenth. The impression they created and the theories they inspired are not without interest.

"In the month of August 1348, after Vespers when the sun was beginning to set," according to Jean de Venette, "a big and very bright star appeared over Paris, toward the west. It did not seem, as stars usually do, to be very high above our hemisphere but rather very near. As the sun set and night came on, this star did not seem to me or to many other friars who were watching it to move from one place. At length, when night had come, this big star, to the amazement of all of us who were watching, broke into many different rays and, as it shed these rays over Paris toward the east, totally disappeared and was completely annihilated. Whether it was a comet or not, whether it was composed of airy exhalations and was finally resolved into vapor, I leave to the decision of astronomers. It is, however, possible that it was a presage of the amazing pestilence to come, which, in fact, followed very shortly in Paris and throughout France and elsewhere, as I shall tell." ³²

---

³⁰ Thorndike, *Latin Treatises*, p. 6.
³¹ C. G. Jung, *Flying Saucers: A Modern Myth of Things seen in the Skies*, London, 1959, pp. 159 ff.
³² *Chronicle*, pp. 48-49. To some modern observers, the sudden outpour of rays would have suggested a jet propulsion and the swift take-off of a disappearing U. F. O. John of Reading relates that in 1366, "stellae conglobatae, ad modum fulguris igneos post se radios relinquentes in terram, prout aspicientibus apparuit, et caelo ceciderunt, quarum fervores vestes itinerantium ac capillos urebant, et consumabantur super terram." *Chronicon*, p. 173. The

The monk of Malmsbury says that on October 8, 1366, "visae sunt faculae ignitae in firmamento convolare, huc et illuc discurrere." These fiery torches which operated between the moon and the earth, seemed as large as a human thigh, from three to twelve cubits in length, sharp at one end but broad at the base, in the shape of a torch. According to two monks who saw the phenomenon, it lasted two hours. Many people who saw the luminary within the concave firmament, compared it to a lighted candle in a house or some hollow space shining through a window or some open cracks; and it appeared within like a beam of fire, very sharp at the surface, much broader at the base, and decreasing to nothing, it crossed slowly from southwest to northeast. [33]

Some extraordinary prodigies foreshadowed the revolt of the Maillotins in 1382, if one is to believe the Religieux de Saint Denis. "Pendant huit jours ...avant le dit soulèvement, on vit jour et nuit un globe de feu brillant voltiger de porte en porte au-dessus de la ville de Paris sans aucune agitation de vent, sans éclair et sans bruit de tonnerre; le temps fut au contraire toujours serein." The same chronicler relates that on July 10, 1395, in the area of Maguelonne, reliable witnesses saw a large and extremely brilliant "comet," and that five other small bodies, which flitted around it in a rapid and continual movement, had hurled themselves against it repeatedly. After this sort of combat, in which these "meteors" repeatedly came together and separated, during a period of half an hour, all of a sudden a flaming man, mounted on a bronze horse and armed with a lance which cast flames, had struck the comet and disappeared. [34]

Henry Knighton describes a phenomenon which took place in 1387, and has intriguing points or resemblance with U.F.O.'s sighted in modern times.

> Quaedam forma in specie ignis in multis locis Angliae apparuit, nunc in una forma nunc in alia, quasi singulis

---

"stellae conglobatae" bring to mind the "due cerchetti" seen in the air in 1325, according to Agnolo di Tura del Grosso, *Cronaca Senese*, p. 418.

[33] *Eulogium*, pp. 241-2. The editor (p. XLVIII), thinks the phenomenon might have been a shower of aërolites, and the moving luminary a large meteor. However, the time of year is against this theory, and meteorites do not move slowly. The suggestion that it could have been the aurora borealis is difficult to accept since is seldom seen in the sounthwest.

[34] *Chronique*, I, 143, 481.

noctibus, in diversis tamen locis, per menses Novembris et Decembris. Et saepe quando quis solus gradiebatur, cum illo ibat, et cum stante stabat. Et quibusdam apparuit in forma rotae volubilis ardentis, aliis autem in forma barelli rotundi flamman ignis superius emittentis, aliis vero in forma longi tigni ardentis, et sic aliis in una forma, aliis vero in alia forma per multum tempus hiemis, praecipue in comitatibus Leycestrias et Northamptoniae apparuit. Cum vero plures simul gradiebantur, non se eis approximaverit sed quasi de longe eis apparuit. [35]

At about the same time, in August 1388, another very strange happening took place, according to John Malverne: "Nam duae stellae circa horam vesperarum coeperunt in partibus austrinis clarescere, et in medio inter eas visum est coelum aperire, ac angelos luciferos quasi per unam horam in aere volitare, demum in coelum subito redierunt." [36] Incredible as this sighting appears to us today, one must admit that the principals are at least as interesting as our little green men from Venus.

Such were the celestial portents witnessed in the fourteenth century, and the reactions of the chroniclers who reported them for posterity. One wonders how the historians of the twenty-sixth century will look back upon the U.F.O.'s of today and the attitudes of the viewers, if humanity has not blown itself up before then. Surely, they will be confused by what they read. On the one hand, Major Keyhoe, director of N.I.C.A.P., has collated the experiences of thousands of reliable witnesses including pilots, technicians, meteorologists, astronomers, etc...., whose testimony is occasionally corroborated by radar sighting and photographs. [37] But all of this is hogwash, according to Professor Donald Menzell of Harvard, a fervent advocate of the empirical method, who wrote a book to disprove the existence of U.F.O.'s without coming to grips with a single sighting, but declaring that all these reliable witnesses suf-

---

[35] *Chronicon*, p. 257. The resemblance between the forma rotae, barelli or tigni, and the modern saucer or cylindrical, cigar-shaped U.F.O.'s is significant. The same phenomenon is related by Holinshed, Chronicles, II, 829. But he relates it under the year 1395.

[36] *Polychronicon*, IX (Continuatio), p. 184.

[37] *Flying Suacers from outer Space*, New York, 1953; *Flying Saucers: Top-secret*, New York, 1960.

fered from delusions induced by natural phenomena.[38] He reflects the views of the United States Air Force, which refuses to admit that U.F.O.'s are real, because — according to Major Keyhoe — it fears the panic that would sweep over this most enlightened nation, if the truth should be revealed. The Air Force, to prove the honesty of its position and the non-existence of the U.F.O., has sponsored a two-year $500,000 study, under the direction of Dr. Edward U. Condon of Boulder, Colorado. However, several scientists have resigned from the project, and complained to Congress that U.F.O.'s are still not getting the profound study they deserve. Meanwhile, Carl Jung, a specialist not on the macrocosmos but on the microcosmos of man's psyche, studies U.F.O.'s for over ten years. He came to the conclusion that the evidence provided by Major Keyhoe and others "leaves no room for doubt," and that Professor Menzell has failed to offer a satisfying scientific explanation of even one authentic U.F.O. report. "It boils down to nothing less than this," he says, "that either psychic projections throw back a radar echo, or else the appearance of real objects affords the opportunity for mythological projections."[39] Jung's personal theory is expressed in the following terms:

> Ufos are real material phonemena of an unknown nature, presumably coming from outer space, which perhaps have long been visible to mankind, but otherwise have no recognizable connection with the earth or its inhabitants. In recent times, however, and just at the momet when the eyes of mankind are turned towards the heavens, partly on account of their fantasies about possible spaceships, and partly in a figurative sense, because their earthly existence feels threatened, unconscious contents have projected themselves on these inexplicable heavenly phenomena and given them a significance they in no way deserve.

But Jung, who was begotten by Freud, also studied the characteristics of U.F.O.'s in dreams. "Sexuality has its share in the structure of the phenomenon," he declares. "It is probably no accident that in one of the dreams a feminine symbol appears, and in the other a

---

[38] *Flying Saucers*, Harvard University Press, Cambridge, Mass, 1953.
[39] *Flying Saucers: A Modern Myth of Things Seen in the Skies*, London, 1959, p. 147.

masculine, in accordance with the reports of lens-shaped and cigar-shaped U.F.O.'s." [40]

But what will historians of the twenty-sixth century think of us, when they read that in this mixed-up generation, where an outlandish growth of hair has obscured the differentiation between sexes, the cigar-shaped U.F.O. is called a "mother-ship"?

---

[40] *Op. cit.*, pp. 151-2; 55.

RAIMON DE LAS SALAS

By Frank M. Chambers
The University of Arizona

"Raimonz de Salas si fo us borges de Marseilla. E trobet cansos et albas e retroenzas. No fo mout conogutz ni mout prezatz."

Apart from his poems, this brief *vida* of the thirteenth or fourteenth century is our only source of information concerning Raimon de (las) Salas, who does not figure in any historical documents. The *vida* occurs in two mss (*I* and *K* [1]) and is printed here in the text of Boutière-Schutz, *Biographies des Troubadours* (Paris: Nizet, 1964), p. 510.[2] "Raimon de Salas was a burgher of Marseilles. He composed *cansos, albas,* and *retroensas*. He was not very well known or very highly esteemed."

The poet's name is given variously in the mss as "de Salas," "de las Salas," "de la Sala," sometimes with the further indication "de Marseilla." Among his preserved poems are three *cansos*, one *alba*, one fictitious *tenso* with a lady, and perhaps one genuine *tenso* (or *partimen*) with another poet. The *retroensa* was rare in Provençal verse, and no composition of this type is ascribed to our poet. The corpus of Raimon's work was established by Karl Bartsch in his *Grundriss zur Geschichte der provenzalischen Literatur* (Elberfeld, 1872), under the number 409; it consists of five poems, all of which are included in the present edition. Besides these, two other poems

---

[1] For the designation of manuscripts and the numbers given to poets and poems, see Pillet-Carstens, *Bibliographie der Troubadours*, Halle, 1933. The manuscripts are listed on pp. vii-xxxv.

[2] This text is that of ms *I*. The variants in *K* (closely related to *I*) are insignificant: *uns* for *us*; *cansons*; *retroenças* (not, as Boutière-Schutz say, *retroensas*); *ni mot*.

are attributed to Raimon de las Salas. The important song *Bels Monruels, aicel que·s part de vos* (now listed under Bernart de Ventadorn: 70,11, although probably not written by him) is given to Raimon only by the unreliable ms *P*; I think we can dismiss this attribution.[3] The second poem in question is the *partimen* with Bertran d'Avignon *Bertran, si fossetz tant gignos*, listed by Bartsch and his successors[4] under Raimon de Miraval, as number 406,16. Topsfield will probably discuss the attribution of this poem (on stylistic and other grounds) in his long-promised edition of Raimon de Miraval. I have included it here among the works of Raimon de las Salas, not because of any real assurance that he wrote it, but because I have no particular reason for denying it to him.

The dates of Raimon de las Salas are highly uncertain. Jeanroy *Poésie lyrique des troubadours* [Paris, 1934] I, 422) places his floruit between roughly 1215 and 1230. These dates go back to Chabaneau's edition of the *vidas* ("Les biographies des troubadours," in *Histoire de Languedoc,* X [Toulouse, 1885], 379); but neither Chabaneau nor Jeanroy nor, as far as I know, anyone else has ever advanced any arguments in support of them. If we accept the *partimen* 406,16 as his work, then he was alive in 1216; and he refers (409,4) to a Rambalda del Baus, unattested in documents but mentioned by Sordello and Bertran d'Alamanon, so he would be their contemporary (approximately 1225-1260). Since none of his other poems can be dated, I do not see how we can be more specific than this. The facts of his life are totally unknown, beyond the presumption that he was a protégé of the Baus family and (if 406,16 is genuine) that he traveled in Lombardy.

Several of these poems have appeared in more or less satisfactory editions, but all are newly edited here. The variants are meant to be complete; even orthographical differences are recorded, since these can be of great interest. The only exceptions are differences that depend on the expansion of abbreviations (for example, I regularly transcribe *dōna* as *donna*, but do not list it as a variant when the text has *domna*; likewise *que* vs. *qe*). All ms readings are

---

[3] For a critical edition of this poem and a discussion of its authorship, see Carl Appel, *Peire Rogier* (Berlin, 1882), pp. 88-94.

[4] Pillet-Carstens (see note 1) and István Frank, *Répertoire métrique des troubadours,* vol. II, Paris, 1957.

taken from or checked against microfilms, except that for *A* I relied on the diplomatic reprint of Pakscher and De Lollis (see poem 6).

I

ANCSE M'AVETZ TENGUT A NONCHALER

409,1

MANUSCRIPTS: *D* (86-312), *F* (48-151).
ATTRIBUTION: *Raimon de las salas d' marseilla* in *D*; *Bernartz del poget* in *F*. To my knowledge, the attribution to Raimon de las Salas, a preference going back to Bartsch's *Grundriss,* has never been seriously questioned, although there is little evidence either to support it or to controvert it. Kolsen (see below) does mention a similar use of *noncaler* (line 1) in another poem by Raimon (409,5); but this is hardly conclusive proof of authorship. It has been assumed that *F*'s "Bernartz del poget" refers to Bertran del Poget, who is correctly named in the heading of the following poem in *F*. This also cannot be taken as proved, though it is possible. At all events, Raimon has as good a claim to the poem as Bernart (or Bertran).
VERSIFICATION: A *canso* (or *mieg-canso*) consisting of three *coblas unissonans* of eight lines each. The metrical pattern (Frank, *Répertoire métrique* [tome premier, Paris, 1953] number 577: 48) is one of the commonest used by the troubadours: decasyllables riming *abbaccdd*. The actual rime sounds (*er, ir, o, e*) are not shared by any other poem in this pattern.
PREVIOUS EDITION: Adolf Kolsen, *Beiträge zur altprovenzalischen Lyrik* (Firenze, 1939), pp. 207-214.
TEXT: That of *F*, also adopted by Kolsen, who however emends the ms in a couple of verses (3, 5) to obtain a "normal" caesura. I have not followed him in this.

1. Ancse m'avetz tengut a nonchaler
   On meillz vos sai de bon talan servir.
   Don veirai s'ab mal m'en porai jauzir,
   Amors, pos bes no m'en pot pro tener;
   E deuri' esser, zo·m par, per razo,   5
   Qe, s'ieu faz mal, n'aia bon guizerdo,
   Pos per be-faitz mi rendetz mal ancse,
   Ez er pecchatz s'al vostre tort m'ave.

2. E poriatz m'ab pauc be retener;
   Mas vos no·n cal, per q'eu vas vos m'azir.   10
   Pero trop faill, qui fai atrui faillir
   Son escien, desqe l'a en poder,
   Ez eu faill plus, qar a vos mou tenzo.
   E no·us cugez qe vostr' oc torn en no,

Amors, anz voill. S'anc jorn vos hai dit re,   15
Qe·us sia greu, ve·us m'a vostra merce!

3. E si merces no·m pot ab vos valer,
Sera pecchatz, qar tan voill obezir
Vostres comanz; e si·m volez aucir,
No·us mi defen, e faz o ben parer: 20
Qe mercejan vos veing querre perdo
Del vostre tort. Gardatz doncs s'anc mais fo
Hom qez ames ab tan de bona fe;
Qe·us qier perdon del tort q'avetz de me!

1. You have always considered me with indifference in the things in which I know best how to serve you faithfully. I shall see therefore if I can have pleasure of you, love, by evil means, since good means avail me nothing; and it should be reasonable, I think, for me to have a good reward if I do ill, since you always render me ill for good deeds, and it will be a sin if I receive (a reward) corresponding to the wrong that befalls you.

2. And yet you could hold me with (only) a little good; but you care nothing for that, and consequently I am angry with you. But he does wrong who intentionally causes another to do wrong when he has him in his power. And I am even more at fault when I pick a quarrel with you; and do not think, love, that I will turn your yes into a no (that I would refuse it); on the contrary, I wish (it). If I have ever at any time said anything to you that is disagreeable to you, behold me (now) at your mercy!

3. And if mercy cannot avail with you in my behalf, it will be a sin, because I wish so much to obey your commands; and if you wish to kill me, I shall not defend myself against you, and I make this plain to you: for I come as a suppliant to seek your forgiveness for your wrongdoing. Consider then if ever there was a man who loved so faithfully; for I seek your forgiveness for the wrong that you have done to me!

Variants in D

1: 1. mauez, noncaler. 2. un meill. sap. talen. 3. donc. poiria. iausir. 4. puois. bes] ren. 5. deuria esser çom. raison. 6. seu. nagues. guezardon. 7. puois. be far. rendez. 8. e es foudaz.

2: 9. porias ma. 10. ma nous en cal. mair. 11. autrui. 13. ez. mas. car. ab uos me tenzon. 14. cuges. torn] tron. non. 15. amors uueill enanz seus ai dig re. 16. quis.

3: 17. e puois merce non. auos. 18. peccaz puois tan. 19. uostre coman. 20. e faz uos aparer. 21. puois merceian uos uenc. perdon. 22. gardaz si anc mais fon. 23. queus ames aitan. 24. quer. de tor cauez.

NOTES

2. *On meillz.* I take this to mean, quite literally, "where best," that is, in that respect in which I can serve you best; and not, as Kolsen explains it, "wenn auch noch so sehr."

3. Kolsen emends this line to: *Adonc veirai s'ab mal m'en posc jauzir.*

5. Kolsen emends to: *E deu esser, so mi par, per razo.*

8. Kolsen cites precedents from Appel's *Chrestomathie* (glossary) for *a* in the sense "according to, in proportion to."

14-16. Kolsen punctuates with an exclamation point after *amors* and a question mark after *greu.* He translates: "And do not believe, love, that your yes will turn into a no. But do I wish, then, if I have ever said anything to you, that it should be disagreeable to you?" This seems strained. I prefer to take *eu* as the subject of *torn* and to connect *anz voill* with what precedes rather than with what follows.

18. Kolsen rejects *F*'s *qar* in favor of *D*'s *puois.*

II

DIEUS, AYDATZ

409,2

MANUSCRIPTS: *C* (373), *R* (30-257), *E* (111).

ATTRIBUTIONS: *R. de la sala* in *R*; *Bernart Marti* in *E*; no heading visible in *C*, which is damaged at this point, but the two tables of contents of *C* (by poems and by authors) give the author as *Raymon de la Sala* and *Raymõ de Salo*, respectively. Bartsch rejected *E*'s attribution in his *Grundriss*, and there has been no doubt expressed since his day that the poem belongs to Raimon de las Salas. Hoepffner excludes it from his edition of Bernart Marti. The statement of the *vida* that Raimon composed *albas* supports his claim to this poem, the only extant *alba* under his name.

VERSIFICATION: An *alba* consisting of three *coblas unissonans* of 22 lines each, the last seven being a refrain, which is given in full only for the first stanza. The metrical pattern is unique (number 188:1 in Frank's *Répertoire métrique*):

```
a a b c a a b c a a b c d d d e e a f f f f
3 3 3 5 3 3 3 5 3 3 3 5 3 4 4 3 4 4 3 4 4 5
```

PREVIOUS EDITION: Bartsch, *Provenzalisches Lesebuch* (Elberfeld, 1855), pp. 101-102.

TEXT: Since *C* is far too badly damaged to serve as a base ms, and since the order of verses seems less good in *E* than in *R* (14-15, 27-34), I have followed the text of *R* (as Bartsch did) with a very few emendations.

1.   Dieus, aydatz,
    S'a vos platz,
    Senher cars
E dos e verays,
    E vulhatz   5
    Que ab patz
    Lo jorns clars
E bels c'ades nays
    Nos abratz,
    Car solatz   10
    E chantars
E voutas e lays
    Ay auzitz
    D'auzels petitz
    Pels playssaditz.   15
(REFRAIN)   L'alb' e·l jorns
    Clars et adorns
    Ven. Dieus, aydatz!
    L'alba par
    E·l jorn vey clar   20
    De lonc la mar
    E l'alb' e·l jorns par.

2.   Sus, levatz,
    Drutz c'amatz,
    Que sem pars   25
Er bels jorns e gays;
    E·l comjatz
    Sia datz
    Ab dous fars
Et ab plazens bays.   30
    Enselatz
    E pujatz,
    Car l'estars
Non es bos hueymays,
    Que·ls maritz   35
    Ay vistz vestitz
    E ben garnitz.
(REFRAIN)   L'alb' e·l jorns
    Clars etc.

3.   Be velhatz   45
    E gaytatz,
    Gayt'; encars
No·ns ven nuls esmays.
    Non crezatz

	Per armatz	50
	Que jogars	
	De mon amic lays,	
	Qu'e mon bratz	
	Jauzen jatz;	
	Mas l'afars	55
	No·us iesca del cays.	
	S'autr' o ditz,	
	Faitz n'esconditz	
	Soven plevitz.	
(Refrain)	L'alb' e·l jorns	60
	Clars et adorns etc.	

1. God, please help, dear Lord and sweet and true, and permit that the clear and beautiful day which is already beginning may surround us with peace; for I have heard in the hedges conversations and songs and trills and lays of little birds. (Refrain:) Dawn and day are coming, bright and pretty. God, help! Dawn is appearing and I see the day clear, along the sea, and dawn and day are appearing.

2. Up, arise, lovers who love each other, for without equal the day will be beautiful and gay; and let parting be made with sweet deeds and with pleasing kisses. Saddle and mount, for it is not good to stay any longer, for I have seen the husbands dressed and well armed. (Refrain.)

3. Be alert and watch, watchman; no anxiety comes to us yet. Do not believe that because of armed men I would leave the pleasures that I have with my beloved, who lies reclining in my arms; but let the matter not come forth from your mouth (do not announce this news). If another says it, make often guaranteed denials of if (say and swear that it is not so). (Refrain.)

Variants and Emended Readings

1: 1. aidatz *C*, aiudatz *E*. 3. quars *E*. 4. E *lacking R*. dous *E*. uerais *E*. 5. uoillatz *E*. 8. nais *E*. 10. Car] que *E*. 12. lais *E*. 13. ai *E*. 14-15. pels plaisaditz dauzels petitz *E*. 14. auzelhs *C*. 15. pel *R*. 16. lalbelhs... *C*. iorn *E*. 17. clar & adorn *E*. 18. Ven] e *E*. aidatz *E*. 20. uei *E*. 22. iorn *CER*.

2: 25. pars] pres *E*. 26. bel iorn e gais *E*, ...elh iorn es clars *C*. Order of verses in *E*: 31-34, 27-30. 29. fars] faytz *R*, faitz *E*, fays *C*. 30. bais *E*. 31. e sselatz *R*, e senhatz *C*. 33. Car] que *E*. 34. nous er pro hueimais *E*. es] er *C*. 36. uist *E*. 37. E ben] uenir *E*. 38 ff. *lacking E*. 38. iorn *R*.

3: 45-46. Ben gaitatz e ueillatz *E*. 47. gaitencaras *E*. 48. que nous er nuill fais *E*. nulhs esmays *C*. 49. no *E*. 50. pels *E*. 51. quel baizar *E*. 52. del mieu amic lais *E*. mos amicx *R*. 53. quen mos *E*. braz *C*. 55. Mas] e *E*. 56. cais *E*. 58. faitz *CE*. 60 ff. *lacking E*. 60. iorn *R*.

Bartsch's edition follows the text of *R*, but prints *ai* regularly for *R*'s *ay* and introduces a few further emendations, most of which I have incorporated in my text (4. E. 15. Pels. 22. jorns. 25. ses [*for* sem]. 29. fars. 38. jorns. 39. celatz. 40. privatz. 52. mon amic. 60. jorns). Bartsch also prints the refrain in full for each stanza, although none of the mss does so. *C* and *R* give a few words of the refrain for the second and third stanzas, then add their symbol for etc. *E* simply omits the refrain in the second and third stanzas.

In order to show how much reliance can be placed on ms *C* for confirmation or contradiction of the readings of *R*, here is the complete text of *C*:

1. ...s aidatz...os platz...her cars E d...s euerays...lhatz Que...z Lo jorns clars...nays Nos abratz...chantars E uou...zitz Dauzelhs...ssaditz Lalbelhs... adorns Ven dieus...ar El iorn uey clar...lalbel iorn par.

2. ...rutz quamatz q̃...elh iorn es clars el...tz Ab dous fays...ays E senhatz e...estars Non er bos...qels maritz Ay...garnitz Lal...

3. ...e gaytatz gayten...nulhs esmays Nõ...atz que iogars...ays Que mon braz...mas lafars Nous...Sautro ditz Faitz...uen pleuitz Lalbel...dorns Ven etc.

NOTES

9. It seems more logical to connect *abratz* with *abrasar* ("to embrace"; Levy, *Petit Dictionnaire* gives the additional meaning "entourer") than with *abrazar* ("to kindle, inflame").

17. *et.* As frequently, the word is not spelled out, but indicated by a special sign. In all such cases, rather than print an ampersand, I have transcribed this sign by *et* before a vowel.

18. *Ven.* The use of a singular verb is justified by the fact that the two subjects *alba* and *jorns* are in a sense one thing.

25. Bartsch emends *sem* to *ses*. I see no difficulty in keeping the reading of the mss; *sen* is a recognized variant of *sens*, and before *p* the *n* could easily be labialized to *m*.

29. *fars.* The three mss read uniformly *fays* (*faytz, faitz*), but *fars* is called for by the rime.

31. *Enselatz.* The ms readings here are divergent (*e sselatz, e senhatz, en selatz*). Bartsch emends *R*'s *e sselatz* to *e celatz* and emends *puiatz* in the following line to *privatz*, which has no ms support at all. I think it makes more sense to connect the two lines with saddling and mounting a horse (in order for the lover to make his escape) rather than with the idea of secrecy.

35. *maritz.* The plural form seems odd, though it is clearly called for by the rime and is the only ms reading.

45. This last stanza is evidently spoken by the woman who is with her lover. The second is spoken by the watchman on the outside. The first is probably also spoken by the watchman, or possibly by the lover.

51. *jogars.* The plural form is surprising, but it is supported by the readings of *CR* and by the demands of the rime.

III

DONNA, QAR CONOISSENZA E SENZ

409,3

MANUSCRIPTS: D^a (179-636), I (108), K (94), d (340-228), L (42).
ATTRIBUTION: *Raimont de salas* in D^a, *Raimonz de Salas* in IK (and d?), anonymous in L.
VERSIFICATION: A *tenso* with a lady (presumably composed entirely by Raimon himself) consisting of four eight-line *coblas unissonans* and two *tornadas* of four lines each. The metrical pattern (Frank 624:60) has a very common rime scheme, *abbacddc*; but the combination of this with the syllable count 8 8 8 8 7' 7 7 7' occurs in only one other poem, the anonymous *cobla* 461,101 *E doncx que val aquestz amars*, which does not have the same rime sounds.
PREVIOUS EDITION: Adolf Kolsen, *Trobadorgedichte* (Halle, 1925), pp. 63-64.
TEXT: That of D^a. I and K are very similar to this, but omit line 22 and offer puzzling readings in line 39. L is substantially different and, it seems to me, less good (lines 19, 20, 21, 28, 31, 39). Kolsen's edition is a rather free mixture of readings from D^a and L, with spellings somewhat regularized, even without ms support (e. g. the rime words *sens, temens*, etc.). I have followed D^a exactly except as noted in the variant readings. I have not been able to check the readings of d, which are probably similar to those of IK.

1. Donna, qar conoissenza e senz
   Son e vos de tot benestar,
   Vos veing chai consell demandar
   De ço dunt estauc en bistenz:
   C'un' amor ai encubida   5
   Tant rica e de gran valor
   Qu'eu no li·aus dir la dolor
   Qe per lei m'es escharida.

2. Raimon, ben sui tant conoissenz
   Qe d'aicho·us sabrai conseill dar;   10
   E s'avez bon cor en amar,
   No·n devez esser trop temenz.
   Que s'es pros ni eschernida
   Cil a cui querez s'amor,
   Ja no·i gardera ricor,   15
   Sol no·i trob autra faillida.

3. Donna, soven me prent talenz
   C'umilmen li·aus merce clamar,
   E quant mir son bel cors e gar
   Sa valor, q'es sobrevalenz,   20

    Estauc cum causa esmarida
    Que ren no·ill dic, per paor
    Que n'agues solaz pejor
    Pois, quant l'auria enquerida.

4. Raimon, ricors e ardimenz   25
    Taing en amor al comenzar,
    Per q'eu vos lau que senz tarjar
    Annes enquerre hardidamenz
    Leis cui jois capdela e guida;
    E s'avez tant de follor   30
    Qe·us en laissez per temor,
    Greu es per vos conquerida.

5. Donna, toz temps a ma vida
    Li volc celar ma dolor,
    Mas pos a vos par meillor,   35
    Dirai·ll mon cor, ses faillida.

6. Raimon, cel que merce crida
    A sidonz, l'en a meillor;
    Et eu prec li per Amor
    Q'en lei no·n trobez faillida.   40

1. Lady, since knowledge and sense of all propriety are in you, I come here to ask your advice about that concerning which I am in confusion: for I have coveted a love so noble and of (such) great worth that I do not dare to tell her the pain which has come to me through her.

2. Raimon, I am indeed knowledgeable enough to be able to give you advice about this; and if you have a good heart in loving, you should not be too fearful of it. For if the one whose love you seek is excellent or discerning, she will not consider (demand) noble birth in you, provided she does not find any other lack.

3. Lady, the desire often seizes me to dare humbly to beg her mercy, but when I look at her beautiful person and consider her worth, which is surpassing, I stand like an afflicted creature without saying anything to her, for fear that I might then be less well received after I had asked for her love.

4. Raimon, daring and boldness are proper in love at the beginning, wherefore I advise you to go without delay to ask boldly for the love of her whom joy conducts and guides; and if you are so foolish as to fail in this through fear, it will be hard for you to overcome her.

5. Lady, all the time in my life I have wished to hide my pain from her, but since it seems better to you I shall speak my heart to her without fail.

6. Raimon, he who begs mercy of his lady has it (mercy) better from her; and I beg her for Love's sake that you may not find any lack of it in her.

Variants and Emended Readings

1: 1. Dompna *I*, Domna *K*. qua *IK*. conoissencha e sen *L*. 2. es en uos *L*. 3. jeu ueing cha consseill *L*. ueni *IK*. conseill *IK*. 4. d' cho don jeu estau enbisten *L*. daisso dont (dunt *K*) estau *IK*. 5. qun *L*. hai *L*. encobida *IK*. 6. tan *L*. richa *L*, ric *IK*. 7. perqieu no *L*, que no *IK*. li·aus] aus *L*. 8. mes per lei *L*. escarida *IK*, encharzida *L*.

2: 9. Raimonsz *L*. soi tan conoissen *L*. 10. daichos *K*, daisso *I*, daicho *L*. 11. eshauesz *L*, essauez *K*. amor D^a 12. no deuesz estre *L*. deuetz *K*. temen *L*. 13. qar ser *L*. pros ez eisernida *L*, pros meschernida *IK*. 14. cella cui *IKL*. queresz *L*. 15. no gardara richor *L*. 16. se no itruoba altra *L*.

3: 17. Dompna *I*, Domna *K*. soue mi *L*. prend *L*, per *IK*. talen *L*. 18. cumilmenz *IK*, qumelmenz *L*. laus *IK*, lan *L*. 19. quan *I*, qan *KL*. mir lacking D^a, remir *L*. e gar] esgar D^a. 20. q'ual *L*. sobrels ualen *L*. 21. jeu estau com res marrida *L*. estau *IK*. com *K*. 22. *omitted IK*. q' re no dic *L*. 23. q' nhaja *L*. solasz *L*, solatz *IK*. 24. puois qant lhaurai *L*.

4: 25. Raimonsz rich cor e hardimen *L*. 26. staing D^aL. comenchar *L*, comĕcar *K*. 27. qieu *L*. ses *L*. 28. anes *IK*, annasz *L*. enquer *IK*. ardidamenz *IK*, hardidamen *L*. 29. lei *L*. joi *L*. capdella *IL*. 30. shauesz tan *L*, sauetz tan *K*. folor *K*. 31. q' or enlaissasz per paor *L*. 32. grieu *L*.

5: 33. Domna *IK*. totz *IKL*. tenps d' ma *L*. 34. uol *IK*. mas dolor *L*. 35. epuois *L*. meior *L*. 36. darail *IK*. mocor *L*.

6: 37. Raimonsz lui qi *L*. 38. asidonsz lau amejor *L*. 39. et eu perdi per amor *IK*, e preg olan peramor *L*. 40. no·n] men *IK*. trobetz *IK*, trobes *L*.

Notes

1. *conoissenza e senz*. Since our mss consistently retain the final nonsyllabic vowel here (*conoissenza*) and in many similar cases, I have followed their practice. Kolsen has *conoissench' e sens*.

2. Kolsen translates *de tot benestar* "ganz höflich" and connects it with what follows: "I come courteously." I prefer to take the expression literally and to connect it with *conoissenza e senz*.

15. Kolsen reads *gardara*, with *L*. Since D^aIK agree in reading *gardera*, I have kept it. It is true that a future, rather than a conditional, seems called for; but Appel (*Chrestomathie*, p. xix) lists several instances of a first-conjugation future in *-era* instead of the commoner *-ara*.

25. *ricors*. Kolsen reads *rich cor*, with *L*, doubtless because the lady had told Raimon (line 15) that *ricor* ("noble birth") would not be required of him. But *ricor* was a word of many meanings, and both Raynouard (*Lexique*

roman, V, 94) and Levy (*Provenzalisches Supplementwörterbuch,* VII, 345) give examples of it in the senses "rashness, temerity, pride," which fit nicely here with the following *ardimenz.*

26. *Taing.* The singular verb is possible with a compound subject consisting of two roughly equivalent expressions. Notice incidentally that D^aL read *staing,* for which I can find no justification at all.

33. *a ma vida.* Kolsen reads (with L) *de ma vida;* but *a ma vida* in the sense "mein Leben lang" is illustrated by Levy (*SW,* VIII, 757) with quotatoins from several poets, including Bernart de Ventadorn (*Ja no·m partrai a ma vida,* from 70,30: *Lo tems vai e ven e vire*).

38-39. These two lines caused the copyists some trouble. I do not understand Kolsen's *lau a meillor* (based on *L*); his version of 39 (*E prec e clam per amor*) is a free emendation of *L*'s *e preg olan per amor.* The reading of *IK* in 39 (stemming as usual from a common source) must have resulted from a confusion of the abbreviations for *per* and *pre,* and a further confusion of *cl* and *d,* so that *prec li* becomes *perdi,* which makes no sense. The text of D^a, on the contrary, seems to me perfectly intelligible: "he who begs his lady for mercy receives it better from her (than one who does not), and I (the lady adviser) beg her (the poet's beloved) for Love's sake that you may not find a lack of it (mercy) in her."

IV

NO·M PUOS PARTIR

409,4

MANUSCRIPT: *D* (87-313).
ATTRIBUTION: *idem.* Raimon (following 409,1, with its heading *Raimon de las salas d' marseilla*).
VERSIFICATION: A *canso,* consisting of four nine-line *coblas capcaudadas* and a *tornada* of three lines. The metrical pattern (Frank, 281:1) is:

```
a    b     a    b     a    b     c    d    e
4    6'    4    6'    4    6'    10   10   10'
```

The *a* rime is new for each stanza (*ir, ort, es, iers*); the *c* and *d* rimes are constant throughout (*is; ans*); the *e* rime of one stanza becomes the *b* rime of the next (e: *ire, enda, ensa, endre;* b: *ansa, ire, enda, ensa*). In this precise form, the poem's metrical structure is unique; but if we take the three introductory pairs of short lines as three decasyllables with internal rime, we arrive at precisely the same metrical scheme (*aaabcd*) as a *canso* of Pons de la Guardia (377,5: *Si tot no·m ai al cor gran alegransa*). Furthermore, the rimes there are also *capcaudatz,* with the same progression from one stanza to the next; and the rime sounds of the two poems are identical. It is evident that one poet imitated the other, or that they had a common model, now lost. Unfortunately, the dates of these poets are only approximately fixed, and they may overlap. It seems, however, from István Frank's edition of Pons de la Guardia (*Boletín de la Real Academia de Buenas Letras de Barcelona*

XXII [1949], 229-336), that Pons was at least a considerably older contemporary of Raimon. In the absence of any other indication, we may therefore conjecture that Raimon imitated Pons's poem, introducing into its form the refinement of internal rimes.

PREVIOUS EDITION: None, aside from a diplomatic reprint of the text of *D* by Mussafia in *Sitzungsberichte der Kaiserlichen Akademie der Wissenschaften, philosophisch-historische Klasse*, Wien, vol. 55 (1867), p. 440.

1. No·m puos partir
De joi ni d'alegranssa,
Puois anc venir
No·m pot mais de pesanza.
E de conssir 5
E de grant malananssa
Pos ben partir, quez anc nuls Serazins
Non soffri tan de pena ni d'afanz
Com faz per leis don m'ausio·ll suspire.

2. Tolt m'a deport, 10
Joc e solaz e rire,
Car l'am tan fort
Del meu plaz escondire
Non ai conort,
Mais enuei e desire 15
Del seu genz cors a cui eu stauc aclinz,
E que me plaz sos bes e sos enanz
Tant qu'eu non ai poder c'aillor m'entenda.

3. Hanc no·m promes
Don savis la reprenda, 20
Ni·m dis ni·m fes
Tant que merses l'en renda,
Ni jamais fes
Ren c'om la·n sobreprenda,
N'anz po ben dir per q'eu l'en stau cap clins. 25
Hanc non s'afrais sos cors e sos talanz
Vas mi puois vi sa plaisen captenença.

4. Domn' anc nulls serfs
No fez major suffrenza,
Qu'eu sai qu'estiers 30
M'a de sa benvolenssa.
E als no quier
Mas sol que Amors venssa
Leis de cui soi leials amics e fins
E de cui sui tot desamatz amanz 35
Tan qu'eu no·m puosc plus en sa onor entendre.

5. Na Rambalda del Baus, vostre pretz fins
   Es tan gradiz entre·ls pros e·ls presanz
   Qu'en l'auzor grat es puzat ses descendre.

1. I cannot depart from joy or gladness, since no more sorrow can ever come to me (than I have already). But from care and great misfortune I can indeed depart, for never did any Saracen suffer so much pain or torment as I do for her whose sighs (i.e., the sighs I breathe for her) kill me.

2. She has taken from me pleasure, amusement, and solace, and laughter; for I love her so much that I have no consolation from concealing (having to conceal) my suit, but care and desire for her noble body, before which I stand bowed; and her good and her advancement please me so much that I have no power to turn my thoughts elsewhere.

3. She never made a promise to me for which a wise man could reprove her, nor did she ever say or do anything to me for which I might give her thanks, nor did she ever do anything for which she might be blamed, nor can she even say why I stand before her with my head bowed. She has never inclined her body or her thought toward me since first I saw her pleasing behavior.

4. Never did a lady inflict greater suffering on any serfs, for I know that she has obliterated me from her good will. And all I wish is that Love may overcome her whose loyal and faithful friend I am, and of whom I am a completely unloved lover, so much so that I cannot think any more of her honor.

5. Lady Rambalda of Baus, your fine merit is so well received among the excellent and the distinguished that it has risen to the highest level without descending.

READINGS EMENDED

8. afan. 19. non. 22. que] ques. 33. *After this line, D has these two superfluous lines, which more or less duplicate 32-33:* E donc quei quer So camors mi uenssa. 34. fis. 38. presaz. 40. lauzors graz.

NOTES

13. *plaz.* This represents, of course, *plag* (*plach, plait*), "suit."
16. *genz.* This should grammatically be *gen*, the oblique case. — *eu stauc.* Perhaps this should be emended to *estauc*, a far commoner form; the same could be said of *en stau* in line 25.
25. *anz.* The sense is not entirely clear; it must be something like "even." — *l'en* (unless we emend *l'en stau* to *l'estau*) is a combination of the indirect object *li* and *en*, the latter meaning approximately "because of any action on her part."

26. *s'afrais*. Preterit of *s'afranher*; singular verb with two subjects, as we have seen elsewhere.

28. *Domn' anc*. Mussafia's transcription is *Dom anc*, but the ms reading is clearly *Dom nanc*. — *serfs*. The *f* is purely graphic and was not pronounced; the word is commonly spelled *ser*, pl. *sers*.

30. *estiers*. Past participle of *esterzer*, "to wipe away."

32. *quier*. The rime demands the ending *-ers*, but this seems impossible for the first person singular present of *querre*. On the other hand, I do not see any way to justify *estier* instead of *estiers* in line 30. Must we simply admit that the rime is defective?

37. *Na Rambalda del Baus*. This member of the famous Baus family does not appear in any document yet discovered. She is named, but without any clues to her identity, by Sordello in a *tenso* with Bertran d'Alamanon (*Doas domnas*: 437, 11) and by Bertran himself in his *planh* (76, 12: *Mout m'es greu*, addressed to Sordello) on the death of Blacatz. The date of the *planh* seems to be ca. 1237; that of the *tenso* is less certain, but probably not far from the same year (see M. Boni, *Sordello* [Bologna, 1954], pp. 159, 108, 101, lxiii).

39. *puzat*. More commonly, *pujat*; cf. *plaz* in line 13.

V

SI·M FOS GRAZIZ MOS CHANZ EU M'ESFORCERA

409,5

MANUSCRIPTS: D^a (179-637), *I* (108), *K* (94), *d* (340-227).
ATTRIBUTION: *Raimonz de salas* in *IK* (and *d*?); no heading in D^a (but it follows 409, 3, which is headed *Raimont de salas*). The lady presented as the author of the reply (the last two stanzas) is probably fictitious.
VERSIFICATION: A *canso* (or two *mieg-cansos*) consisting of five eight-line *coblas unissonans*. The metrical pattern (Frank 577:138) is the same as that of 409, 1: decasyllables riming *abbaccdd*. This is one of the commonest used by the troubadours, but the rime sounds (*era, atz, er, an*) are not shared by any other poem in this pattern.
PREVIOUS EDITIONS: O. Schultz (-Gora), *Die provenzalischen Dichterinnen* [Altenburg, 1888], p. 30; C. Chabaneau, *Revue des langues romanes*, XXXIII, 107-108. Chabaneau's readings are more reliable than Schultz's.
TEXT: That of D^a, which seems slightly preferable to that of *I* (and *K*), followed by Schultz and Chabaneau: cf. lines 28, 36. I have not been able to check the text of *d*.

1. Si·m fos graziz mos chanz eu m'esforcera
   E dera·m gauz e deporz e solaz;
   Mas issi·m sui a nonchaler gitaz,
   Que ma domna, que a toz jorz esmera,
   Ço qu'eu li dic non deigna en grat tener,   5
   Qu'apenas sai entre·ls pros remaner,

Ni non sui ges cel qe era antan:
Aissi me volf mos covinenz e·ls fran.

2. Ha las! cum muor quant mi membra cum era
   Gais e joves, alegres, envesaz!   10
   E quant m'albir qu'eu sui de joi loignaz,
   Per pauc mos cors del tot no·s desespera.
   E dunc mei hueill cum la pogron vezer?
   Car n'ai perdut d'els e de mi poder.
   Ço m'an ill faz, don mos cors vai ploran,   15
   Qu'eu non puos far conort ni bel semblan.

3. Ha, bella donna, res, cum be·m semblera
   Que, on que fos, degues humilitaz
   Venir en vos, que tant humil semblaz
   Vers mi, que ja a mos jorz no·s camgera.   20
   Amors n'a tort, que·us fai dur cor aver,
   E vos sabez qar l'en donaz poder;
   Qar si Amors e vos es a mon dan,
   Las! ges longas non puos soffrir l'afan.

4. Bel dolz amis, ja de mi no·s clamera   25
   Vostre bels cors cortes et ensignaz
   Si saubessez qals es ma voluntaz
   Ves vos, de cui sui mellz hoi q'er non era;
   E non creaz qu'e·us meta e nonchaler,
   Car gauz entier non puesc sens vos aver,   30
   A cui m'autrei leialmen senz engan,
   E·us lais mon cor en guage on qu'eu m'an.

5. Mas una genz enojosa e fera,
   Cui gauz ni bes ni alegrers non plaz,
   Nos guerrejan, don mos cors es iraz,   35
   Car per ren als senes vos non estera.
   Pero en mi avez tant de poder
   Q'ab vos venrai quant me·l farez saber,
   Mal grat de cels q'enqueron nostre dan,
   E pesa·m fort car senz vos estauc tan.   40

    1. If my song were welcomed, I would make an effort and would give myself joy and pleasure and solace; but I am treated here with indifference, for my lady, who daily becomes more perfect, does not deign to show gratitude for what I say to her, so that I can scarcely remain among the good, and I am not the man I used to be: thus she turns aside my agreements (the agreements I had with her) and breaks them.

    2. Alas, how I die when I remember how gay and young, merry and joyful I used to be; and when I consider that I am far from joy, I (*lit.*, my

body) almost give way completely to despair. And then how could my eyes see her? For I have lost control over them and over myself. This they have done to me, wherefore my body goes weeping, so that I cannot take courage or make a good appearance.

3. Ah, fair lady, (fair) creature, how good it would seem to me if, wherever it might be, kindness had to come to you, who *seem* so kind toward me, (kindness) that during my whole life would never change. Love is to blame, who makes you have a hard heart, and you know why you give him power to do so; for if Love is in you to my harm (*or* if Love and you are to my harm), alas, not long can I endure the torment.

4. Fair sweet friend, never would your fair body (you), courtly and well bred, complain of me, if you knew what is my wish concerning you, to whom I belong more today than I did yesterday; and do not believe that I am indifferent to you, to whom I give myself loyally, without deceit, and I leave you my heart in pawn, wherever I may go.

5. But certain annoying and hateful people, to whom neither joy nor good nor happiness is pleasing, make war on us, whereat my body is (I am) sad, because for no other reason would I be without you. Yet you have so much power over me that I shall come with you when you tell me, in spite of those who seek our harm, and it grieves me greatly that I am without you so long.

Variants and Emended Readings

1: 1. grazitz *IK*. 2. gaug *IK*. deportz *K*. solatz *IK*. 3. aissim *IK*. gitatz *IK*. 4. Q'a madõna *D^a*, Q'ama dõpna *I*, Que a ma domna *K*. totz *IK*. iornz *I*. 5. So *IK*. deĩgna *IK*. 6. entres *D^a*. romaner *IK*. 8. uol *IK*. el *D^{a}IK*.

2: 9. hailas *I*. menbra *I*. 10. enuesatz *IK*. 11. loingnatz *IK*. 12. no·s] nom *D^a*. 13. donc *IK*. miei *K*. oill *IK*. 14. quar *I*, qar *K*. 15. so *IK*. fatz *I*. 16. posc *I*, puosc *K*. senblan *I*.

3: 17. a *IK*. dõpna *I*, domna *K*. 18. humilitatz *IK*. 19. semblatz *IK*. 20. iornz *IK*. camiera *IK*. 22. sabetz *I*. quar *IK*. 24. quar *IK*. longuas *IK*. posc *I*, puesc *K*. laffan *I*.

4: 25. Bels douz amics *IK*. nous *D^a*. 26. enseingnatz *IK*. 27. saubessetz *I*, saubesetz *K*. cals *IK*. uoluntatz *IK*. 28. uos es de cui sui mielz hoi que non era *IK*. 29. creatz *IK*. 30. gaug *IK*. puosc *IK*. ses *IK*. 31. ses enian *IK*. 32. gatge *IK*.

5: 34. gautz *I*, gratz *K*. alegres *K*. platz *IK*. 35. iratz *IK*. 36. quar *IK*. vos *lacking IK*. 37. per so *IK*. tan *IK*. 38. cab *IK*. mil *IK*. faretz *I*. 40. pesan *D^a*, pesã *I*. ses *IK*. tant *D^a*.

NOTES

4. I follow Schultz and Chabaneau in emending the *q'a* (or the equivalent) of all three mss to *Que*.

8. *volf*. From *volver*: "she turns aside, turns away, my agreements." Raynouard (*Lex. rom.* V, 568) gives the meanings "tourner, retourner, renverser, rouler"; Levy (*SW* VIII, 841) "wenden, umwenden, abwenden." Schultz emends *I*'s *uol* to *tol*, Chabaneau to *tuol*, which seem less clear than *D^a*'s *uolf*. I follow Schultz and Chabaneau, however, in emending *el* to *e·ls*.

17. Chabaneau suggests emending *domna* to *doussa*, which would make the construction of *res* a little clearer.

25-40. The lady's reply could be considered a separate *mieg-canso* in answer to the first, and following the same metrical pattern; but these two stanzas are in all likelihood the work of Raimon himself.

VI

BERTRAN, SI FOSSETZ TANT GIGNOS

406,16

MANUSCRIPTS: *A* (183), *D* (148-515), *I* (157), *K* (143). Bartsch's statement (*Grundriss*) that the poem occurs also in *L* is apparently erroneous.

ATTRIBUTION: *Raimonz* in *D*, *Bertrans dauignon e Raimons delas salas* in *A*, *Raimons de miraual e den beltran* in *I*, *Raimons de miraual e den bertran* in *I* index, *Raimons de miraual* in *K* and *K* index. Paul Andraud (*La vie et l'œuvre du troubadour Raimon de Miraval* [Paris, 1902], pp. 180-182) denies the poem to Raimon de Miraval because (he says) *IK* list the authors as Raimon de Miraval and Bertran de Lamanon (d'Alamanon); since the latter poet lived too late to have participated in this *partimen*, and since *A* ascribes the poem to Raimon de las Salas and Bertran d'Avignon (the latter of whom *could* have participated in it), therefore *both* attributions of this ms stand a better chance of being right. This argument, unfortunately, has no weight at all, because *IK* nowhere ascribe the poem to Bertran d'Alamanon: *K* names only Raimon de Miraval, and *I* lists Bertran or Beltran, with no further identification. Andraud may be right in giving the poem to Raimon de las Salas, but not for this reason. Jeanroy accepts the attribution to Raimon de las Salas (*Poésie lyrique* I, 350 and 422), but gives no arguments in its favor. The date of the poem (1216; see note to line 24) may be a little late for Raimon de Miraval, but I do not know that it is impossible. As I see it, then, the attribution of the poem to Raimon de las Salas rests on our willingness to put more faith in the testimony of *A* than in that of *IK*, and possibly on a subjective conviction that the style is not that of Raimon de Miraval. I personally am not at all sure about the authorship of this *partimen*, as far as the first participant is concerned. For Bertran d'Avignon, the only claimant in any ms to the other half of the poem, see the note on line 22.

VERSIFICATION: A *partimen* consisting of eight *coblas doblas* (that is, with new rimes at the end of every two stanzas); the first six lines have eight syllables each, the last two have ten. The rime scheme is peculiar in that the first two stanzas follow the pattern *abbaccaa* (Frank 549:4), while the remainder of the poem follows the pattern *abbaccbb* (Frank 599:3). This sloppy craftsmanship might be an argument for ascribing the poem to Raimon de las Salas rather than to Raimon de Miraval, who is a better poet. No other poem combines either of these rime schemes with lines of this syllable count.

PREVIOUS EDITION: E. Monaci, *Testi antichi provenzali* [Roma, 1889], col. 85.

TEXT: That of *A*, taken fom the diplomatic reprint by Pakscher and De Lollis in *Studj di filologia romanza* III, 567-568. The differences between *A* and the other mss are not great (lines 11, 13, 37). Monaci also follows *A*.

1.   Bertran, si fossetz tant gignos
     Que saubessetz lo mieils triar
     D'aisso qez e·us vuoill demandar,
     Tenssons fora ben de nos dos.
     Digatz: cal ant plus pretz cabal,   5
     Li Lombart o li Provensal;
     Cals razonatz ni tenetz per plus pros,
     Per mieils faire gerra, conduich ni dos?

2.   Raimon, destas doas razos
     Qe·m partetz, la cals mieiller par,   10
     L'una pren, l'autra lais estar.
     Lombartz vuoill esser ad estors,
     Car de Proenssa no me cal;
     Per q'ieu chausisc sai, que mais val
     Lombardia, on trob cavalliers bos,   15
     Francs e cortes; e·m platz lor messios.

3.   Bertran, al mieu entendemen
     Chausit avetz la sordejor.
     Trop son plus ric gerrejador
     Li Proensal e plus valen   20
     Per gerra e per message.
     Tolon la terra a·N Symon,
     E·il demandon la mort a lor seignor,
     E al comte cuich que rendra s'onor.

4.   Raimon, trop lor datz d'onramen,   25
     Q'a Belcaire en lor honor
     Lor fetz Symons tant de paor,
     E si eron dos tans de gen.
     En apres, a gran mespreison,
     Renderon li sa garnison;   30

Per q'en totz faitz sont li Lombart meillor
E plus honrat e mieils combatedor.

5. Bertran, a doble vos envit
   De la tenzon que razonatz,
   Que lai es proesa e barnatz 35
   Mantengutz, larguesa e convit;
   Lai dona hom cavals e destriers
   E fant rics conduitz e pleniers.
En Lombardia podetz ben, si·us platz,
Morir de fam si deniers non portatz. 40

6. Raimon, fort avetz joc marrit,
   Que qand es perdutz, l'envidatz.
   Sai son plus donador assatz,
   E·il Lombart son mais issernit,
   Qu'il dan cavals, draps e deniers, 45
   E·ls tenc d'armas plus fazendiers
Qe·ls Proensals que vos tant me lauzatz,
E sai es hom plus soven convidatz.

7. Bertran, de tot avetz gran tort,
   Qe lai a trobadors prezans 50
   Que sabont far e vers e chans,
   Tenssos, sirventes e descort;
   E lai son las dompnas de pretz,
   Que l'una cuich qe·n val ben detz
De Lombardas, mas, qe sont femnas grans 55
C'apenas neis sabon far bels semblans.

8. Raimon, aissi non a conort
   Q'ieu ja·us en sia contrastans,
   Car li Lombart d'aitals bobans
   No·is plazon, ni d'aital deport; 60
   Car vos mezeus, si vos voletz,
   Atressi conoisser devetz
Que de las dompnas nais lo grans engans,
C'als maritz fant noirir autrui enfans.

1. Bertran, if you were clever enough to be able to choose the better (side) in what I wish to ask you, there could well be a *tenso* between us. Tell me: which have more excellent worth, the Lombards or the Provençaux; which do you consider or esteem more noble and better at making war, hospitality, and gifts?

2. Raimon, of these two choices that you give me to decide which seems better, I take one and leave the other alone. I wish to be a Lombard

in battles, for I care nothing for Provence. Therefore I make my choice *here*, for Lombardy is better, where one finds good, noble, courtly knights; and I like their liberality.

3. Bertran, in my opinion you have chosen the worse (side). The Provençaux are much bolder warriors and more meritorious in war and in liberality. They are taking the land away from Sir Simon and are asking their lord for his death, and I think he will return his fief to the Count (of Toulouse).

4. Raimon, you do them too much honor, for at Beaucaire in their fief Simon frightened them so, and yet they had twice as many men. Afterward, with very bad judgment, they gave him back his garrison. Therefore in all matters the Lombards are better and more honored and better fighters.

5. Bertran, I challenge you to a double stake (I double the bet) in the *tenso* that you are defending, for prowess and nobility, generosity and hospitality are maintained *there* (in Provence); there one gives horses and steeds, and they offer rich and lavish entertainments. In Lombardy, if you please, you can easily starve to death unless you carry money with you.

6. Raimon, you have a bad (position in the) game, for when it is lost you challenge it (you raise the stake). *Here* are many more patrons, and the Lombards are more discerning, for they give horses, clothes, and money, and I consider them better men at arms than the Provençaux that you praise to me so much, and here one receives more frequent invitations.

7. Bertran, you are completely wrong about the whole thing, for *there* (in Provence) there are distinguished troubadours who know how to compose *vers* and songs, *tensos, sirventes,* and *descorts*; and *there* are the worthy ladies, for I think one of them is easily worth ten Lombard ladies, furthermore they (the Lombard ladies) are big women who scarcely even know how to make a good appearance.

8. Raimon, here there is no encouragement for me to argue with you about that, for the Lombards take no pleasure in such ostentation or in such amusements; for you yourself, if you will, must also admit that from ladies comes the great deceit, for they make their husbands feed other men's children.

VARIANTS AND EMENDED READINGS

1: 1. Bertrams *D.* foses *D,* fossez *I,* fosses *K,* tan *I.* 2. saubeses *D.* meillz *D,* meill *IK.* 3. daiso *I.* q̄u uos *D.* uoill *DIK.* 4. tensos *DK,* tessos *I.* be *DIK.* 5. digaz *D.* an *DIK.* prez *D.* 6. lombrat *K.* proençal *D,* proensal *I.* 7. quals *IK.* rasonaz *D,* rasonatz *IK.* tenez *D.* per plus plus *D* (*in margin in modern hand,* pros). 8. meillz *D,* mielz *I,* miellz *K.* guerras *DIK.* condug *DIK.* dons *K,* don *I.*

2: 9. Raimonz *D,* Raimons *IK.* rasos *DIK.* 10. partez *D.* qual *IK.* meillor *I. Order in D:* 12, 11. 11. prenc e lautra lais uos estar *IK.* pren e lautra *D*. 12. lombraz *D*, lombratz *K*, lonbart *I*. uoill *DIK*. aestors *IK*, destors *D*. 13. quar *IK*. proensa *IK*. no men cal *D*, mi non cal *IK*. 14. qeu *D*. chausic *DI*. chai *DIK*. que] car *D*, quar *IK*. 15. lonbardia *I*, lombaria *K*. cauailliers *D*, caualiers *I*. 16. em plaz *D*, e platz *IK*. meissios *IK*.

3: 17. Bertrams *D*, Bertrans *K*. entendimen *I*. 18. auez *DIK*. lo sordeior *A*. 19. guerreiador *DIK*. 20. proensal *DIK*. 21. guerre e *D*, guerra e *IK*. meission *IK*. 22. toillon *DIK*. simon *DK*. 23. eill *DIK*. seingnor *DIK*. 24. e *DIK*. cuit *IK*, cui *D*. renda *DIK*.

4: 25. Raimonz *DK*. daz *D*. 26. ca *D*, qua *IK*. 27. fez *D*. symonz *I*, simonz *DK*. tan *IK*. 28. eran *D*. tanz *D*. 29. grant *IK*. mesprisson *I*, mesprison *K*. 31. toz *D*. faiz *D*. son *DIK*. lombrat *K*. 32. meillz *DIK*.

5: 33. Bertrams *D*, Bertrans *IK*. 34. tenson *DIK*. rasonaz *D*, rasonatz *IK*. 35. lai] sai *A*. barnaz *D*. 36. manteguz *DK*. largesa *K*. couit *D*. conuitz *A*, couitz *IK*. 37. dona hom] donon *DIK*. destres *D*, destres *K*. 38. fan *DI*, fai *K*. *co*nduz *D*, condutz *IK*. pleners *IK*. 39. podez *D*. plaz *D*. 40. se *DI*. deners *IK*. no *K*. portaz *D*.

6: 41. Raimonz *D*, Raimons *IK*. forz auez *D*. iuec *IK*. marit *I*. 42. qant *DK*, quant *I*. perduz *D*. leuidaz *D*. 43. chai *DIK*. assaz *D*. 44. E·il] li *IK*. plus esernit *DIK*. 45. qill *D*, qeill *I*, queill *K*. dan] don *IK*. deners *IK*. 46. eills *IK*. fasendiers *DIK*. 47. prouensals *DIK*. tan *D*. mi *DIK*. lauzaz *D*. 48. chai *DIK*. conuidaz *D*, couidatz *IK*.

7: 49. Bertrams *D*, Bertrans *IK*. toz *I*. auez *DI*. tor *D*. 50. trobators *D*. prezanz *D*, presanz *IK*. 51. sabon *DIK*. far e vers] far uers *D*, ben far uers *IK*. chãz *DI*, chãtz *K*. 52. tensos *IK*. tensons *D*. seruentes *D*. descortz *AIK*, descorz *D*. 53. domnas *K*, dõnas *DI*. prez *D*. 54. cuit *DIK*. qe ual *D*. dos *D*. 55. mar que son *DIK*. granz *DIK*. 56. semblanz *DIK*.

8: 57. Raimonz *DIK*. aici *DIK*. 58. q'uia uos sia contrastanz *D*, queuia uos en (eu *I*) sia contrastanz *IK*. 59. Car] mas *DIK*. bobanz *D*. 60. nos *DIK*. plason *IK*, plaison *D*. ni *lacking IK*. daitals deportz (deporz *D*) *AD*. 61. quar *I*, qar *K*. mizeus *D*. uolez *D*. 62. atressi *IK*, atreissi *D*. deuez *D*. 63. las *lacking A*. domnas *IK*. lo *lacking A*. granz *DIK*. enganz *D*, enianz *IK*. 64. quals *IK*. mariz *D*. fan *DIK*. autruis *IK*. enfanz *DIK*.

NOTES

12. *estors*. For a somewhat similar confusion of *-ors* and *-os* in rime, see my article "Imitation of Form in the Old Provençal Lyric," *Romance Philology* VI (1953), p. 118.

14. *sai*. From their use of *sai* in speaking of Lombardy, *lai* in speaking of Provence, it is clear that the poets composed this *tenso* in Italy.

16. *messios*. I have borrowed the translation "liberality" from Linskill's edition of Raimbaut de Vaqueiras (392, 15: *Senher n'Aymar, chauzes de tres baros,* line 19); the meanings given by Raynouard and Levy ("mise, émission, dépense," "Wette, Ausgabe, Aufwand") seem less appropriate here.

18. *la sordejor*. Either *la*, the reading of the majority of the mss, or *lo*, the reading of *A*, could be justified: *lo* representing a vague neuter, *la* referring back specifically to the word *razo*.

22. *Symon*. Simon de Montfort. The reference is to events of the year 1216. Simon had received Beaucaire in fief from the Archbishop of Arles in 1215, during the Albigensian Crusade, to the detriment of its former lord, Count Raymond VI of Toulouse. In the summer of 1216, Raymond set out for Spain to enlist help, leaving his son, the future Raymond VII, at the head of a devoted band of Provençal followers to attempt the reconquest of this land. They actually did retake Beaucaire, except for a garrison of Simon's men who held out in the donjon of the castle. One of the knights who accompanied young Raymond on this expedition was Bertran d'Avignon, presumably the poet named as one of the participants in the present *tenso*. (*La Chanson de la croisade albigeoise*, éd. par E. Martin-Chabot [Paris, 1957], vol. II, p. 137. The siege of Beaucaire occupies *laisses* XVII to XXII.)

23. This line seems to mean "And they ask of their lord (Raymond) death for him (Simon)."

24. "And I think he (Simon) will return his fief to the count (Raymond)." This line dates the poem between the siege of Beaucaire and the death of Simon de Montfort in 1218. — The form *renda* (*DIK*) is perhaps better than *rendra*, since the subjunctive is probably commoner after *cuidar*, but I think that *A*'s reading is not impossible.

26-30. When Simon learned what was happening at Beaucaire, he hastened to the town and made an unsuccessful effort to dislodge the conquerors and free his garrison, which was slowly starving. Seeing that he could not do so, he agreed to give up his siege and withdraw from Beaucaire if young Raymond would release the men of the garrison. This proposal was accepted, the men were released, and Simon marched off to plunder Toulouse.

42. *envidatz*. For this verb, which refers back to *envit* (line 33), see Levy, *SW* III, 110.

52. *descort*. The sense calls for *descortz*, the reading of all the mss; but the rime demands *descort*.

55. *mas*. For the meaning, see Levy *SW* V, 32 (15).

BREVI PROSE IN VOLGARE PIEMONTESE DEL QUATTROCENTO:

I *TESTI CARMAGNOLESI*

Di GIANRENZO P. CLIVIO
University of Toronto

In un codice della Biblioteca Nazionale di Torino segnato N. V. 37, che malauguratamente andò distrutto in un incendio nel 1904, si contenevano, oltre alle Laudi di Carmagnola, alcuni brevi passi in prosa scritti in dialetto piemontese del Quattrocento. Essi furono trascritti e pubblicati da Ferdinando Gabotto e Delfino Orsi nella prefazione alla loro edizione delle *Laudi del Piemonte* (Bologna, 1891, pp. xvii-xix), ma non sono finora stati mai esaminati dal punto di vista linguistico e sono rimasti, a quanto parrebbe, pressoché ignoti ai romanisti. Atteso il rinnovato interesse che si nota da qualche tempo per lo studio dei dialetti piemontesi sia antichi che moderni,[1] non parrà dunque inutile che ci si occupi qui brevemente di queste prose e che si trattegggino i caratteri principali del volgare in cui furono stese. Invero, nella relativa scarsità di attestazioni scritte del piemontese antico, questi passi sono un documento ben

---

[1] Si vedano ad esempio, per il piemontese antico gli studi di Giuliano Gasca Queirazza tra i quali citiamo la serie dei *Documenti di antico volgare in Piemonte* (Torino 1965-) giunta oggi al terzo fascicolo; per i dialetti moderni, la monografia di Corrado Grassi, *Correnti e contrasti di lingua e di cultura nelle valli cisalpine di parlata provenzale e franco-provenzale* (Torino 1958) e quella recente di Ilia Griset, *La parlata provenzaleggiante di Inverso Pinasca (Torino) e la penetrazione del piemontese in Val Perosa e in Val San Martino* (Torino, 1966); per la letteratura dialettale piemontese, si veda la recente ed amplia antologia *La letteratura in piemontese* a cura di C. Brero e R. Gandolfo (Torino, 1967).

prezioso. Mancando ad essi un nome, li chiameremo per comodità *Testi carmagnolesi*, poiché erano contenuti nello stesso manoscritto delle Laudi di Carmagnola.

Si tratta di tre passi, di cui il primo e l'ultimo sono brevi sermoni pronunciati da un rettore, e il secondo un'orazione rivolta a Cristo ed alla Madonna. Mentre i due sermoncini sono in una prosa sintatticamente normale, l'orazione, pur non essendo in metro, devia in qualche caso dai costrutti ordinari e sembra tradire nell'ignoto autore l'aspirazione verso un certo ritmo che servisse a nobilitare il volgare.

Prima di procedere all'analisi linguistica, trascriviamo qui di seguito i tre passi, distinguendoli coi numeri romani e numerando i righi in volgare.

I

Officium comune quod fieri debet
in dominicis que sont (*sic*) inter primam et ultimam
dominicam mensis. Rector dicit credo
parvum totum completum post
carnis resurectionem
Rector.

1 Benet, laudà he regratià ora he sempre may sea
  el nom del nost sacratissimo signor Benet misèr
3 Iesu Christ. R. Semper laudà he regratià.
  Rector.
5 Frateli mei carissimi, perseverant in le nostre
  bonne usanze, in questa present matina noy si
7 farema canter officij, priere, laude he oration,
  le qual saran cantà a lo honor he gloria de Dio
9 he in solemnità della festa de ancoy he a corexion
  de li defet he manchament nustr, e a ciò che
11 noi semo più tost exaudy, noi si arema recors
  a quella fontana de grati confort he speranza
13 di li maiori peccator Marì, e si la saluterema
  con quela angelica salutatione.

II

Post dicitur preces post salutatio (sic) crucis.

1 Ayturi eine nostr signor benet misèr Iesu Christ,
  voi che sei vras salvator,

2 Signor de vras, mandene de la vostra sanctissima
gratia, pas e beneta benedition,
3 He sempre abi marsì e misericordia de noi,
De noi miseri e meschin pecator,
5 De tuti e deli altri chi per lo mond son,
Signor Iesu Christ, parè voi chi save la vita nostra,
7 Se noi auson fait o dit cosa chi contra
Li vost sant commandament sea.
9 Signor de vras, mandene pantiment innans
Ch'el dì de la nostra fin sea,
11 Azò che dapres la nostra mort requesta non sea.
Ave Maria, ho tsteilla (*sic*) Diana,
13 Madona, del pareis voi sei la sovrana.
Desfendene, madona, de rea fin de morb
15 He de mort subitanna.
Sancte Deus, sancte fortis, sancte et immortalis,
miserere nobis.

III

Rector

1 Belli freli chi sei vegnù in questa present matina, ave fait el vostr debit; queli chi son nent
3 vegnù, ne poeno pa dir ansì. Tuta volta noi
prierema lo nost signor benent miser Iesu Christ
5 chi li piasa demeterli in lo cor de fer antender
quel chi li an promis, azò che Christ non sea
7 scrit in peccà; d'altra part chi n'è stait al
principi de lo officio si voglia dir X pater noster
9 e X ave Maria; ancora 3 pater noster e 3 ave
Maria per tute le anime che son in purgatorj,
11 azò che Dio si ne voglia aver misericordia;
ancora 3 pater noster e 3 ave Marie a ciò che
13 Dio si ne voglia vardè de ogni adversità.

Abbiamo seguito scrupolosamente la trascrizione data dal Gabotto, ma dobbiamo avvertire che il testo ci pare palesemente guasto in III 5-6. Infatti, se si mantiene la lettura *demeterli* il senso non torna: l'emendazione, ovvia e oseremmo dire sicura, è di leggere *de meterli*, cioè "di metter loro". Così anche al rigo successivo la frase *azò che Christ non sea scrit in peccà* par richiedere un'emendazione, giacché così com'è non avrebbe senso. Proponiamo dunque che in luogo di *Christ* si legga un pronome dimostrativo maschile singolare, la cui forma potrà esser stata *quest* o *quist*,[2] ma terminante in ogni caso col nesso *st*. A parte questi due particolari, la lettura è chiara e non par dare adito a dubbi.

Il carattere piemontese della lingua di questi testi balza agli occhi in maniera evidentissima. A riprova di questo fatto, basterà far rilevare il part. pass. *cantà* I 9 cui corrisponde l'inf. *canter* I 8. Come è noto, la corrispondenza nei verbi di prima coniugazione dell'infinito in -*e(r)* al participio passato in -*à* è un fatto tipico del Piemonte, e anzi più precisamente della parte occidentale (a sud della Stura di Lanzo) e meridionale (a sud del Po) dell'attuale regione pedemontana. Inoltre, l'esito *it* di CT come in *fait* II 7 e *dit* (<*diit*) II 7 (che in altre zone del Piemonte è č palatale o semplicemente *t*), conferma che la lingua dei nostri testi è da assegnarsi al Piemonte occidentale.

Nel complesso, siamo qui di fronte ad un piemontese schietto che risente sorprendentemente poco delle lingue di cultura. Tuttavia, non mancano, come del resto ci si può aspettare per la natura semiculta dei testi stessi, alcune forme da ascriversi all'influsso del latino ecclesiastico o del volgare illustre. L'influsso attribuibile al toscano si riduce, invero, a poca cosa anche perchè, nei casi dubbi, è più plausibile, data la natura ecclesiastica dei testi, pensare all'azione del latino. Possiamo citare come toscaneggiante la forma *frateli* I 5, del resto sostituita più sotto da quella schiettamente locale *freli* III 1 con la *l* forse già intaccata e dunque da leggersi modernamente *frei*. L'influsso toscano si fa sentire anche nella conservazione eccezionale (talora forse soltanto grafica) di alcuni -*o* finali di parola che, per norma, in piemontese cadono. Citiamo *sacratissimo* I 2, che è evidentemente culto; *Dio* I 8 (e passim) accanto al quale però si ha più volte la bella forma piemontese *Dé* II 2, 9, oggi quasi scomparsa; ed infine *officio* III 8 col plurale *officij* I 7 entrambi del linguaggio chiesastico. Un caso di grafia toscaneggiante è la *z* di *usanze* I 6 e di *speranza* I 12 che ha però valore di *s* sorda, come del resto la *x* di *corexion* I 9 e di *exaudy* I 11 (cfr. ital. ant. *essaudire*).

Un discorso a parte meritano le forme degli aggettivi e pronomi dimostrativi, che farebbero pensare a tutta prima all'invadenza del

---

[2] Forme attestate altrove nel piemontese antico, per esempio nei *Sermoni Subalpini*.

volgare illustre. Nei nostri testi troviamo infatti *quel* III 6, *quella* I 12 e *quela* I 14, *queli* III 2, e *questa* I 6, mentre sono affatto assenti le forme locali piemontesi nelle quali il *que-* passa a *co-*. Purproppo, la conoscenza che abbiamo oggi del piemontese antico e, sopratutto, della cronologia dei cambi fonologici piemontesi è ancora molto imperfetta. È certo, comunque, che ad un dato punto *que-* passò a *co-*, dando luogo a forme di dimostrativi come *col, cola, cost, costa,* ecc., ma non è possibile dire con certezza quando tale cambio sia avvenuto, nè se abbia avuto luogo simultaneamente in ogni parte del Piemonte.[3] Nel caso dei *Testi carmagnolesi*, siamo portati a pensare che le forme dei dimostrativi siano genuinamente piemontesi e risalenti ad un tempo anteriore alla data del cambio succitato. Giova, a questo proposito, un rapido sguardo agli altri documenti di piemontese antico che ci sono pervenuti. Nei *Sermoni Subalpini*, attribuiti di solito al secolo dodicesimo, troviamo soltanto forme con *qu-*.[4] Lo stesso di può dire per gli *Ordinamenti di Dronero*,[5] di incerta datazione ma anteriori al 1500 e per le *Recomendaciones* di Saluzzo,[6] che sono della fine del secolo XV. Si penserebbe, dunque, di poter affermare che il passaggio *que-> co-* sia da porsi dopo il 1500, nel qual caso non stupirebbero le forme in *que-* dei *Testi carmagnolesi*. Tuttavia, altri documenti, alcuni databili con precisione e tutti anteriori alla data suddetta, recano le forme in *co-*. Basterà citare i noti testi trecenteschi di Chieri, datati 1321,[7] e la *Sentenza di Rivalta* del 1446.[8] Anche i quattro-

---

[3] La maggior parte dei dialetti piemontesi hanno oggi forme inizianti in velare sorda del tipo *kus(t)-kas(t)* e *kul-kal* (vedi AIS, carta 1587), ma forme con *kw-* sopravvivono in pochi punti, per esempio a Vico Canavese (punto 133).

[4] Cfr W.. Foerster, "Galloitalishe Predigten," *Romanische Studien* 4. 1-92 (1879-1880), p. 76.

[5] Cfr. G. Gasca Quirazza, *Documenti di antico volgare in Piemonte*, II: *Gli Ordinamenti dei Disciplinati e dei Raccomandati di Dronero*, Torino, 1966, p. 96.

[6] Se ne veda l'edizione del Gasca Queirazza, *Documenti di antico volgare in Piemonte*, I: *Le "Recomendaciones" del Laudario di Saluzzo*, Torino, 1965.

[7] Se ne veda l'edizione del Salvioni, "Antichi testi dialettali chieresi," nel volume miscellaneo *In memoria di Napoleone Caix e Ugo Canello*, Firenze, 1886, pp. 345-355.

[8] Edita da F. Bollati ed A. Manno, "Documenti inediti in antico dialetto piemontese," *Archivio storico italiano*, serie 4, 2. 375-388 (1878).

centeschi *Parlamenti ed epistole* hanno alcune forme in *co-*,[9] e la forma *col* si trova nella breve *Lamentazione di Torino*.[10] Da citare è anche l'interessante *quost* in un testo del secolo XV di cui il Cipolla pubblicò due brevi passi e che è per il resto ancora inedito.[11] Allo stato attuale delle nostre conoscenze, possiamo dunque soltanto formulare l'ipotesi che il passaggio di *que-* a *co-* sia avvenuto prima in una zona del Piemonte che comprenderebbe tra l'altro Chieri e Rivalta (il Monferrato?), e solo più tardi in una seconda zona, comprendente Saluzzo, Dronero e Carmagnola. Nella prima zona il cambio deve aver avuto luogo già nella prima metà del secolo XIV, mentre nella seconda bisognerà scendere al secolo XVI.

All'influsso del latino ecclesiastico sono dovuti alcuni vocaboli che non trovano rispondenza nel lessico locale. Citiamo *grati* I 12, *salutatione* I 14, *subitanna* II 15 che è però ben assimilato se —com'è probabile— la doppia *n* indica velarizzazione, e le grafie *mn* di *solemnità* I 9, *ct* di *sanctissima* II 2 e *dv* di *adversità* III 13.

Procediamo ora ad un'analisi linguistica che ci permetta di cogliere i fatti essenziali.

Dal punto di vista fonologico, rileviamo che quasi tutti i caratteri tipici del piemontese sono già presenti, seppure non tutti in modo costante. Si nota lo scempiamento delle doppie in *matina* I 6, *pecator* II 3 (ma *peccador* I 13), *tuta* III 3 ecc., ma in alcuni casi esse sono conservate: *commandament* II 8, *innans* II 9, ecc. L'intacco velare della *n* intervocalica pare attestato dalle grafie *bonne* I 6 e *subitanna* II 15 dove *nn* rappresenterà la fase ʋn (che oggi è ridotta a ŋ eccetto che in parti del Monferrato), ma bisogna notare che più spesso manca l'indicazione grafica di questo fatto: *matina* I 6, *fontana* I 12, *sovrana* III 13. La lenizione delle occlusive intervocaliche è ben attestata nelle forme di tradizione diretta, e la si nota anche nella voce semidotta *pareis* II 13 da confrontarsi col *pareyso* della lauda "La dona del pareyso" di Fra Columba da Vinchio.[12] Si notino *benet* I 1 e passim, *priere* I 7 e *prierema* III 4,

---

[9] Cfr. G. Bertoni, "Annotazioni e correzioni all'antico testo piemontese dei 'Parlamenti ed Epistole'," *Romania* 39.305-314 (1910), p. 311.

[10] *La letteratura in piemontese*, cit., p. 123.

[11] C. Cipolla, "Antichissimi aneddoti novaliciensi," *Memorie dell'Accademia delle Scienze di Torino*, serie 2, 50.127-135 (1901), p. 128.

[12] F. Levi, "Inni e laudi di un frate piemontese del secolo XIV," *Archivio storico italiano*, serie 7, 10.91-100 (1928), p. 98.

freli III 1, *ave* III 2; ma le eccezioni non mancano e sono dovute all'influsso latino: il *pecator* II 4 dei nostri testi è altrove in piemontese antico *pecaor*.

Notiamo anche l'assibilazione delle palatali davanti a vocale anteriore, attestata in *vras* II 1, *pas* II 2, *marsì* II 3, *piasa* III 5, mentre in *principi* III 8 abbiamo un caso di conservatismo grafico.

Difficile dire se la *-r* degli infiniti *canter* I 7 *dir* III 3 *fer* III 5 *antender* III 5 sia da ritenersi meramente grafica e avente solo valore etimologico. Induce anzi a pensare il contrario la forma *demeterli* III 5 dove la *r* si mantiene malgrado il pronome enclitico, ma va presa in considerazione la forma *vardè* III 13 senza *r*, che ha valore di indizio. Notiamo, infine, per il consonantismo il passaggio della fricativa bilabiale di origine germanica alla labiodentale nello stesso *vardè* III 13, e rileviamo che la vocalizzazzione di *l* implicata non è attestata: *altri* II 5, *altra* III 7.

Per il vocalismo, mentre è giustificato pensare che l'esito di *u* lungo latino sia qui *ü*, nulla si può dire con certezza circa l'esito fonetico di *u* breve ed *o* lunga latine, rappresentate costantemente da *o*, eccetto che in *ayturi* III 1 che è da confrontarsi con le forme *aytorij* e *ayturior* delle *Recomendaciones*.[13] Uguale è la grafia di *o* breve in sillaba chiusa (*mort* II 11, *morb* II 14, ecc.) e in sillaba aperta dove oggi troviamo *ö* (*cor* III 5, *voglia* III 8, ecc.). Come al solito, è impossibile determinare con certezza il valore del grafema *o* in piemontese antico, giacché gli esiti moderni sono tre, e cioè *o*, *u* ed *ö*, e non sono distinti graficamente prima dell'Alione. Si noti la tipica dittongazione in *tsteilla* II 12.

Per il vocalismo atono, oltre alla normale caduta delle vocali finali diverse da *a* o *e* del plurale femminile, si deve notare la caduta della *e* protonica in *vras* II 1 e passim, e la tendenza di *e* a diventare *a* davanti alle liquide, come in *marsì* II 3 e in *pantiment* II 9, fatto che si osserva ancora nel piemontese rustico.

Per la morfologia, ci limiteremo a segnalare soltanto i fatti di maggior rilievo.

In quanto alla flessione nominale, sono da rilevare alcuni casi di maschile plurale in *-i* da ritenersi latinismi di tipo ecclesiastico, ma per lo più il plurale maschile non si distingue dal singolare. Casi misti sono le frasi *de grati confort* I 12 e *de li maiori peccator* I 13.

---

[13] Gasca, *Le "Recomendaciones,"* cit., p. 32.

Nel plurale femminile si conserva sempre la *-e* di prima declinazione, come per esempio in *le nostre bonne usanze* I 5-6, ma la *-i* di terza declinazione cade in *oration* I 7.

La flessione verbale è solo parzialmente documentata. Si noti la tipica desinenza *-ema* della prima plurale in *farema* I 7, *arema* I 11, *prierema* III 4 ecc., desinenza qui attestata solo nel futuro.[14] Ha carattere eccezionale *semo* I 11. Oltre ai frequenti participi in *-à*, se ne trovano alcuni forti, oggi in parte normalizzati, come *promis* III 6 e *scrit* III 7 (ora *prometù* e *scrivù*, ma *scrit* vive ancora), oltre a *fait* e *dit* II 7 e *stait* III 7 che sono anche moderni. Da ricordare anche *exaudy* I 11 e *vegnù* III 3.

Particolarmente interessanti sono le forme della seconda plurale dell'imperativo che mostrano il passaggio della desinenza *-ate* ad *-e*: con pronome enclitico abbiamo *mandene* II 2 e *desfendene* II 14, oltre alla bella forma *parè* II 6 (se pure non è da leggere *pàre*).

Per le altre forme verbali rimandiamo al glossario.

Non richiede particolare commento in una analisi sommaria come la presente, il resto della morfologia che non offre fatti di speciale interesse.

Per il lessico rimandiamo ancora al glossario che segue, limitandoci qui a richiamare alcune forme tipicamente piemontesi come *ancoy* I 9 e *freli* III 1; e vocaboli oggi scomparsi, ma frequenti in piemontese antico, come *vras* I 1 e *ayturi/* II 1. Per altro, data la loro brevità e il carattere semidotto, questi testi non ci offrono gran che dal punto di vista lessicale.

Lessico.

Le forme verbali sono ordinate sotto la forma dell'infinito. Quando quest'ultima non è documentata nei *Testi Carmagnolesi*, viene data tra parentesi la forma ricostruita basata su altri testi piemontesi antichi o sul latino volgare. In qualche caso di particolare interesse, si citano forme attestate in altri documenti o forme del piemontese moderno. Con Gasca I e II si fa riferimento ai glossari contenuti nei due studi di G. Gasca Queirazza, citati più sopra;

---

[14] la desinenza *-ema* è oggi passata ad *-uma*.

per i *Sermoni Subalpini* (Serm. Sub.) si fa riferimento per pagina e riga all'edizione datane da Francesco Ugolini in *Testi antichi italiani* (Torino, 1942). Le forme moderne sono quelle date dal *Gran dizionario piemontese-italiano* (Torino, 1859) di Vittorio di Sant'Albino.

a prep. I 8, 9, 10, 12; *a ciò che* I 10; III 12.
adversità III 13
al prep. art. III 7
altra III 7; altri II 5
ancora III 9, 12
ancoy I 9 (mod. *ancheuj*) Gasca I *encoy*, Serm. Sub. *oi* p. 18 l. 3.
angelica I 13
anime III 10
ansì III 3
antender III 5
Ave II 12; III 9, 10
aver III 11 ind. pres **5** *avé* III 2 **6** *an* III 6; fut. **4** *arema* I 11. imper. **2** *abi* II 3; cong. imperf. **4** *auson* II 7
ayturi II 1, Serm. Sub. *aitori* p. 27, l. 17
azò che II 11; III 6, 11

benedition II 2
belli III 1
benet I 1, 2; III 1 (*benent* III 4); *beneta* II 2
bonne I 6

carissimi I 5
canter I 7 part. pass. f. p. *cantà* I 8
che I 10; II 1; III 10; *ch'* II 10
chi II 5, 6, 7; III 1, 2, 5, 6, 7
Christ I 3; II 1, 6; III 4, 6
ciò I 10; III 12
commandament II 8
con I 14
confort I 12
contra II 7
cor III 5
corexion I 9
cosa II 7

dapres II 11
de prep. I 8, 9 ecc.; II 2,3 ecc.; III 5,7
de (< *Deus*) II 2, 9
debit III 2
defet I 10

del prep. art. II 13; *deli* II 5; *della* I 9
(*desfender*) imper. 1 con pron. encl. di 1ª pers. p. *desfendene* II 14
dì II 10
Diana II 12
Dio I 8; III 11, 13
dir III 3, 8; part. pass. m.s. *dit* II 7

e I 10, 13; II 2, 3, 4 ecc. *he* I 1; II 15 ecc.
el art. I 2; II 10; III 2
(*esser*) ind. pres. 3 *è* III 7; 4 *semo* I 11; 5 *sei* II 1, 13; III 1;
    6 *son* II 5; III 2, 10; Fut. 6 *saran* I 8; cong. pres. 3 *sea* II 8,
    10, 11; III 6; imperat. 3 *sea* I 1; *eine* II 1 (forma non chiara).
(*exaudir*) part. pass. m.p. *exaudy* I 11

fer III 5; fut. 4 *farema* I 7; part. pass. m.s. *fait* II 7; III 2
festa I 9
fin II 10, 14
fontana I 12
frateli I 5; *freli* III 1

gloria I 8
grati I 12
gratia II 2

ho (voc.) II 12
honor I 8

Iesu I 3; II 1, 6; III 4
in I 5,6 ecc.
innans II 9 (mod. *anans*)

la art. II 2, 6, 10, 11, 13
la pron. I, 13
laude I 7
(*lauder*) part. pass. m.s. *laudà* I 1, 3
le art. I 5, 8; III 10
li art. I 10, 13; II 8
li pron. dat. s. III 5, 6
lo art. I 8; II 5; III 4, 5, 8

Madona II 13; *madona* II 14
maiori I 13
manchament I 10
mandene imper. con pron. encl. di 1ª pers. p. II 2, 9
Marì I 13; *Maria* II 12; III 9, 10; *Marie* III 12
marsì II 3, Serm. Sub *marcì* p. 17, 1. 44
matina I 6; III 1

may I 1
mei agg. poss. I 5
meschin II 4
meterli inf. con pron. encl. di 3ª pers. p.m. II 5
miser I 2; II 1; III 4
miseri II 4
misericordia II 3; III 11
mond II 5
morb II 14
mort II 11, 15

ne pron. III 11, 13
ne negaz. III 3; *n'* III 7
nent III 2
noi I 11; II 3, 4, 7; III 3; *noy* I 6
nom I 2
non II 11; III 6
nost I 2; III 4; *nostr* II 1; *nustr* I 10; *nostra* II 6, 10; 11; *nostre* I 5

officio III 8; *officij* I 7. Anche in Gasca II, in diverse varianti grafiche.
ogni III 13
ora avv. I 1
oration I 7, Serm. Sub. *oracium* p. 31 1. 105.

pa III 3
pantiment II 9
(*parer*) imperat. 5 *paré* II 6
pareis II 13
part III 7
pas II 2
pecator II 4; *peccator* I 13
peccà III 7
per prep. II 5; III 10
(*perseverer*) ger. *perseverant* I 5
(*piasir*) cong. pres. 3 *piasa* III 5
più I 11
(*poer*) ind. pres. 6 *poeno* III 3
present I 6; III 1
(*prier*) fut 4 *prierema* III 3
priere I 7
principi III 8
(*prometer*) part. pass. m.s. *promis* III 6
purgatorj III 10

qual I 6
quel III 6; *quela* I 14; *quella* I 12; *queli* III 2
questa I 6; III 3

rea II 14
recors I 11
(*regratier*) part. pass. m.s. *regratià* I 1, 3
(*requer*) part. pass. f.s. *requesta* II 11. l'infinito è attestato nei Serm. Sub. p. 28 1. 32.

sacratissimo I 2
salutatione I 13
(*saluter*) fut. **4** *saluterema* I 13
salvator II 1
sant II 8
(*saver*) ind. pres. **5** *save* II 6
(*scriver*) part. pass. m.s. *scrit* III 3
se II 7
semper I 3; *sempre* I 1; II 3
si I 6, 11, 13; III 7, 11, 13
signor I 2; II 1, 2, 6, 9; III 4
solemnità I 9
sovrana II 13
speranza I 12
(*ster*) part. pass. m.s. *stait* III 7
subitanna II 15

tost I 11
tseilla II 12
tuta III 3; *tute* III 10

usanze I 6

vardé III 13
(*venir*) part. pass. m. p. *vegnù* III 1, 3
vita II 6
voi II 1, 6, 13
(*voler*) cong. pres. **3** *voglia* III 8, 11, 13
volta III 3
vost II 8; *vostr* III 2
vras II 1, 2, 9

MONTAIGNE HUMANISTE ET FOLKLORISTE

Par MARCEL FRANÇON
Harvard University

Nombreuses sont les définitions que l'on a données des termes *Renaissance, humanisme, humanistes*. Examinons ce qu'entendait Montaigne quand il s'est servi de ce dernier mot. On ne trouve ce terme qu'une seule fois dans les *Essais*; c'est dans le chapitre I, lvi ("Des Prières"); qui est un de ceux auxquels Montaigne a fait le plus grand nombre d'additions, en 1582, en 1588, et sur l' "Exemplaire de Bordeaux." Nous verrons, ensuite, que Montaigne, tout humaniste qu'il ait été, appréciait ce que nous appelons le folklore.

* * *

En 1582, Montaigne ajouta, au chapitre "Des Prières," un préambule:

> Ie propose icy des fantasies informes et irresolues, comme font ceux qui publient des questions doubteuses a debattre aus escoles, non pour establir la verité, mais pour la chercher, et les soubmetz au iugement de ceux a qui il touche de regler non seulement mes actions et mes escris, mais encore mes pensées. Esgalement m'en sera acceptable et utile la condemnation, comme l'approbation; et pourtant, me remettant tousiours a l'authorité de leur censure, qui peut tout sur moy, ie me mesle ainsin temerairement a toute sorte de propos, comme icy.[1]

---

[1] *Essais de Michel de Montaigne. Texte original de 1580 avec les variantes des éditions de 1582 et 1587* publié par R. Dezeimeris & H. Barckhausen (Bordeaux, 1870-1873), I, 264, n. 1. — *Les Essais de Montaigne. Reproduc-*

Sur l' "Exemplaire de Bordeaux," Montaigne a ajouté, entre *approbation* et *et pourtant*, le passage suivant :

> tenant pour execrable, s'il se treuve chose dicte par moy ignoramment ou inadvertament contre les sainctes prescriptions de l'eglise catholique, apostolique et Romeine, en la quelle je meurs et en la quelle je suis nai.

Relevons, aussi, cette addition qui se lit dans l' "Exemplaire" :

> il se voit plus souvent cette faute que les Theologiens escrivent trop humainement, que cett' autre que les humanistes escrivent trop peu theologalement [...]. [2]

et la suivante :

> Je propose les fantasies humaines et miennes [...] d'une maniere laïque, non clericale, mais tres religieuse tousjours. [3]

Ces citations suffiront à notre propos : Montaigne indique, ici, très nettement qu'il emploi des expressions (comme *fortune, destinée, les dieux*) qui n'ont qu'une valeur littéraire et poétique, que ce sont des termes vulgaires et non approuvés, et que, lui-même, il discourt "comme les enfans proposent leurs essais." [4]

Pour Montaigne, être *humaniste*, c'est être ce que nous appelons *un homme de lettres*, et l'opposition est marquée entre les *lettres humaines* —"le dire humain"— et le "parler divin." [5] Montaigne n'a pas l'ambition d'enseigner, n'ayant aucune qualité pour cela ; il présente, simplement, ses réflexions, ses "fantasies" ; elles sont "matiere d'opinion, non matiere de foi."

Montaigne s'intéresse à la littérature, plus qu'à la philosophie. Une des sources principales des *Essais* se trouve chez les poètes. De la poésie, Montaigne a dit : "Je l'ayme infiniment." [6] De même

---

tion typographique de l'Exemplaire annoté par l'Auteur... avec un avertissement... par M. Ernest Courbet (Paris, 1906-1931), I, 131-134. — *Œuvres complètes de Michel de Montaigne. Les Essais,* par le Dr. A. Armaingaud (Paris, 1924), II, 486-487.

[2] *Les Essais,* éd. Armaingaud, II, 498.
[3] *Id.*, p. 499.
[4] *Id.*, pp. 498-499.
[5] *Id.*, p. 498.
[6] *Les Essais,* éd. Armaingaud, IV, 195 (Livre II, chap. xvii).

qu'il a déclaré: "J'ayme les Historiens ou fort simples ou excellens,"[7] il a fait l'éloge de la poésie populaire comme celui de la poésie d'art:

> La poësie populere et purement naturelle a des naïfvetez et graces par ou elle se compare a la principale beaute de la poësie parfaicte selon l'art; comme il se voit es villanelles de gascouigne et aus chançons qu'on nous raporte des nations qui n'ont conoissance d'aucune sciance, ny mesmes d'escriture. La poësie mediocre qui s'arrete entre deus, est desdeignee, sans honur et sans pris.[8]

Montaigne cite deux chansons des "Cannibales"; voici la première:

> qu'ils viennent hardiment trétous et s'assemblent pour disner de luy; car ils mangeront quant et quant leurs peres et leurs ayeux, qui ont servy d'aliment et de nourriture à son corps. Ces muscles, dit-il, cette cher et ces veines, ce sont les vostres, pauvres fols que vous estes; vous ne recognoissez pas que la substance des membres de vos ancestres s'y tient encore: savourez les bien, vous y trouverez le goust de vostre propre chair.[9]

Montaigne cite un autre trait des Cannibales:

> Outre celuy que je vien de reciter de l'une de leurs chansons guerrieres, j'en ay un' autre, amoureuse, qui commence en ce sens: Couleuvre, arreste toy; arreste toy, couleuvre, afin que ma sœur tire sur le patron de ta peinture la façon et l'ouvrage d'un riche cordon que je puisse donner à m'amie: ainsi soit en tout temps ta beauté et ta disposition preferée à tous les autres serpens.[10]

Entre juin et septembre 1789 fut publiée la traduction que fit Goethe de ces deux passages:

---

[7] *Les Essais*, éd. Armaingaud, III, 201 (Livre II, chap. x).
[8] *Les Essais*, éd. Armaingaud, II, 479 (Livre I, chap. liv).
[9] *Id.*, pp. 260-261 (Livre I, chap. xxxi).
[10] *Id.*, p. 263. Voir J. G. Frazer, *The Golden Bough* (New York, 1941), p. 32: "The Huichol Indians admire the beautiful markings on the back of serpents."

Todeslied eines Gegangenen.

Kommt nur kühnlich, Kommt nur alle,
Und versammelt euch zum Schmause!
Denn ihr werdet mich mit Dräuen,
Noch mit Hoffnung nimmer beugen.
Seht, hier bin ich, bin gefangen,
Aber noch nicht überwunden.
Kommt, verzehret meine Gleider,
Und verzehrt zugleich mit ihnen
Euere Ahnherrn, eure Väter,
Die zur Speise mir geworden!
Dieses Fleisch, das ich euch reiche,
Ist, ihr Thoren, euer eignes,
Und in meinen innern Knochen
Stickt das Mark von eueren Ahnherrn.
Kommt nur, kommt! Mit jedem Bissen,
Kann sie euer Gaumen schmecken.

* * *

Liebeslied eines Amerikanischen Wilden

Schlange, warte, warte, Schlange,
Dass nach deiner schönen Farben,
Nach der Zeichnung deiner Ringe,
Meine Schwester Band und Gürtel
Mir für meine Liebste flechte.
Deine Schönheit, deine Bildung
Wird vor allen Schlangen
Herrlich dann gepriesen werden. [11]

Evald Christian von Kleist, lui aussi, a donné une traduction de la chanson de la couleuvre:

Lied der Kannibalen

Montagne B. I. Kap 30

Verweile, schöne Schlange,
Verweile! meine Schwester
Soll in ein Band von Golde

---

[11] V. Bouillier, "Montaigne et Goethe," *RLC*, V. 4 (1925), 572-593. Cf. J. W. Goethe, *Gedenkausgabe der Werke, Briefe und Gespräche* (Artemis-Verlag, Zürich, 1953), II, 327-328.

Dein Bild für Isen wirken.
Für Isen, meine Freundinn;
Alsdann wird deine Schönheit,
Vor allen andern Schlangen
Der Welt, gepriesen werden. [12]

Herder avait, de son côté, traduit la même chanson:

AN EINE SCHLANGE.

Brasilianich

Verweile Schlange,
Verweile Schlange.
Es soll die Schwester
Nach deinen Farben
Ein Halsband sticken,
Ein reiches Halsband
Für meine Freundin.
So, schöne Schlange,
Wird deine Schönheit
Und deine Farben
Vor allen Schlangen
Der Welt gepriesen. [13]

En 1826, Goethe fit une nouvelle traduction de cette même chanson:

Brasilianisch

Schlange, halte stille!
Halte stille, Schlange!
Meine Schwester will von dir ab
Sich ein Muster nehmen;
Sie will eine Schnur mir flechten,

---

[12] Des Herrn Ewald Christian von Kleist, *Sämtliche Werke* (Berlin, 1771), I, 41. Remarquons que le chapitre I, xxxi ("Des Cannibales") des éditions publiées pendant la vie de Montaigne, fut numéroté xxx à partir de l'édition parisienne de 1595 et ce n'est qu'en 1906 que l'on a rétabli l'ordre primitif (voir mes *Leçons et Notes sur la littérature française au XVIe siècle*, 4e éd. [Cambridge, 1967], p. 166). Les traductions ont, jusqu'au XXe siècle, suivi l'ordre des chapitres de l'édition de 1595, donnée par Marie de Gournay.
[13] *Herders Werke herausgegeben von Dr. Heinrich Meyer* (Stuttgart), I, 505-506.

> Reich und bunt, wie du bist,
> Dass ich sie der Liebsten schenke.
> Trägt sie die, so wirst du
> Immerfort vor allen Schlangen
> Herrlich schön gepriesen.[14]

V. Bouillier a noté que les vers 3 à 6 de la traduction de la première chanson, par Goethe, sont une interpolation d'après un autre passage du même chapitre des *Essais*:

> Ils ne demandent à leurs prisonniers autre rançon que la confession et recognoissance d'estre vaincus; mais il ne s'en trouve pas un, en tout un siecle, qui n'ayme mieux la mort [...].[15]

On a dit que Goethe avait probablement pris "deux ou trois mots" à Titius, l'auteur de la première traduction allemande des *Essais* (1753). Bouillier rapporte aussi que Chuquet avait vu, dans la première traduction de la chanson de la couleuvre par Goethe, une "imitation frappante" de la version de Kleist; mais si "l'imitation ou la réminiscence des trois derniers vers paraît peu contestable," "la version de Kleist, infidèle et maniérée [...] demeure manifestement inférieure à celle de Goethe." Quant à la traduction de Herder, elle était restée inédite jusqu'en 1885.

Dans ses "Réflexions sur Térence" (1762), Diderot examine le cas de ce poète: "Térence a peu de verve [...]," mais "il porte dans son sein une muse plus tranquille et plus douce [que celle qui inspire Molière ou Aristophane]. C'est sans doute un don plus précieux que celui qui lui manque; c'est le vrai caractère que nature a gravé sur le front de ceux qu'elle a *signés* poètes, sculpteurs, peintres et musiciens. Mais ce caractère est de tous les temps, de tous les pays, de tous les âges et de tous les états. Un Cannibale amoureux qui s'adresse à la couleuvre et qui lui dit: 'Couleuvre, arrête-toi [...]'; ce Cannibale a de la verve, il a même du goût [...]."[16] Dans la

---

[14] V. Bouillier, p. 577. Cette poésie fut publiée dans le recueil *Kunst und Alterthum* (année 1826). Dans l'édition donnée par Ernst Beutler (Artemis-Verlag Zürich, 1953), p. 338, on lit la date de 1825, qui doit être celle de la composition de cette poésie.

[15] *Essais*, éd. Armaingaud, II, 256.

[16] *Oeuvres complètes de Diderot*, éd. Assézat (Paris, 1875), V, 233-234.

"Lettre sur les sourds et muets" (1751), Diderot discute l'inversion des mots: "Par exemple, si de ces deux idées contenues dans la phrase *serpentem fuge*, je vous demande quelle est la principale, vous me direz, vous, que c'est le serpent; mais un autre prétendra que c'est la fuite; et vous aurez tous deux raison." [17] Dans le treizième *Fragment sur la littérature allemande moderne* (publié en 1767), Herder "traite à son tour du problème des inversions en français et en allemand et utilise largement les suggestions de Diderot, sans avoir toujours la franchise de le citer. Tout ce qu'il dit de la valeur émotive de l'inversion, jusqu'à l'exemple 'Fleuch die Schlange!' pour exprimer la fuite et 'Die Schlange fleuch' pour désigner le serpent est tiré de la *Lettre sur les sourds et muets*." [18]

Dans la "Préface de l'édition de 1729" de sa tragédie d'*Œdipe*, Voltaire écrivit: "tous les peuples de la terre, excepté les anciens Romains & les Grecs, ont rimé & riment encore. Le retour des mêmes sons est si naturel à l'homme, qu'on a trouvé la rime établie chez les Sauvages, comme elle l'est à Rome, à Paris, à Londres & à Madrid. Il y a dans Montaigne, une chanson en rimes américaines, traduite en français [...]." [19] Comme le remarque M. Dréano, ces "rimes américaines" sont une invention de Voltaire.

Thomas Warton père traduisit la chanson de la couleuvre et cette version fut publiée après sa mort. Ses fils annoncèrent la traduction en ces termes: "An American Love-Ode. *Taken from the Second Volume of Montaigne's Essays.*" L'édition de 1801 était intitulée: "Address of an Indian Girl to an Adder. Written in the year 1740, by a Scholar of Winchester College." On peut s'étonner de cette interprétation: dans le texte de Montaigne, la personne qui s'adresse à la couleuvre exprime le vœu suivant: "que ma sœur tire [...] la façon et l'ouvrage d'un riche cordon que je puisse donner à m'amie." Voici le texte de Thomas Warton père:

---

[17] *Id.*, I, 364.

[18] Roland Mortier, *Diderot en Allemagne* (Paris, 1954), pp. 348-349. Cf. *Herders Sämmtliche Werke*, éd. Suphan (Berlin, 1877), pp. 191-192. Cf. M. Dréano, *La renommée de Montaigne en France au XVIIIe siècle* (Angers, 1952), p. 302.

[19] *Oeuvres de Voltaire*, nouv. éd. par M. Palissot (Paris, 1792), I, 21. Cf. Dréano, p. 319. Voltaire continuait en disant: "on trouve dans un des spectateurs de M. Addisson une traduction d'une ode lapone rimée, qui est pleine de sentiment." Voir *The Spectator*, éd. Donald F. Bond (Oxford, 1965), III, 376-378, 518-520; IV, 18.

> Stay, stay, thou lovely, fearful snake,
> Nor hide thee in yon darksome brake:
> But let me oft thy charms review,
> Thy glittering scales and golden hue;
> From these a chaplet shall be wove,
> To grace the youth I dearest love.
>
> Then ages hence, when thou no more
> Shall creep along the sunny shore,
> Thy copy'd beauties shall be seen;
> Thy red and azure mix'd with green,
> In mimic folds thou shalt display;—
> Stay lovely, fearful adder, stay. [20]

Miss Norton a une note qui se rapporte au vers 6: "It may be noted that the speaker is changed from a man to a woman."

Commentant "les deux morceaux de la poésie des Indigènes de l'Amérique," Moët a dit: "L'un est un chant de défi d'un prisonnier de guerre à ses bourreaux, l'autre un chant d'amour. Rien n'égale la sauvage énergie du premier et le charme pénétrant du second; mais rien aussi n'est plus opposé au goût régnant du temps de Montaigne et même à ce qui fut, jusqu'au commencement de ce siècle, le goût français." [21]

Pour Miss Gracey, les jugements de la Pléiade sur "la poésie provinciale et américaine" auraient été: "manque de culture, manque d'art." Elle précise: "Ces poètes, aristocrates de famille et de tempérament, ne pouvaient pas goûter la beauté naïve d'une chanson populaire; ils ne voyaient que la grande poésie savante et artistique de la Grèce et de Rome, et, un peu plus bas sur l'échelle, la poésie italienne. Que Montaigne, l'élève de la grande poésie [...] ait pu

---

[20] *Montaigne. His personal relations to some of his contemporaries, and his literary relations to some later writers. A compilation by Miss Grace Norton* (Boston et New York, 1908), p. 140. Miss Norton donne les dates suivantes: Thomas Warton (1687-1745). Eric Partridge a donné une autre date pour la naissance de Thomas Warton père: 1688; et Clarissa Rinaker, une autre: 1690. Cf. Thomas Warton *The Elder, Poems on Several Occasions,* reproduced from the Edition of 1748 (New York, 1930), pp. 139-140. Voir mes notes: "De Montaigne à Hegel," *BSAM*, 3ᵉ série, Nº 27 (Juillet-Septembre 1963), pp. 50-52; et "Montaigne et les deux Thomas Warton," *BSAM*, 4ᵉ série, Nº 7 (Juillet-Septembre 1966), pp. 96-98.

[21] E. Moët, *Des opinions et des jugements littéraires de Montaigne* (Auch, 1850), pp. 72-73.

en même temps goûter les petites chansons de sa province, ou remarquer le caractère anacréontique de certaine chanson rapportée de l'Amérique du Sud — voilà ce qui nous le met à part de ses contemporains." [22]

On voit les objections que nous ferions. Il a été de tradition, pendant longtemps, en effet, de nier le goût que les poètes du seizième siècle ont eu pour le folklore. Clément Marot, Marguerite d'Angoulême, et Ronsard ont, pourtant, manifesté l'intérêt qu'ils portaient à l'art populaire, [23] si bien que les jugements de Montaigne sont bien moins insolites que le prétend Miss Gracey. Mais c'est, là, la marque de ces simplifications, de ces généralisations et de ces oppositions chères aux manuels: d'un côté, le folklore; de l'autre, le classicisme. De même voit-on des contrastes tranchés entre *Moyen Age* et *Renaissance*. Montaigne, pourtant, est un exemple d'écrivain qui a pour le *Moyen Age* beaucoup d'estime, [24] ce qui ne l'empêche pas d'admirer aussi et surtout —il est vrai— Lucrèce, Horace, Virgile, Ovide, et tous les écrivains latins que, sauf, en particulier, Lucrèce et Tacite, [25] le *Moyen Age* avait pratiqués et dont il était pénétré.

Si, donc, Montaigne apprécie la poésie populaire, cela peut surprendre les critiques modernes qui ont été formés par un enseignement en partie erroné, mais les contemporains de Montaigne n'ont probablement pas été surpris de son attitude. On a encore trop tendance, aujourd'hui, à voir en Rabelais et Montaigne des précurseurs de la pensée moderne. [26] Les écrivains du seizième siècle sont, plutôt, les descendants et les héritiers du *Moyen Age*, et, souvent, ils rappellent le passé, plus qu'ils n'annoncent l'avenir. Mais

---

[22] Phyllis Gracey, *Montaigne et la poésie* (Paris, 1935), p. 29.

[23] Voir ma note *BSAM*, N° 27 (1963), 50-52, et celles que j'ai publiées ailleurs: "Rappels d'une chanson populaire faits par Marot et par Ronsard," *BFIF*, XXI, 3ᵉ sér., N° 4 (octobre-décembre 1956), pp. 109-110, et "Ronsard et la poésie populaire," *BFIF*, XXII, 3ᵉ sér., N° 8 (octobre-décembre 1959), page 230.

[24] Parmi les sources des *Essais,* on relève Joinville et Froissard que Montaigne cite plusieurs fois (voir Pierre Villey, *Les sources et l'évolution des Essais de Montaigne,* 2ᵉ éd. [Paris, 1933], I, 145-147, 167-168, 281.

[25] Voir John Edwin Sandys, *A History of Classical Scholarship*, 3ᵉ éd. (Cambridge, 1921), t. I, et Simone Fraisse, *L'influence de Lucrèce en France au XVIᵉ siècle* (Paris, 1962).

[26] Voir ma note: "Thélème," *Annali dell Istituto Universario Orientale,* VIII, 2 (Juillet 1966), 257-259.

ce qui est intéressant à signaler, c'est que Montaigne semble être le premier à avoir distingué ce que les romantiques allemands ont appelé *Natur- und Kunstpoesie,* quand il a dit:

> La poësie populere et purement naturelle a des naïfvetez et graces par ou elle se compare a la principale beaute de la poësie parfaicte selon l'art [...]. [27]

C'est ce passage qu'a traduit Herder:

> Die Volkspoesie, ganz Natur, wie sie ist, hat Naivetäten und Reize, durch die sie sich der Hauptschönheit der kunstlichvollkommensten Poesie gleichet. [28]

En conculsion, je dirai qui'l y a eu un *humanisme* du *Moyen Age,* [29] comme il y a eu un *humanisme* du seizième siècle: ce sont, d'ailleurs, les mêmes auteurs, Virgile, Ovide, en particulier, qui eurent la plus grande influence au Moyen Age comme au seizième siècle.

Je dirai ensuite qu'il n'y a pas d'opposition radicale entre l'*humanisme* —en entendant ce terme comme s'appliquant au culte de la littérature antique— et la tradition médiévale et populaire.

---

[27] *Essais,* éd. Armaingaud, II, 479, comme nous l'avons déjà dit. Voir Benedetto Croce, *Poesia popolare e poesia d'arte,* 2ᵉ éd. (Bari, 1946), p. 22.

[28] *Herders Werke,* éd. H. Meyer (Stuttgart), I², 3.

[29] Voir Étienne Gilson, *Héloïse et Abélard,* 3ᵉ éd. (Paris, 1964): "La leçon des faits," pp. 147-168. Voir aussi Roland Mousnier, *Leçons sur l'humanisme et la Renaissance de la fin du XVᵉ siècle au milieu du XVIᵉ* (Paris: CDU, 1966), et Thérèse Goyet, *L'Humanisme de Bossuet. I. Le goût de Bossuet* (Paris, 1965), p. 130, n. 156, cite l'abbé Claude Fleury qui, en 1686, définissait le terme *humaniste*: "Les *humanistes* [...] méprisaient le commun des docteurs [...]. Les docteurs de leur côté, je dis les théologiens et les canonistes, regardaient ces nouveaux savants comme des grammairiens et des poètes qui s'amusaient à des jeux d'enfants et à de vaines curiosités." C'est presque en termes pareils que Montaigne opposait les humanistes et les théologiens. Relevons, en outre, le premier emploi en français du terme *humaniste,* comme s'appliquant aux érudits qui s'occupaient des langues et des littératures grecques et romaines: c'est Th. Gerold qui, rendant compte, dans la *Revue critique d'Histoire et de Littérature,* N° 36 — 5 sept. 1874 (huitième année), p. 156, de l'ouvrage suivant: *Johann von Wiclif und die Vorgeschichte der Reformation* von Gothard Lechler, 2 vol. (Leipzig, 1873), a traduit le mot allemand *Humanismus* (forgé en 1808, par Niethammer), par le mot français *humanisme.* Ce mot s'était employé, en 1765, avec le sens d'amour des hommes en général.

Ce qui est, pourtant, nouveau au seizième siècle, c'est une tendance plus marquée vers la dissociation qui se produit entre la littérature savante et la littérature populaire. Je vois, là, une marque de la séparation qui tend à devenir plus nette entre les classes sociales: à partir du XVIe siècle —et jusqu'à la fin du XVIIIe siècle— la littérature et l'art, deviennent, en France, de plus en plus aristocratique ou, plutôt, ils s'adressent de plus en plus à un public oligarchique et ploutocratique que favorise le pouvoir grandissant de la bourgeoisie. [30]

---

[30] J'aimerais ajouter les références suivantes: Giuseppe Cocchiara, *Storia del folklore in Europa* (Turin: Einaudi, 1952). — Grace Norton, *Studies in Montaigne* (New York, 1904), pp. 205-206: "Ampère has remarked that the phrase 'la poésie populaire' is used by Montaigne for the first time in French letters." — Bertram Barnes, *Goethe's knowledge of French Literature* (Oxford, 1937), pp. 32-33. — Marianne Bockelkamp, "Montaigne et Goethe en Italie," *BSAM*, 4e sér., N° 12 (1967), 25-36. — G. Feugère, *Erasme* (Paris, 1874), emploie le terme *humanisme*. — M. Françon, "Humanisme," *RenQ*, 21, 1968, 300-303.

PRELIMINARIES TO A STUDY OF GALLICISMS IN OLD SPANISH

By Steven Hess
University of Pittsburgh

Linguists have long remarked that loan-words mirror the imprint that one culture makes upon another. Edward Sapir postulated that although the nature and extent of the borrowing depend entirely on the historical facts of cultural relation, the psychological attitude of the borrowing language itself has much to do with its receptivity to foreign words. Thus, he explained, in the case of German, vast numbers of French and Latin words, borrowed at the height of certain cultural influences, could not maintain themselves in the language.[1] Less psychologically oriented, but writing almost simultaneously, Otto Jespersen insisted that the most thoroughgoing speech mixtures were due, not to racial mixture, but to continued cultural contact, especially of a literary nature, as in the case of Anglo-Saxon and Norman French.[2] The influence of Gallo-Romance, i.e. the Old French and Old Provençal literary languages, on early Spanish may well illustrate the ideas of both illustrious pioneers, without invalidating either. The borrowings clearly resulted from prolonged cultural contact, but the subsequent loss of many of the early Gallicisms remains to be explained.

The only comprehensive study of Gallicisms in Old Spanish, undertaken more than a half-century ago by John B. De Forest,[3]

---

[1] *Language. An Introduction to the Study of Speech* (New York, 1921), pp. 194-195.
[2] *Language. Its Nature, Development, and Origin* (London, 1922), p. 210.
[3] "Old French Borrowed Words in the Old Spanish of the Twelfth and Thirteenth Centuries, with Special Reference to the *Cid*, Berceo's Poems,

endeavored to isolate only borrowings from Old French, attempting with varying success to exclude possible loans traceable to Old Provençal. In the specific area of morphemic borrowing, Anita Katz Levy has carefully analyzed the fate of the "suffixoids" -*el* (-*er*) and -*aje* in the Iberian Peninsula, providing an exhaustive bibliographic apparatus, but only the first part of her fine-grained analysis has yet appeared in print.[4] The interaction of cultural and linguistic factors in the transmission of Gallicisms to medieval Spanish remains to be studied. The present work will attempt to place the lexical evidence in its historical context and to outline certain principles of methodology which may be used in the identification and analysis of this specific family of loan-words.

The historical explanation for the presence of ultra-Pyrenean borrowings in early Spanish texts encompasses the main trends of the medieval history of Western Europe. Well known in Romance literatures is the first of these Gallo- (perhaps, more accurately Franko-) Iberian contacts, the defeat of Roland at Roncesvalles in 778, after which epic disaster the emperor Charlemagne began a systematic conquest of northeastern Spain. Toward the end of his reign, his sons established as a dependency of the Frankish empire the *Marca Hispanica,* a territory which would later become the kingdom of Navarre, northern Aragon, and the county of Barcelona.[5] Some two centuries later, the Count of Barcelona, Borel, became a vassal of Hugh Capet in 987, in exchange for assistance in his struggle against the Muslims. However, for the present study, the continuing close relation between France and Catalonia is not of primary consideration, since it is the medieval Spanish language,

---

the *Alexandre,* and *Fernán González," Romanic Review,* VII (1916), 369-413. See the unsigned review, frequently ascribed to Américo Castro, in *Revista de Filología Española,* VI (1919), 329-331. The doctoral dissertation of Rudolf Soellner, "Die galloromanischen Lehnwörter im Altspanischen von der Entstehung der Sprache bis 1500," (Munich, 1949), is a monograph of some 194 pages whose contents does not support its ambitious title.

[4] "Contrastive Development in Hispano-Romance of Borrowed Gallo-Romance Suffixes," *Romance Philology,* XVIII (1964-65), 399-429.

[5] Stewart C. Easton and Helene Wieruszowski, *The Era of Charlemagne: Frankish State and Society* (Princeton, 1961), pp. 38-39.

not Catalan, which is under scrutiny here.[6] Aside from direct military intervention, the Cluniac reform was the major source of Gallic influence in Iberia. Alphonse VI of Castile, the king who plays a capital role in the *Poem of the Cid*, asked the abbot Hugh of Cluny to send some of his monks to reform the Castilian monasteries. One of them, Robert, became abbot of Sahagún, and his successor, Bernard de Sédirac was chosen the first Archbishop of Toledo when the city was wrested from Muslim control in 1085. Named Primate of Spain (1088) by Pope Urban II, he entrusted many ecclesiastical offices to his fellow Aquitanian immigrants. Another compatriot, Raymond, Bishop of Osma, who succeeded Bernard as Primate (1124-1151), became the patron of the *escuela de traductores* at Toledo.[7]

Another wave of trans-Pyrenean immigration, of a more transient nature, came in the persons of multitudes of devout pilgrims who undertook the journey to Santiago de Compostela to venerate the relics of St. James the Apostle. The most dedicated of these travelers was the most powerful feudal lord of Southern France, William X of Aquitaine, who ended his days in the habit of a pilgrim. Perhaps the most famous of all was Louis VII, who likewise followed the path leading to distant Galicia, now called the *camino francés,* in honor of its early Gallic itinerants. Gallo-Romanic loan-words which mirror these extensive peregrinations are found in Spain's earliest known poet, Gonzalo de Berceo, who

---

[6] Joan Corominas, in his monumental *Diccionario crítico etimológico de la lengua castellana* (*DCELC*) (Madrid, 1954-57), has a decidedly Catalan slant in its treatment of possible loan-words from Gallo-Romance. Without entering into the forty year-old controversy as to whether Catalan is essentially a Gallo- or Ibero- Romance language, suffice it to state that Corominas has exaggerated the role of Catalan in the transmission of loan-words into Spanish, so far as the early period (twelfth and thirteenth centuries) is concerned. The fact the troubadours from Catalonia used the *lemosí* standard rather than their native vernacular shows that medieval Catalan was long subject to the influence of its more prestigious contiguous sister, Provençal. To label a loan a "Catalanism" at this period, one would have to give convincing phonological and historical reasons for excluding Old Provençal as a possibility in any given case.

[7] Marcellin Defourneaux, *Les Français en Espagne aux XIIe et XIIIe siècles* (Paris, 1949), pp. 23-35; 113-114; 157-158. This work is a most comprehensive history of the French intervention, covering political and ecclesiastical, as well as cultural contacts.

lived in La Rioja, quite close to the *camino*. In his works, all religious and primarily hagiographic, one finds the borrowings *añel* 'lamb' (Sp. *cordero*), *fraire* 'brother' (Sp. *hermano*), and *domage* 'pity, damage' (Sp. *daño*). (The first two of these will be analyzed closely later to illustrate how Gallicisms are identified.)

Dynastic marriage and compelling alliances fostered cooperation between French and Spanish crusaders. Alphonse VI married Constance of Burgandy, the niece of Robert the Pious. Their daughter Urraca (an early rival of El Cid) and her half-sisters Teresa and Elvira were wedded to French barons. His successor Alphonse VII, attempting to reconquer Saragossa, received immeasurable assistance from a papal proclamation of a Crusade; the French heeded the call and triumphed as a separate army under Gaston of Béarn, who received the title *señor de Zaragoza* from Alphonse for his services. French military intervention ended with the decisive campaign of Las Navas de Tolosa (1212), when the united Spanish Christian armies achieved victory without foreign reinforcement. Resulting loan-words referring to chivalry and warfare are numerous; the following appear in the first monument of Spanish literature, the *Poem of the Cid*: *barnax* (OF. *barnage, bernage*) 'prowess, noble need', *batalla* (OProv. *batalha*) 'battle', *bloca* (OF. *bocle*; OProv. *bocla*, *bloca*) 'buckle (found in the center of a shield)' *brial* (OProv. *blialt*) 'tunic' *espolon* (OProv. *esporon* < Frankish *SPORO) 'spur', *fardido* (OF. *hardi* < Frankish *HARDJAN 'to harden') 'intrepid', *omenaje* (OProv. *omenatge*) 'homage' *prez* (OProv. *pretz*) 'worth, honor', *palafre* (OF. *palefrei*, OProv. *palafre(n)*) 'palfrey' and *derranchar* (OF. *desrengier*) 'to break rank'. In other semantic areas, the *Poem* has *cascavel* (OProv. *cascavel*) 'bell', *cuita* (a derivative of *cuitar* < OProv. *coitar*, *cochar*) 'trouble, worry', *cosiment* (OProv. *causiment*) 'favor; discretion', *deleite* (OProv. *deleite*) 'delight, pleasure', *derrocar* (OProv. *derrocar*) 'to throw down', *enplear* (OF. *empleiier*; OProv. *emplegar*, *empleiar*) 'to use, employ' *esquila* (OProv. *esquila* < Gothic *SKILLA (German *Schelle*)) 'bell', *follon* (OProv. *felon, felhon*; OF. *fel, felon*) 'traitor, coward, braggart' *fonta* (OF. *honte*) 'shame', *mensaje* (OProv. *messatge*, OF. *message*) 'message, messenger', *sobregonel* (OProv. *gonel*) '(kind of) tunic' *solaz* (OProv. *solatz*) 'pleasure', *tacha* (OF. *tache*) 'fault, defect', *usaje* (OProv. *usatge*, OF. *usage*) 'custom', *vergel* (OProv. *vergier*) 'meadow, garden', and *vianda* (OF. *viande*) 'food, provisions'. Possible loans from Gallo-Romance, often attributed to "Vulgar Latin," are *blanco* 'white', *franco* 'free', both of Germanic origin, and *rebtar* (Latin REPUTARE) 'to accuse, challenge' and *pleito* (Low Latin PLACITUM) 'decree; argument', both legal terms which are either Gallicisms or semi-learned adaptations of Merovingian Latin legal terminology. [8]

The influence of the Provençal troubadours in Spain was first studied by the eminent nineteenth century literary historian, Manuel Milá y Fontanals (*De los trovadores en España*, Barcelona, 1861). The first troubadour definitely known to have visited Spain is Marcabru. His crusade song, "Pax in nomine Domine" was a futile attempt to encourage his compatriots to join the Crusade against the Almoravids in 1137. Visiting the court of Alphonse VII, he admired the qualities of the young emperor in his eulogistic poem "Empeeraire, per mi mezeis / sai quant vostra proeza creis." [9] The marriage of Alphonse VIII to Leonore, sister of Richard the Lion Hearted, made the Castilian court a haven for wandering minstrels. Ramon Vidal de Besalu witnessed a program of troubadour entertainment in which an unknown poet achieved instant success in the court: "Unas novas vos vuelh comtar / que auzi dir a un joglar." [10] The court at Toledo received warm praise from another one of its honored guests, Peire Vidal: "Mout es bona terra Espanha / E'l rei que senhor en so." [11] The legacy of the Provençal lyric is evident in the typically troubadour terminology found in the corpus of early Gallicisms. The names of musical instruments (although ultimately of Germanic origin) *giga* and *rota* are clearly imported from Provence. The tradition of the courtly love song carried concepts such as *cosiment, cuita, gento, losenja, sen,* and *solaz* beyond the Pyre-

---

[8] For an analysis of some 150 early loan-words, with extensive textual citation, one may consult the author's unpublished dissertation, "Gallicisms in Old Spanish of the Twelfth and Thirteenth Centuries," (Harvard University, 1966).

[9] For the poems, see J. M. L. Dejeanne, *Poésies complètes du troubadour Marcabru*, Toulouse, 1909. (*Bibliothèque Méridionale, 1re série, tome 12*). Ramon Guthrie constructs his biography in *Marcabrun*, New York, 1926.

[10] Ramón Menéndez Pidal, *Poesía juglaresca y orígenes de las literaturas románicas*, 6th ed. (Madrid, 1957), p. 211.

[11] J. Anglade, *Les poésies de Peire Vidal* (= *Classiques français du Moyen Age*, no. 11) 2nd ed., Paris, 1923.

nees, clearly echoing the most common *topoi* of the troubadours. This influence began to wane almost simultaneously with the end of French military participation in the Spanish crusades; the suppression of the Albigensian heresy, ordered by Pope Innocent III early in the thirteenth century, concomitantly destroyed the political and cultural autonomy of Southern France, reducing the prestigious literary *lemosí* to a local patois.

Turning to the strictly linguistic aspect of this survey, the first task is to define the criteria by which loan-words or borrowings (*Lehnwörter, emprunts, préstamos*) are distinguished from "native" words (*Erbwörter, mots populaires, palabras auctóctonas*). For the Romance languages the task is simplified by the documentation of an extensive corpus in the parent language, Latin. However, the spoken form of the latter, somewhat at variance with what the written records reveal, must be partially reconstructed through a comparative study of the off-shoots ("reflexes") in the successor vernaculars of the Romance-speaking territory. This proto-language, most traditionally and still most frequently designated "Vulgar Latin," provides the etyma of a majority of the vocabulary in each of the Romance languages. The phonological development of these words seems to follow definite patterns, which were once called sound-laws (*Lautgesetze, lois phonétiques, leyes fonéticas*), but are perhaps better named phonological correspondences.[12] Words which follow these patterns are considered "native", while others of Vulgar Latin origin which have not undergone some or all of these developments are either (1) later adaptations from Late or Medieval Latin (often called "learned" or "semi-learned", according to the degree of deviation from the attested Latin) or (2) adaptations from other Romance vernaculars. The latter group may be called "inter-Romance loans," since a Vulgar Latin etymon is attested but does not follow the patterns of phonetic correspondence typical of the borrowing lan-

---

[12] A succinct clarification is given in the most recent authoritative manual on Romance linguistics: "Hay 'leyes fonéticas' no ciertamente en el sentido de series de fenómenos de validez universal (para todas las lenguas) y previamente calculables conformes a leyes naturales, sino en el sentido de complejos de fenómenos comprobables a posteriori y que dentro de una lengua acusan una sorprendente analogía." In Heinrich Lausberg, *Lingüística románica* (I *Fonética*) (Madrid [1965]), p. 171.

guage, but the pattern which typifies another Romance vernacular ("sister-language"), which is the lender. In a completely separate category are those words which do not have Latin etyma, such as the vast Arabic lexicon in Old Spanish; these Arabisms are *by definition* loan-words, since by historical circumstance they cannot be descendants of Vulgar Latin.

In this study GALLICISMS mean loan words from Old French and Old Provençal [13] which appear in Old Spanish texts. The term OLD SPANISH refers to the language of the early texts used for documentation, and is neither synonymous nor co-extensive with Old Castilian. However, in nearly all the principal texts of the twelfth and thirteenth centuries, Castilian forms already are predominant. [14] Recalling the examples of ultra-Pyrenean influence in the medieval Spanish lexicon which were adduced in the historical part of this survey, let us examine the linguistic criteria which prove their Gallo-Romanic provenance.

The first item mentioned was *añel* 'lamb,' found in Gonzalo de Berceo. [15] The item is not recorded by Corominas in his DCELC. The source is Lat. AGNĔLLUS, a diminutive of AGNUS 'lamb,' whose Romance reflexes include OF. *agnel* (Mod. Fr. *agneau*), OProv. *anhel*, Cat. *anyel* and Ital. *agnello*, which all mean 'lamb' in the most general sense. In Iberia, however, the same animal is designated by Sp. *cordero*, Port. *cordeiro*, reflexes of a hypothetical noun *CORDARIUS, postulated by Latin CORDUS 'late-born,' used

---

[13] Words of Old Provençal origin are often studied separately. De Forest thought he had excluded them from his compilation of early Gallicisms, but many of the items were incorrectly or inconclusively ascribed to Northern French. The most recent treatment is by G[ermán] Colón Doménech, "Occitanismos," *Enciclopedia Lingüística Hispánica* (= *ELH*) II (Madrid, 1967), pp. 153-192, but the author warns that the survey, rather hastily prepared, must not be considered more than a tentative assessment. In the same volume, B[ernard] Pottier has examined "Galicismos" (pp. 121-151), modern as well as medieval, but offers neither etymologies nor textual citations.

[14] "El hecho de que los copistas no generalizasen el dialectalismo muestra cómo la recitación de poemas épicos, ya secular entonces, había afirmado el predominio del castellano sobre sus vecinos laterales, que desde el primer momento evitan manifestarse en la literatura." Rafael Lapesa, *Historia de la lengua española*, 4th ed. (Madrid, 1959), pp. 145-146.

[15] "assado lo comiessen, non cocho el annel/ celebrassen su pascua pueblo de Israel" *El sacrificio de la misa* (149b), ed. Antonio G. Solalinde, Madrid, 1913.

in the expression AGNUS CORDUS, found in Varro and Pliny.[16] OSp. *añel* must be a Gallicism because of the development of the suffix -ĔLLU > *él* (cf. native results: CASTĔLLU > *castillo*, ROTĔLLA > *rodilla*). In general, accented short *ĕ* of Latin (or open *ę* of Vulgar Latin) diphthongizes to *ié* in Old Spanish; before a palatal consonant, the *ié* is reduced to *i* in Modern Spanish (cf. SĔLLA > *siella* > *silla*);[17] Berceo's *añel* does not show the result of this dipthongization that one would expect in Old Spanish, but follows the Gallo-Romanic phonological pattern which retains the open *ę* of Vulgar Latin in a syllable ending in a consonant ("closed syllable"). Thus, OSp. *añel* is a borrowing of OF. *agnel* or OProv. *anhel*, and since both Gallo-Romanic congeners represent [añél] one cannot distinguish which one is the immediate source. In addition, the semantic context of the Spanish example is literary, specifically Biblical; the infrequent occurrence of OSp. *añel*, as well as its subsequent disappearance is characteristic of a borrowing.[18]

The second item under consideration is *fraire*, 'brother, friar,' first attested in a document of 1174,[19] and later throughout the works of Berceo. The etymon is Lat. FRATER, FRATRE(M), whose reflexes include Fr. *frère*, OProv. *fraire*, OItal. *fratre*, *frate* (with a religious connotation only, in contrast to *fratello* 'male sibling')[20] The popular OSp. *fradre* (cf. *padre* < PATRE(M)) is also found in Berceo.[21] The lender is OProv. *fraire*, where the evolution -TR- > -*ir*- is regular (*peira* < PĔTRA). In Spanish, the borrowing referred exclusively to an ecclesiastical function; the idea 'brother' = 'male sibling' was probably always *hermano* < GERMANŬ, an adjective remaining from the binominal expression

---

[16] W. D. Elcock, *The Romance Languages* (London, [1960]), p. 164.

[17] R. Menéndez Pidal, *Manual de gramática histórica española*, 10th ed. (Madrid, 1958), § 10.2.

[18] Only one other example is found in the early period, in the *P* MS. of the *Libro de Alexandre* (ed. Raymon S. Willis, Jr., Princeton and Paris, 1934): "el tau e las puertas de sangne del aynel/ las plagas de Egibto el angel cruel (1222d).

[19] R. Menéndez Pidal, *Documentos lingüísticos de España, I, Reino de Castilia* (Madrid, 1919). Document 13, line 8 (Aguilar del Campó, 1174).

[20] Carlo Battisti and Giovanni Alessio, *Dizionario etimologico italiano*, III (Firenze, 1952), pp. 1709b, 1710b.

[21] "Si los otros sos fradres lo quisiessen soffrir" *Vida de Santo Domingo de Silos*, ed. John D. Fitzgerald, (Paris, 1904), line 91a.

FRATER GERMANUS, 'full- (as opposed to half-) brother'. Thus, the typically OProv. -ai- provides indisputable phonological evidence for the source of OSp. *fraire*, to the exclusion of OF. *frere*. The importation of the term may be safely ascribed to the reformers from Cluny.

Exhibiting a different type of Gallo-Romanic phonology is the troubadour concept *solaz*, found as early as the *Poem of the Cid*.[22] The etymon is Lat. SOLACIŬ 'consolation,' a noun formed on the verb SOLARI 'to comfort.' (*DCELC*, IV, 257). OSp. *solaz* [soláts] is borrowed from OProv. *solatz*. Meyer-Lübke (REW[3] § 8060) considered. Ital. *solazzo*, Cat. *solas*, and Sp., Port. *solaz* as borrowings from Old Provençal, but listed OF. *solaz* as an independent, rather than borrowed, congener. However, OFr. *solaz* is actually also a loan-word, because Lat. *o* in countertonic position (ie. as the vowel of the initial syllable in a polysyllabic word) regularly develops to *ou* (sometimes found as *u* in the texts) very early in the Old French period, cf. OF. *mourir, murir* < V. L. *MORIRE (Classical Latin MORIRI); thus the normal development would have been *soulaz*.[23] In addition OSp. *solaz* must be a loan because of the evolution of the suffix — ACIŬ > — *az*, where -*azo* would be expected; the loss of final unaccented -*o* < Lat. -*ŭ* is often a clue to Gallo-Romance origin. Another borrowing, also from the troubadour vocabulary, which follows the same foreign pattern is OSp. *prez*, from OProv. *pretz* < Lat. PRĔTIŬ 'price.' Here, in addition to the Gallo-Romanic "suffixoid," the non-dipthongization of accented *ĕ* likewise points to a Gallicism.[24] A native congener *priezo* is wanting in Spanish; only the semilearned *precio* is attested in addition to the borrowed *prez*. The phonological evidence rules out OF. *pris* (Mod. Fr. *prix*) as a possible source, clearly pointing once again to Old Provençal. The task of identification of loan-words if often alleviated, as in the cases of *solaz* and *prez*, by the presence of more

---

[22] "vere a la mugier a todo mio solaz," ed. R. Menéndez Pidal (Madrid, 1913), line 288b.

[23] The loan-word *solas*, later *solace*, in Middle English is concrete evidence that countertonic vowel of OF. *solaz* was still [o] in the twelfth century.

[24] Accented open *ę* diphthongizes to *ié* in Spanish, even before the "first class of *yod*," i.e. [-tj̣-] or [-kj̣-]. Cf. Menéndez Pidal, *Manual*, § 10.3 and 53.4.

than one Gallo-Romanic phonological development in the same word.

Although comparative phonology perhaps offers the most salient clues, some loan-words reflect morphological patterns as well which are foreign to Ibero-Romance. The most frequent is the suffix *-aje* < —ATĬCŬ, whose native counterpart is *-adgo,* > *-azgo* in Castilian, and *-algo* in Leonese. (e.g. *portazgo, hallazgo.*) In the *Cid* alone one finds *mensaje, omenaje,* and *usaje.* Elsewhere, not really a suffix (i.e. an independent morpheme), but perhaps better labeled, as Yakov Malkiel suggests, "suffixoid," *-er, -el* < -ARĬŬ are typically Gallo-Romanic in opposition to the native Sp. *-ero,* Port. *-eiro.* Again, returning to the *Cid,* one finds the very first occurrence of this type, *vergel.*[25] The source is OProv. *vergier* < V. L. *UĬRĬDĬARĬŬ 'grove,' presumed to have replaced the Classical Latin UĬRĬDARŬM 'grove' (*DCELC,* IV, 708). In addition to the final *-el,* (resulting from a dissimilation *verger* > *vergel*) ther are other clues to Gallo-Romance origin: the development of cons.DĬ- to *-g-* [dž], in contrast to the native *-ç-* [ts]. One may compare the reflexes of Lat. HŎRDĔ(ŎL)ŬM 'barley': OSp. *orçuelo,* OF. *orge,* OProv. *ordi.* The source of OSp. *vergel* may be either Old French or Old Provençal.[26] However, the importance of this concept as a *locus amoenous* in the troubadour lyric may favor Provence as the immediate source. Ony may postulate that the native Spanish reflex of *UIRIDIARIU would have been *berçero,* on the basis that Lat. UĬRĬDĬA > OSp. *berça* (Mod. Sp. *berza*) 'cabbage.'

In another morphological category are the relatively few borrowings which relect the survival of the nominative case of Latin, which flourished in Gallo-Romance at least until the fourteenth century, but is rarely attested even in the earliest vernacular documents of the Peninsula. OSp. *chantre*[27] 'choir-master' reproduces OF. *chantre,* the reflex of the Latin nominative CANTOR, whose accusative CANTORE(M) gave the "oblique" *chanteur,* the form

---

[25] "Fallaron un vergel con una limpia fuont," ed. cit., line 2700.

[26] OProv. *-ier* as a suffix may even have been borrowed from *langue d'oïl.* The "native" *langue d'oc* result of -ARIU seems to have been *-eir*; thus, the variants *premier—premeir,* See Lausberg, *Lingüística románica,* p. 259.

[27] "tenie el logar de chantre e leuantaua el coro," *Primera Crónica General,* ed. R. Menéndez Pidal (Madrid, 1906), p. 490a25.

which has survived in modern times. Wartburg (*FEW*, II, 236) notes that CANTOR 'singer' retained only a religious denotation 'choirmaster' in the Romance languages, and that the reflexes show a regular phonological evolution only in Gallo-Romance and Ital. *cantore*, while Sp., Port. *chantre* are Gallicisms. However, he does not consider Sp. *cantor*, whose accentuation [kantór] shows it to be a popular descendant of the Latin [kantóre], and cannot reflect the nominative [kántor], unless one were inclined to consider *cantor* a learned word borrowed directly from Latin with a shift in accent. One is attracted more by the first hypothesis, since the magistral *FEW*, only tangentially concerned with Ibero-Romance and often negligent in its coverage in that area, does not record Sp. *cantor* at all. Phonologically OSp. *chantre* points clearly to Northern French, given the evolution CAN- > *chant-* in a closed syllable (V. L. CANTARE > OF. *chanter*, OProv. *cantar*; Lat. CANE(M) > OF. *chien*, OProv. *can*, in an open syllable). Thus, *cantor* and *chantre* are doublets in Spanish, the latter a loan-word from northern France. OSp. *chantre* also indicates that although ecclesiastical terms probably arrived in Spain with the Cluny monks, the loans themselves may be of either Northern or Southern French origin.

Thus far we have examined some of the criteria for identifying loan-words which have an ultimately Classical Latin origin. Much more complex is the identification of Gallicisms which descend from the Germanic superstratum which overlay the Latin base of the medieval Romance vernaculars. Germanicisms may have arrived in the Peninsula in any of three successive waves of diffusion: (1) those belonging to Vulgar Latin, and thus developing according to the same phonological patterns as other Latin etyma; (2) adaptations from the Germanic tongues brought to Spain by the Suevi, Vandals, or, most significantly, the Visigoths; (3) borrowings from Frankish, romanicized in Old French or Old Provençal, and consequently classified as Gallicisms. The pioneering thesis of Josef Brüch (*Der Einfluss der germanischen Sprachen auf das Vulgärlatein*, Heidelberg, 1913), that approximately one hundred Germanicisms were already present in Vulgar Latin before 400 A. D., has been rejected by almost all subsequent researchers. The presence of so many loan-words in spoken Latin before the fifth century, when the Eastern and Western Empire became definitively separated, would have to be confirmed by the reflexes of those early borrowings in Eastern Romance (Rumanian), as well as in Western Romance. Challenging Brüch's postulation, Eugen Lerch demonstrated that Rumanian does not share any early Germanic loan-words with the West.[28] Gerhard Rohlfs went even further, asserting that many of the so-called Germanicisms of Vulgar Latin were actually of Frankish origin, and spread beyond the Gallo-Romance territory either through Old French or the medieval Latin of the Merovingian period[29] (sometimes designated "Gallican Low Latin").

In order to be considered an "Iberian" rather than "Gallican" Germanicism, a borrowing must be traceable to the tribes which invaded the Peninsula, the most important of which, both historically and linguistically, was the Visigoths. Even if a word is traeceable to Gothic rather than Frankish, the proof is not really definitive, according to the outstanding expert on the Germanic superstratum in Romance, Ernst Gamillscheg.[30] He states that it is difficult to distinguish accurately between Frankish loans, romanicized in the North of France, and those which came into Spain from the Visigothic kingdom, which first based in Toulouse, later expanded southward toward Toledo. The loans of Frankish origin, latinized before 600 A. D., and later borrowed by Spanish show the same phonological development as words of Latin ancestry. On the other hand, later Frankish loans, borrowed through the intermediary of Gallo-Romance vernaculars, show traces of the phonology of the language in which they were romanicized.

An exemplary case of a Germanic loan transmitted to Iberia via Gallo-Romance is OSp. *fonta*, 'insult, offense,' found in the *Cid*.[31] The source is OF. *honte*, whose etymon is a hypothetical Frankish *HAUNITHA, reconstructed on the basis of Old High German *honida*, Middle Dutch *hoonde*, and is first attested latinized in the

---

[28] "Germanische Wörter im Vulgärlatein?" *Romanische Forschungen*, LX (1947), 247-284.

[29] "Frankische und franko-romanische Wanderwörter in der Romania," *Festgabe Ernst Gamillscheg* (Tübingen, 1952), pp. 111-128.

[30] Gamillscheg's latest synthesis partially modifies many of his earlier observations in regard to Ibero-Romance. See "Germanismos," *ELH* II, pp. 79-91.

[31] "porque dan parias plaze a los de Saragoça/ de Mio Çid que non temien ninguna fonta," ed. cit., lines 941-942.

Reichenau Glossary as *haunta*. (*FEW*, XVI, 183.) There is another reflex in Gallo-Romance, OProv. *anta* (< **aunta*, with a reduction of the diphthong before a nasal consonant), but it is less frequent than *onta*, a loan from Northern French.[32] The phonological indication of the *langue d'oïl* origin of OSp. *fonta* is the orthographical initial *f-* (representing [f] ∿ [h] in early medieval Spanish, when there was vacilation in the evolution of the aspirate from the fricative). Old French is the only Romance language to retain the initial aspirate of Germanic; thus the early borrowing HĔLMŬ 'helmet' yields OF. *helme* (Mod. Fr. *heaume*, where the aspiration has disappeared, but its history is indication by the failure to elide with the definite article, i.e., *le heaume*), in contrast to Sp. *yelmo*, Ital. *elmo*. In the adaptation of OF. *honte* [hõntə] as OSp. *fonta* (hónta), there has been a change in the final unaccented vowel: OF. *-e* appears as OSp. *-a*. This adjustment is typical of feminine nouns of Northern French origin: *colche* > *colcha*; *dame* > *dama*; *tache* > *tacha*. The adaptation is probably morpho-syntactic as well as phonetic: (1) OF. *-e* was [ə], thus just as similar (or dissimilar) to OSp. *-e* [e] as to OSp. *-a* [a]. (2) the borrowings were all feminine nouns and were adopted into Spanish as feminines; since the most frequent marker of feminines is *-a* in Spanish, the process of analogical formation aided the phonetic possibilities. Thus, OF. *la honte* [lahõntə] became OSp. *la fonta* [lahónta]. In addition, it is precisely at the time of this extensive ultra-Pyrenean cultural and linguistic influence that Old Spanish shows the loss of final *-e*, even after consonantal clusters (in the *Cid*, *nuef*, *noch*, *art*, for earlier and later *nueve*, *noche*, *arte*). This tendency toward *apócope extrema* continued until the triumph of the anti-Gallicist reaction under Alphonse X in the second half of the thirteenth century.[33] Therefore, the phoneme /e/ was unstable, if not entirely expendable, in word-final position when many of the Old French feminines with their characteristic final *-e* were borrowed. In addition, the analogical tendency to substitute final *-a* in Old Spanish, thus preserving the morphological pattern

---

[32] Joseph Anglade, *Grammaire de l'ancien provençal* (Paris, 1921), p. 92.

[33] For the historical and linguistic contexts of the loss and subsequent restoration of final *-e* in Old Spanish, see Rafael Lapesa, "La apócope de la vocal en castellano antiguo. Intento de explicación histórica," *Estudios dedicados a Menéndez Pidal*, II (Madrid, 1951), pp. 185-226.

of the majority of feminine nouns, plus the "foreignness" of OF. *-e*
[ə], in are all factors which, considered collectively and interdependently, explain the shift OF. *-e* > OSp. *-a*.

A clear-cut division between Iberian and Gallican Germanicisms in Old Spanish is exemplified by two interchangeable designations for 'spur,' *espuela* and *espolón*, both of which are attested in the *Cid*. North of the Pyrenees, both OF. *esperon* (Mod. Fr. *éperon*) and OProv. *esporon* point to a Frankish *SPORO, SPORON. Although it is unclear whether *SPORO dates from the Frankish invasion of Gaul or is an earlier borrowing, on purely linguistic grounds, it is certain that the Franks brought the spur to Gaul, and so the material evidence points to a Frankish loan-word.[34] OSp. *espolon* indicates OProv. *esporon*, while the synonym *espuela* reflects a Gothic *SPAURA (in Gothic *au*=ǫ). Both the Frankish and Gothic hypothetical etyma are postulated on the basis of their attested congeners: Old High German *sporo* (Ger. *Sporn*), Anglo-Saxon *spura, spora*. The vitality of the Gothic, rather than Frankish, source on the Penininsula is confirmed by Port. *spora*. Thus, only *espolon* is considered a Gallicism, while *espuela* is a "native" (i.e. *in situ*) adaptation. OF. *esperon* may be ruled out on phonological grounds as a source of the Spanish loan, but it does appear elsewhere in Romania as Ital. *sperone*. Of related interest is the change of intervocalic *-r-* > *-l-* in the Old Spanish borrowing; although more frequent in "implosive" (end of syllable) position, this alternation is not unknown in intervocalic position as well, cf. *andolina*⌢*andorina, voltereta*⌢*volteleta*.[35] From the example of *espolón*, it is evident that Frankish origin does not necessarily require that a loan word be borrowed from Northern French, as De Forest believed. Here *espolon* is obviously modeled on OProv. *espolon*, rather than on OF. *esperon*. However, in other cases, phonological identity makes it difficult, if not impossible to choose between Old French and Old Provençal as the immediate source of transmission. OSp. *estoque* 'dagger,' first found in Spanish in the description of the assassination of Julius Caesar in the *Primera Crónica General*[36] may have been

---

[34] Ernst Gamillscheg, *Romania Germanica I* (Berlin and Leipzig, 1934), p. 180.

[35] Menéndez Pidal, *Manual*, § 72.3.

[36] "eran y todos venidos con sendos estoques so los mantos," ed. cit., page 96b, line 27.

borrowed from either OF. *estoc* or from the geographically more contiguous OProv. *estoc,* without excluding the possibility of a "joint transmission," since the French who came to Spain were from the North as well as the South.

Returning to the significant observations of Sapir about the nature of linguistic borrowing, it is notable that many of the examples used in this study have indeed disappeared from Spanish in modern times. Jespersen underlined the importance of literary contacts in the transmission of loan-words. In conclusion, and thus unintentionally but perhaps felicitously integrating the principles elaborated by the two pioneers, it seems probable that most of the Gallicisms which did disappear were literary borrowings, in the sense that they were adopted, possibly even aurally, for the purposes of literary creation, as Berceo's *añel*. A further study, beyond the scope of this survey, will show that the greatest number of ephemeral Gallicisms appear in the *Libro de Alexandre,* a direct imitation of the Old French *Roman d'Alexandre* and the medieval Latin *Alexandreis*. Perhaps many of these loan-words never did achieve general acceptance in the spoken language and consequently disappear in the same century of their borrowing. No doubt *fraire* was a reality to the masses, while *fonta* remained an abstraction which yielded to the more current *vergüenza*. However, the importance of Gallicisms, whether passing or permanent, cannot be neglected as evidence in any discussion of the French literary influence on Spanish. It is a relationship that Spanish literary historians themselves are reluctant to discuss; the *Diccionario de literatura española*[3] (Madrid, 1964), devotes long articles to English, German, and Italian sources for Spanish literature, but does not have one line on French! Perhaps cultural Gallophobia may yield to greater objectivity in subsequent studies of the French in Spain.

Yakov Malkiel stated a decade ago that "What little work has ben done on early Gallicisms and Provençalisms... is so inadequate as to clamor for prompt replacement."[37] The task would be greatly aided by the appearance of the long-awaited revision of the *Medieval*

---

[37] "Distinctive Features in Lexicography. A Typological Approach to Dictionaries Exemplified with Spanish" (II), *Romance Philology,* XIII (1959-60), 114-115.

Spanish Dictionary, which would at least provide a ready-made corpus, and thus avoid the time-consuming first-hand gleaning of the texts which is now required. Meanwhile, the present study has endeavored to outline the panorama of French influence in Spain as mirrored in the Gallo-Romance loan-words in Iberia and to outline a number of linguistic criteria which may aid in identifying a significant strain within the medieval Spanish lexicon.

THE MONKEY IN MEDIAEVAL LITERATURE

By Urban T. Holmes
The University of North Carolina

The people of the Renaissance and the Middle Ages were fond of wild animals. Francis the First of France had a zoo at Amboise where there were lions and tigers under the care of an Italian named Giovanni Antonio. He had also bears, civet cats, leopards, martins, boars, and some sheep from India. Sometimes when the King moved about he took the lions and tigers with him. Belon the naturalist even claims that he kept these in his bed chamber, but this is hardly likely.[1] Lions were expensive to maintain, but they were popular. Louis XII gave a lion to the city of Tours which the city authorities could not afford to keep. In the mid-thirteenth century Villard de Honnecourt sketched a lion with accuracy, remarking below his sketch that this should be good since he had drawn it from life.[2] It has been suggested by etymologists that our expression "to lionize" can be traced to the fact that town lions received much attention from curiosity seekers.

Our present concern is with monkeys. Henry III of France bought monkeys and parrots (or popinjays) at Dieppe, which came unquestionably from North Africa. He had a bad dream early in 1583 which influenced him to have these killed.[3] Henry IV also had a fondness for monkeys and often carried about with him, in his travels, four monkeys and a parrot. In the twelfth century menagerie

---

[1] Hélène Naïs, *Les animaux dans la poésie française de la Renaissance* (Paris: Didier, 1961), 145.

[2] Villard de Honnecourt, *Album de V. de H., architecte du XIIIe siècle* (Paris: Alfred Darcel, 1968).

[3] Naïs, p. 146.

animals of the exotic kind were not very plentiful. The earliest attested zoo was that of Frederic of Sicily.[4] But many gentry in France and England —probably all of them— had hawks, falcons, dogs of various kinds and, in many instances, monkeys and parrots.

The merchant ships did a brisk trade in monkeys. A Middle English document remarks: "The grete galees of Venees and Florence Be wel ladene Wyth swete wynws, all manere of chaffare (goods), Apes and japes, and marmusettes tailede."[5] But the vast majority of these monkeys were not "tayled"; they were Barbary apes which used to be very prevalent along the whole North African coast — and are found now principally in Gibraltar. Our statement here is not guesswork. The sketches of monkeys which are so frequent in marginal designs on mediaeval manuscripts were examined for us by Professor Buettner-Janisch of Duke University, who is a distinguished simiologist.[6] He identified these without hesitation as representations of the Barbary ape. This ape is about as large as a moderate-sized dog, and has no external tail at all. In captivity it is rather nervous and irritable and often bites.

Giraldus Cambrensis describes a rich procession which accompanied the English chancellor Thomas Becket in September 1158 when he went to Paris to fetch the little bride for Young King Henry. This procession was led by two hundred and fifty male servitors on foot who were singing English songs. Next came huntsmen with fine dogs on double leashes. These were followed by eight carts each drawn by five horses with a driver walking beside each cart, leading a dog. The contents of the carts were covered by leather tarpaulins; these were the furnishing of the room which the Chancellor would be occupying. Behind the carts came twelve pack animals, and on the back of each of these was a rider and a monkey. There were other fantastic things, but we will stop with these monkeys, who had been taught to ride the horses.[7]

---

[4] Gustave Loisel, *L'histoire de la Ménagerie de l'antiquité à nos jours* (Paris, 1912).

[5] See under APE in the *Middle English Dictionary* (Ann Arbor: University of Michigan Press, 1956—).

[6] These sketches are in Lilian M. C. Randall, *Images in the Margins of Gothic Manuscripts* (Berkeley and Los Angeles; University of California Press, 1966).

[7] Geraldus Cambrensis, *Opera*, ed. Brewer, III, 27-31.

It is not easy, when animals are listed in the twelfth and thirteenth centuries, to know whether remarks about them come from actual observations or whether they represent folk motifs, bestiary lore, or material gained from Oriental tale collections. It would seem that the ape is not widely found in folk motifs. The Motif Index of Stith Thompson and his associates has a number of monkey tales but they are drawn from the Motif Index for India compiled by Thompson and Balys.[8] A few are from China. These are tales of the noisy monkey, the monkey king, the army of apes, the helpful monkey, and the monkey as an imitator of man. There is a specific tale from western Europe about the monkey who commits suicide by imitating a cobbler. This comes from Bonaventure des Périers in the sixteenth century.[9] It is evident that the ape or monkey is hardly a folk animal in western Europe. In that area he was kept as a pet only among well-to-do people. In certain of the bestiary MSS there are drawings of the animal which suggest that the artists had not actually seen such a creature.[10]

Bestiary stories about the ape show little observation drawn from life; they continue motifs from the remote past. We are including the *Livre dou Tresor* of Brunetto Latini in this category. There are the common bestiary themes: when a female monkey has two babies she carries the one which she loves more in her arms; the less loved one is on her back. When pursued she is obliged to throw away the one she loves most and save the one on her back. This is because she must flee on all four feet. (This could have been an actual observation.) Another bestiary story is about the huntsman who brings a pair of shoes with him. He puts these on, where his victims can see him. He leaves behind a shoe that will fit a simian. The monkey comes out of the thicket, puts on the shoe, and then cannot escape easily. Still another observation — monkeys rejoice at full moon and are sad when it wanes. Some of the bestiaries say there are five varieties of monkeys: the *cercpithecus* which has a hard tail; those that have long hair and are call sphinxes; the

---

[8] Stith Thompson and Jonas Balys, *The Oral Tales of India* (Bloomington, Indiana: Indiana University Press, 1958).

[9] J. Woodrow Hassell, *Sources and analogues of the Nouvelles récréations et joyeux devis of Bonaventure des Périers* (Chapel Hill, 1957).

[10] Florence McCulloch, *Mediaeval Latin and French Bestiaries,* 2nd ed. (Chapel Hill, N. C.: University of North Carolina Press, 1960).

cinocephali or dog-heads, which have long tails and dog-like faces; the *satyrus* which has a pleasant expression and attractive gestures, and last of all the *callitrices* which have pointed faces, long beards, and wide tails. Presumably these peculiar descriptions go back to some sort of observations made in the dim past. For the many Europeans in the Middle Ages who had seen imported apes these names could have made little sense; but the mediaeval man attached symbolic meaning to the monkey. Cicero had said: "the monkey resembles the most filthy beast for us." For the Christians he symbolized the Devil, and the Devil was thought of as grotesque.

Among Oriental tale collections the most widespread was the *Panchatantra*. This has four monkey *exampla*: the monkey and the wedge, the monkey and the crocodile, the unteachable monkey, and the monkey who does not forget vengeance. The Spanish *Calila e Dimna* (13th century) has two of these. Two workmen are cutting a log and have inserted a wedge into a split. When they leave to eat, a monkey who has been watching removes the wedge and his testicle are caught. He dies. In another tale monkeys who have been warming themselves with a firefly will take no advice on the subject. The Spanish *Calila* has a monkey tale that is not present in the *Panchatantra*; but it is in the Arabic intermediary. A monkey who has the itch is advised by a friend that he should eat the brain of a black serpent. The snake is not dead as the friend believes, and he kills the friend.

It seems then that a mediaeval man could learn from such available tales that the this animal was imitative of man, over-curious, and filthy in his behavior. But there are other details which the mediaevals must have learned from actual observation. Here ancient tradition and first-hand experience went hand in hand. An important reference which is concerned mostly with monkey folklore in the Renaissance is H. W. Janson, *Apes and Ape Lore in the Middle Ages and the Renaissance* (London: Warburg Institute, 1952).

Alexander Neckham in his *De Naturis Rerum* undoubtedly knew the ape from actual observation, but the stories which he repeats err in assuming a power of reasoning which the animal could not possess.[11] Alexander tells how the ape likes to imitate humans. He will put gloves on his paws, tie shoes on his feet, fastening these firmly with straps. A hunter can trap a monkey by getting him to do these things, slowing down his flight. This comes from traditional monkey lore. But Alexander goes further than that: A certain rich man kept a variety of birds and animals; among these were a monkey and a bear. The female monkey had a baby which she showed proudly to every one, man and animal, including the bear who was fastened to an iron rod. The bear tore the baby into pieces and ate it. The mother was greatly disturbed and ran whimpering to her mate. The two proceeded to gather dry wood and deposited it around the bear, in a circle. They set fire to this and blew up the flames. The bear was destroyed. When the owner learned about this he approved and did not punish the apes. Still another tale from Alexander Neckam. A certain monkey lived in the crennels of a castle and often watched a shoemaker who had his shop in a lean-to close by. The animal observed closely the tools and the procedures of the shoemaker. When the man would leave his shop to attend to household chores the ape got the habit of entering his shop through the front opening, grabbing leather and knife and ruining the man's work. The shoemaker had to protect himself. When he saw he was being watched he passed the blunt edge of his knife across his own throat, as though sharpening it on a whetstone. He then left his shop unguarded. The animal came down and imitated the act, with results that can be imagined. (This tale has been told elsewhere, in the vernacular.)

Alexander has other episodes. An old, decrepit minstrel used to exhibit a dancing monkey on a chain. On one occasion he annoyed the beast who hid his rage until a proper occasion. The old man was on his horse and pulled his hood over his head to protect him from the weather. The monkey was riding behind on the crupper, where a satchel was usually placed. He jumped on his master's hood, very quickly, and brought him to the ground. The poor man was rescued by a passer-by; otherwise he could have suffocated. Alexander wants to compare the monkey with Hypocrisy in Man. According to present-day experts the macaque ape, of which the

---

[11] *De naturis rerum*, chapter XXIX.

Barbary ape is one, is generally silent when angry, expressing deep rage by a low monotone "heu."

There is another narrative told by Alexander. A certain minstrel was able to teach two apes to tourney like knights. He took them to view many tourneys, which made this task more easy. Then he trained two dogs to perform as horses in a battle. The simian riders would dig in with their spurs. They broke lances and then drew swords, raining blows on their helmets. Those who looked on had a good laugh. (Possibly Alexander was intentionally mocking the knight class. Most clerks had little love for knights.)

The monkey is not featured in the *Roman de Renart,* and is seldom a character in the French fabliaux. We can explain this by assuming that monkeys were upper-class pets and did not figure largely among the people. Marie de France has more to say about them. She has three monkey fables.[12] In her no. 28 a monkey meets a fox and asks to share some of the fox's bushy tail. He says that the little foxes have too much and the little monkeys have none. The fox refuses and Marie's moral is that a miserly man when he has more than he needs will not allow some one else to enjoy it. This is a strange *exemplum.* Marie's so-called source (LBG) does not have it. She probably thought this up herself.

There is Marie's no. 29 which follows directly after the one just mentioned. Here the wolf is proxying for King Noble, the lion. He has promised not to eat any of his subjects, but hunger prevails. He summons a goat and asks his opinion about his (the wolf's) halitosis. The goat tells the truth and all the subjects grant permission for the wolf to devour the culprit. The next victim who is questioned swears that the wolf king has a lovely breath. He is massacred and eaten for being a liar. The wolf next picks a fat, wellfed monkey. This creature is wise and gives an equivocal answer. The king persists. He says he is ill and the doctors promise him any food he desires. He chooses the monkey. Marie's moral is that one cannot escape from a bad overlord. Her final monkey story is no. 34, about a monkey who became emperor. A pet monkey escaped to the woods and set himself up as emperor over the wild apes. He imitated the household which he knew among the humans. He had

---

[12] *Die Fabeln der Marie de France,* ed. Karl Warnke (Halle: Niemeyer, 1898).

knights, counsellors and sergeants. He took a wife and had progeny. He held great feasts. Two humans became lost in his wood: the one was honest, the other was a liar. The monkeys captured them and they were led before the king. They were asked what they thought of the monkey Court. The honest fellow saw only ugly monkeys. The liar claimed that he had never seen such a beautiful court. The good man was badly beaten and hurt. The moral is that an honest man can hardly survive in a Court where there is tricking and lying.

Another tale that occurs in various sources [13] is of the monkey who had a habit of watching for bald men in a crowd who would be wearing a bonnet. He would jump towards such a man immediately and remove the covering. This was an ill-natured beast, not like those that Marie seemed to favor. Odo de Cheriton in his *Fabulae* also has a monkey narrative. Monkeys have a habit of eating the inside part of any tree that is sweet; but when they crunch a green nut that is bitter they throw the whole thing away, not ascertaining whether the kernel is pleasant or not. The moral is that many men avoid unpleasant tasks, not realizing that the joy of Eternal Life can be gained through penetrating them. [14]

In Chapter IX of his book H. W. Janson remarks on the sexuality of apes. He discusses the eroticism of the ape-bear combination, and those legends which have been present in later centuries about the ape who has raped a human female, or of a gorilla who is the lover of an insatiable woman. This evil reputation did not prevail in the actual Middle Ages, if we can believe the marginal drawings which were executed in the thirteenth and fourteenth centuries, which we designate as *babouines*. These are to be found on many richly illustrated manuscripts. [15] In them the monkey is depicted as being very obscene and filty, but not in a sexual way. Undoubtedly in real life the monkey, not having any sense of right and wrong, could be influenced to do some dreadful things. There must have been many humans who gave them evil encouragement. In the sixteenth century Calvin remarked: La fin [of a certain book] est comme le derrière d'un singe. Car il n'y a petit enfant qui ne voie une turpitude

---

[13] At this time of writing I cannot recall the source for this.
[14] Odo of Cheriton, No. 50.
[15] See Note 6 above.

honteuse." Marnix says something similar: "A chasque sault ils descouvrent leur menterie comme un singe le cul." [16]

In the Gothic marginal drawings to which we have just been referring there are various sketches where the ape or monkey is pictured as a doctor, school master, judge, or thief, performing acts that resemble humans at their worse. In this way it was possible to ridicule all the serious professions.

Our purpose in this essay has been to illustrate the popularity of the Barbary ape as a pet in the Middle Ages. Our mediaeval man liked gross humor, and a monkey could be superior to a human jester in that respect. But "scientists" and reflective people of that period saw in the natural, instinctive behavior of animals a reflection of higher laws of the Universe, unspoiled by Man's free will, which is often in error. Usually it was the evil which they saw reflected in the monkey. Marie de France was not quite so severe. We have still another narrative which attributes instinctive preference of good over evil to an ape. We will close with this.

Jacques de Vitry tells of a merchant on his way to Acre, the chief port of the Holy Land. Some of his wealth had been earned honestly; some he had acquired by fraud. There was a monkey running free about the ship who observed this merchant spending much time in counting the money in his purse. On one occasion the monkey snatched the purse and climbed to the top of the mast. There he opened it and smelled each piece of money. Some he threw into the sea; other silver pennies he kept. The sailors brought him down, and then it was discovered that he had thrown away the money earned in dishonesty and had kept only the good money.

---

[16] Examples are from E. Huguet, *Dictionnaire de la langue française du seizième siècle* (Paris: Didier, 1925-67) under SINGE.

[17] This is No. 102 in *Die Exempla aus den Sermones feriales et communes des Jakobs von Vitry*, ed. Joseph Greven (Winter: Heidelberg, 1914).

INFERNO XV: *Se tu segui tua stella*...

By Nicolae Iliescu
Harvard University

Uno dei fatti più notevoli di tutta la *Divina Commedia* è che nessuno spirito viene incontrato, dall'autore, nel Purgatorio o nel Paradiso per meriti acquistati esclusivamente tramite la ragione. Tutte le anime salvate devono passare attraverso la Chiesa, oppure, se fuori da essa, devono umiliarsi davanti al Dio della Chiesa. Ogni tentativo di Dante e di Virgilio di superare le forze del male, basandosi unicamente sulla capacità e sufficienza della facoltà razionale, finisce sempre col fallire e quasi in disperazione. Solo l'atto di fede, nato dal riconoscimento dei limiti della ragione, può condurre al di là del fiume Lete, il quale è, in un certo senso, termine fisso tra il profano e il sacro.

Quando Virgilio ammonisce Dante che per sfuggire le tre categorie del male, indicate dalle tre bestie, "convien tener altro viaggio" (*Inf.* I, 91), in realtà egli esprime il bisogno di un ridimensionamento interamente nuovo del processo della conoscenza. Il viandante pensava di aver semplicemente smarrita la strada, "la diritta via", per apprendere, in seguito, che nè "il lungo studio e'l grande amore" per Virgilio, nè l'orgoglio del "bello stile" che gli aveva procurato onore potevano, da soli, salvarlo dalla dannazione. S'era resa necessaria la discesa di Beatrice, "anima più degna", affinchè cessasse il pericolo. Il viaggio avrà proprio lo scopo di porre in giusta luce il rapporto tra la ragione e la rivelazione.

Nel terzo canto dell'*Inferno* è detto, con chiarezza, che il problema del viaggio riguarda "il ben dell'intelletto (v. 18), inteso da un duplice punto di vista: dell'attività cioè razionale, in quanto prerogativa di bene naturalmente insita nell'uomo, e della mèta ultima dell'esistenza verso la quale tale attività deve diriggersi. Sotto questo aspetto, quei critici che ancora insistono su un Dante poeta disposto ad attribuire dignità e grandezza a certi personaggi dello *Inferno* trascurano l'importanza fondamentale che ha nella *Commedia* la sostituzione di Aristotele con Virgilio. Ogni episodio delle due prime cantiche del poema rappresenta una tappa giustificatrice della necessità del cambio. Per rendersi conto di tale situazione, bisogna sempre tener presente che la filosofia aristotelica proponeva quale mèta della felicità umana il raggiungimento mondano della autosufficienza razionale. La contemplazione filosofica della realtà costituiva l'ultima felicità. Per Dante, al momento della stesura della *Commedia*, tale assunto si rivelava spiritualmente impossibile: il viaggio che dovrà intraprendere avrà come scopo di "non esser più cieco" (*Purg*, XXVI, 58). Il posto occupato da Aristotele nel *Convivio* e nella *Commedia* convalida, crediamo al di là di qualsiasi dubbio, quanto stiamo dicendo. Nel *Convivio*, l'autore dell'*Etica* e della *Fisica* non solo è il filosofo per antonomasia, ma la sua dottrina viene anche considerata come sinonimo di verità. Nel quarto libro Dante, seguendo Uguccione da Pisa, afferma che la parola 'autore' vale quanto 'degno di fede e d'obedienza', e la persona alla quale si applichi 'si prende per ogni persona degna d'essere creduta e obedita'. Poi aggiunge: 'Questi è Aristotele: dunque esso è degnissimo di fede e d'obedienza'. Inoltre, Aristotele è additato come 'maestro e duca della ragione umana' (*Conv*. IV, 6, 5-8). La conoscenza razionale, cioè la 'scienza', viene definita dallo scrittore, nel primo capitolo del *Convivio*, quale 'ultima perfezione della nostra anima, nella quale sta la nostra ultima felicitade'. Su questa base Dante allarga, in seguito, il significato della ragione fino al punto da far dipendere anche il perfetto ordine civile, concretizzato nella monarchia universale, solamente dalla ragione. Le promesse di pensiero su cui Dante tenta di giustificare la completa autosufficienza e indipendenza dell'impero dal potere spirituale riflettono, certamente, una condizione di eresia; non solo da un angolo prospettico puramente religioso, ma dal punto di vista stesso della ragione. Se nel periodo avanti Cristo l'impero aveva potuto esaudire la sua funzione appoggiandosi massimamente sulla facoltà razionale, con l'avvento della Rivelazione anche la legge umana subiva nella storia una radicale trasformazione, entrando a far parte della riconquistata unità dell'uomo.

Infatti, nella *Commedia* si assiste ad un totale rovesciamento della posizione assunta nel *Convivio*. Gli epiteti 'duca e maestro' si riferiscono fin dall'inizio del poema esclusivamente a Virgilio: "Tu sei lo mio maestro e 'l mio autore" (*Inf.* I, 85); "tu duca, tu segnore, e tu maestro" (*Inf.* II, 40). Aristotele, che il viandante incontra "in prato di fresca verdura" nel Limbo, è definito con tono impersonale come "il maestro di color che sanno" (*Inf.* IV, 131). L'espressione implica, evidentemente, un certo tipo di sapere, anzi un modo specifico di ragionare. Si tratta, è ovvio, di una conoscenza puramente intellettuale, logica, nel senso in cui si parla nel *Convivio*. Aristotele è un libro, non la via della storia. Omero, invece, greco come Aristotele, elogia adesso Virgilio, poeta latino, con voce e parole quasi sacramentali: "Onorate l'altissimo poeta: L'ombra sua torna ch'era dipartita" (vv. 80-81). Come se con la partenza dell'autore dell'*Eneide* qualchecosa della maestà del nobile castello venisse a mancare. Dante non manifesta alcun desiderio di avvicinarsi o di parlare al filosofo greco, e, difatti, a nessum filosofo; narra soltanto ciò che vede:

> Poi ch'innalzai un poco più le ciglia,
>   vidi'l maestro di color che sanno
>   seder tra filosofica famiglia.
> Tutti lo miran, tutti onor li fanno;
>   quivi vid'io Socrate e Platone
>   che 'nnanzi alli altri più presso li stanno;
>
> (*Inf.* IV, 130-35)

Vista panoramica e nulla più. Il senso di questa sottile impostazione dialettica dell'episodio del Limbo si chiarirà soltanto nel *Purgatorio*, nel regno, cioè, dove la natura è integrata dalla grazia scesa nella storia con Cristo. Sono parole che Virgilio rivolge contro la ragione *sibi relicta*:

> Matto è chi spera che nostra ragione
>   possa trascorrer la infinita via
>   che tiene una sostanza in tre persone.
> State contenti, umana gente, al quia,
>   chè se potuto aveste veder tutto
>   mestier non era partorir Maria;
> e disiar vedeste sanza frutto
>   tai, che sarebbe lor disio quetato,
>   ch'eternalmente è dato lor per lutto.

> Io dico d'Aristotele e di Plato
> e di molt'altri;
>
> (*Purg.* III, 34-44)

È l'ultima volta che di Aristotele venga fatta menzione nella *Commedia*: ai piedi del monte penitenziale, e per accentuare l'impossibilità della filosofia di mostrare, da sè, la via del riscatto. Nella configurazione del destino umano, dal punto di vista dell'eternità, il miglior posto che alla ragione spetti, quando è priva dalla grazia, sarà soltanto il Limbo.

* * *

L'episodio di Brunetto Latini rappresenta, per molti aspetti, il risultato tragico di un deliberato tentativo di restare ancorati, nell'era della Rivelazione, ai principi e alle conclusioni della filosofia aristotelica. Qui, come del resto in tutti gli episodi del poema, Dante tratta un problema di ordine universale in una specifica istanza. Ciò che caratterizza, infatti, l'arte del poeta è la facoltà straordinaria di collegare in una visione coerente ed oggettiva i molteplici aspetti di un episodio. Cerchiamo di metterne in luce i punti salienti.

Dante e Virgilio hanno lasciato dietro a loro la nera foresta dei suicidi; alla loro destra si trova l'apocalittica landa bruciata incessantemente dalla pioggia di fuoco; a sinistra scorre Flegetonte, fiume di sangue; sopra stanno immobili le nuvole di fumo che proteggono la diga sulla quale i due viandanti camminano. Questo duro margine, come opportunamente lo nomina il poeta, non può certamente essere molto comodo; la caduta può dipendere dalla più insignificante mancanza di attenzione. Il luogo è di un'asprezza paurosa: è la contronatura. Il groviglio delle allusioni —fumo, fuoco, acqua, fiotto, mare, s'avventa—, la rima, estremamente difficile nella sua struttura fonica e nella simmetrica distribuzione di consonanti e vocali aspre, aumentano lo sgomento.

I particolari, secondo il modo solito dello scrittore, servono ad un doppio proposito: di fornire dei paragoni concreti, atti a facilitare la comprensione della vicenda narrata, e di avvertire il lettore sul contenuto morale dell'episodio. Consideriamo il primo elemento del racconto, la diga. Il riferimento testuale agli argini costruiti dai fiamminghi e dai padovani è sufficiente a chiarire la funzione e l'aspetto immediati di essa. Ma nella concretezza stessa del fatto, scrive Dante a Cangrande della Scala, è incluso un significato superiore, riguardante l'essenza morale di ciò che la lettera esprime. Il senso morale della presente similitudine è il seguente: l'opera dell'uomo, del costruttore, nella materia come nella parola, si giustifica soltanto se riesce a proteggere dalle forze fisiche distruttrici, o dal male. Infatti, per mettere in risalto l'utilità delle dighe fiamminghe Dante, usando un verso assai caratteristico ("temendo il fiotto che'nver lor s'avventa") spinge in primo piano il pericolo e la paura, l'avventarsi della marea (va notato che la parola 'fiotto' appartiene anche al *Tesoretto* di Brunetto Latini). È la prima indicazione (conclusiva allo stesso tempo) del tema e della prospettiva dell'incontro: la diga, il sistema etico che Brunetto con tanta industria aveva costruito nella sua opera *Le trésor* non aveva resistito all'avventarsi del fiotto del male. Il difetto non può essere che nella ideazione del sistema.

Alla descrizione iniziale segue un'altra, di significato ancor più complesso e involuto. La schiera d'anime incontrata dai due, dice il protagonista Dante, "ci riguardava come suol da sera Guardare uno altro sotto nuova luna; E sì ver noi aguzzavan le ciglia Come'l vecchio sartor fa nella cruna" (vv. 18-21). Dal punto di vista del senso letterale le due parti della similitudine si integrano a vicenda e non pongono nessun ostacolo interpretativo. Nell'Inferno non vi è luce in ogni modo, tranne quella riverberata forse dalle dilatate falde di fuoco, e l'autore, nel descrivere gli spiriti di questo cerchio, insiste sul fatto che il viso di ognuno di essi era 'cotto' e 'abbruciato', al di là quasi di qualsiasi possibilità di riconoscimento. È solo naturale, quindi, che non vedano bene, maturati dal martirio del fuoco, come il vecchio sarto da quello della travagliata vita. Ancora una volta, però, il poeta non è interessato soltanto a rendere, con la massima precisione ed oggettività, la situazione.[1] Il lettore accorto avrà già osservato, alla fine della lettura del canto, che i peccatori, fisicamente vedono, assai bene e lontano. Nella terzina 115 è proprio Brunetto Latini a fare la seguente osservazione:

---

[1] Ci pare superfluo lo sforzo del Sapegno (cfr. le note di commento nell'edizione Ricciardi) di voler associare l'oscurità della notte con le "esperienze comuni e famigliari del poeta: le bue notti di una città medievale, la bottega di un vecchio artigiano".

> Di più direi; ma 'l venire e 'l sermone
> più lungo esser non può, però ch'i' veggio
> là surger novo fummo del sabbione.

Quel *là* non ammette interpretazioni.

Il problema della similitudine è, allora, soprattutto di ordine morale. La luna, si sa, rappresenta la ragione umana, anzi la saggezza naturale, ma con tale significato positivo non viene mai menzionata nell'*Inferno,* dove appare soltanto come un semplice astro notturno. Sarà solo nel *Purgatorio* che la luna, piena "com'un secchion che tutto arda" (XVIII, 78), verrà a significare lo splendore più alto della facoltà razionale dell'uomo. Ma si tratterà di Virgilio.[2] Qui potrebbe indicare, se mai, soltanto il grado minimo conoscitivo, nell'ordine delle cose fisiche, rimasto al personaggio, in seguito all'enormità accecante del peccato.

L'altra parte della similitudine —"como 'l vecchio sartor fa nella cruna"— richiama subito alla mente il Vangelo di San Marco dove si dice che sarà più facile far pasare per la cruna dell'ago una grossa fune di nave, che far entrare un uomo ricco nel regno di Dio. Noi non sappiamo quanta richezza materiale Ser Brunetto abbia posseduto, ma sappiamo che egli chiama "il mio tesoro" il libro nel quale aveva accumulato il frutto delle sue risorse intellettuali. Ed è proprio la natura intellettuale delle sue ricchezze, la sua forma mentis a proibirgli l'andata al paradiso; allo stesso modo in cui la preoccupazione esclusiva per i beni materiali impedirà al personaggio del vangelo di raggiungere Dio. L'inferno non fa che fissare, intensificare ed estendere per l'eternità l'attitudine dell'uomo in questa vita. Una lettura attenta dell'episodio mette a fuoco, con precisione, il vero significato della doppia similitudine iniziale: Brunetto ha ristretto la sua prospettiva esistenziale ad una interpretazione immanentistica della realtà, diventando così cieco al problema della immortalità dell'anima. Dante, nell'analizzare la figura del "maestro," non fa che notare con oggettività il fatto che se l'uomo pone tutta la sua fiducia nell'ordine mondano sarà, di necessità, definito e limitato da esso: "ciascun si fascia di quel ch'elli è inceso" (*Inf.* XXVI, 48), spiega Virgilio. In tal senso anche la saggezza più popolare, nota al Latini, è vera:

---

[2] Seguiamo l'interpretazione data da Rocco Montano nella sua eccellente *Storia della poesia di Dante* (Napoli, 1962), vol. II, p. 146.

ed è ragion, chè tra li lazzi sorbi
si disconvien fruttar lo dolce fico.

(vv. 65-66)

Nell'inferno, la pretesa sapienza di Brunetto Latini non è che la negazione della luce. Certo, quando si parla del Latini s'intende dire l'opera del vecchio maestro, nata nel secolo più drammatico della storia italiana delle origini. Vissuto tra il 1220 e il 1294, il cosidetto maestro di Dante era stato testimone di straordinari eventi: il regno e la morte di Federico II, la battaglia di Montaperti (Farinata vi era stato vincitore), quella di Benevento, la morte di Manfredi, l'ascendere della personalità di San Tommaso d'Aquino, le dispute e le condanne delle tesi averroistiche, la lotta continua tra la Chiesa e l'impero. Alla luce di tali fermenti storici, come pure della natura didatitca dello'pera del Latini, l'incontro con Dante non può non rispecchiare il grande dibattito che nel Duecento ebbe luogo tra il naturalismo filosofico, di origine aristotelica, e la teologia. Infatti, tutto il canto si svolge per allusioni e per rimandi a posizioni dialettiche. Quando il pellegrino Dante vuol dirci d'aver riconosciuto l'antico maestro, non si esprime in maniera diretta e in parole piane ma, assai obliquamente, egli parla di "conoscenza sua al mio intelletto" (v. 28). Il verso, è chiaro, ha la funzione di mettere in luce il rapporto, la tensione esistente tra la semplice percezione delle cose e la selezione che la facoltà intellettiva deve operare. Dal mondo in cui il peccatore accoglie Dante e da quello nel quale questi esprime la sua sorpresa di aver trovato il venerato maestro nell'inferno, noi capiamo come tale rapporto sia del tutto errato nel sistema di Brunetto. "Qual maraviglia" (v. 24), grida questi; "Siete voi qui, ser Brunetto?", risponde non meno stupito Dante. Maraviglia, dobbiamo domandarci, rispetto a quale livello di conoscenza intellettiva? La riposta la troviamo anche questa volta solo nel *Purgatorio*. Anche le anime del secondo regno si mostrano altrettanto stupefatte di incontrare Dante vivo camminare tra le loro ombre; ma la meraviglia che esse dimostrano assume la forma di una lode a Dio, a cui ogni cosa è possibille: "Su, Currado! Vieni a veder che Dio per grazia volse" (*Purg.* VIII, 65-66). Forese Donati, nel viso sconvolto del quale si osserva il castigo per la colpa della gola, grida anch'egli il suo stupore nel nome di Dio: "Qual grazia m'è questa?" (*Purg.* XXIII, 42). Nella sorpresa, invece, di Brunetto

Latini, noi leggiamo come Dio non abbia avuto posto nella visione della realtà che egli s'era formato. "Maraviglia" significa qui, innanzitutto, inabilità intellettiva di penetrare al di là delle cose viste, nella zona del principio informativo dove avrebbe potuto scoprire, nelle cose stesse, l'ordine sapienziale di Dio.

Ma se di inabilità si tratta, non però essa è in qualche modo dovuta all'ignoranza. Al contrario, il suo linguaggio di fronte a Dante rivela un deliberato esclussivismo. "Perchè, nota l'Anonimo, era convinto di possedere ogni conoscenza". D'altra parte, il comportamento umile e riverente del pellegrino dà alla figura del peccatore un grandissimo rilievo. Nella *Cronaca* di Giovanni Villani [7] Brunetto è detto 'gran filosofo', 'maestro in digrossare i fiorentini, e farli scorti in bene parlare e in sapere guidare e reggere la nostra repubblica secondo la politica'. Il cronista aggiunge, però: 'fu uomo mondano'; espressione concorde a quella del *Tesoretto* dove Brunetto si autodefinisce e definisce i suoi versi come 'un poco mondanetti'. Nel linguaggio del tempo ciò si diceva di chi, non credendo in Dio, spiegava ogni aspetto dell'universo visibile, e l'uomo stesso, in termini naturalistici. Nell'episodio, non potendo credere che la presenza di Dante, vivo ed incolume, nell'inferno possa essere dovuta ad un intervento divino, ne assegna la causa alla fortuna e al caso: "qual fortuna o destino Anzi l'ultimo dì quaggiù ti mena?" (vv. 46-47). E come da vivo s'era rifiutato di riconoscere Virgilio, vale a dire la presenza della divinità nel progresso della storia, così non lo riconosce ora. Lo scambia, anzi, per una qualsiasi altra anima dell'inferno la quale, pratica del luogo, mostra al viandante la strada: "e chi è questi che mostra il cammino?" (v. 48).

Nell'intendimento del poeta, tuttavia, il verbo 'mostra' rivela la grande differenza che c'è tra l'intelligenza che Virgilio ha dimostrato rispetto alla natura e alle vicende umane, e quella del fiero Brunetto. Per Virgilio, 'mostrare' la strada significa prima di ogni altra cosa ubbidire ad un piano e ordine divini, come aveva fatto Enea. Quando il pellegrino gli dice dello smarrimento "in una valle", "là su di sopra, in la vita serena" (v. 49) Brunetto, che pure l'allegoria della valle e della foresta l'aveva utilizzata nel *Tesoretto*, e Dante non parla qui a caso, resta sordo, tanto al senso letterale della vicenda quanto a quello morale. Ciecamente egli punta verso le stelle (che non

---

[3] *Cronaca*, VIII, 10.

vedrà mai più), additando in esse la forza generatrice e governatrice della sorte dell'uomo. Come se leggessse un oroscopo, dice a Dante:

> Se tu segui tua stella,
> non puoi fallire a glorioso porto,
> se ben m'accorsi nella vita bella.
>
> (vv. 55-57)

Tutte le cose alle quali egli si riferisce, ogni termine di paragone adoperato provengono interamente dalla zona della conoscenza fisica delle cose, e in essa si concludono. Così, parla di rocce, di piante, di erba, di capre, di bestie, di semi e perfino di letame, rivelando una banalissima concezione del mondo, rispetto alla varietà e complessità della realtà visibile. Il suo intelletto pare si sia ridotto ad una fase embrionaria e perciò, sempre, alle leggi meccanicistiche della materia elementare. In verità appaiono assai strane ed ironiche le espressioni d'affetto che il Latini usa verso Dante:

> e s'io non fossi sì per tempo morto,
> veggendo il cielo a te così benigno,
> dato t'avrei a l'opera conforto.
>
> (vv. 58-60)

Il libero arbitrio è totalmente assente dalla sua visione dell'uomo, mentre il cielo non viene visto come la sede della grazia di Dio, bensì come un elemento di astrologia.

Anche quando si riferisce alla storia, nell'intricata invettiva contro Firenze, Brunetto non riesce a superare un didatticismo minore. Egli si limita a pesare il "ben fare" e il male, che sempre risultano dal conflitto delle fazioni, nella vita della città, e che potrebbero alterare la sorte del caro ex-allievo. Il livello intellettuale è quanto più lontano si possa immaginare dalla mèta soprannaturale del viaggio dantesco. Storia e vita sono da lui interpretate semplicemente come una tensione tra la passione e la virtù, e solo rispetto ad un effetto contingente. Dante, il poeta, dimostra d'aver letto con molta attenzione il *Tesoro* e di averne profondamente compresi il contenuto stoico e l'immanentismo.

Il tema del "ben fare" (v. 64) è introdotto dal poeta deliberatamente in questo canto, come pure nel seguente (il quale riguarda, in gran parte, la stessa categoria di peccatori), ed è ripreso dal canto sei. In quest'ultimo, infatti, Dante aveva chiesto a Ciacco notizie su alcuni concittadini deceduti, i quali, secondo i canoni di valutazione morale del pellegrino, "fuor sì degni" e "a ben far poser li'ngegni" (*Inf.* VI, 79-81). La immediata risposta del goloso fiorentino

> ... ei son tra l'anime più nere:
> ....
> se tanto scendi, li potrai vedere.
>
> (vv. 86, 88)

ha, nell'economia del viaggio, la funzione di mettere in risalto quanto distorto sia nella mente del viandante il criterio dei valori e come, quindi, esso non debba essere attribuito al poeta. Questi racconta la sua esperienza solo dopo la ristorazione del "ben dell'ntelletto" e dopo la visione di Dio. Due degli spiriti sono con Ser Brunetto "sotto la pioggia dell'aspro martire" (*Inf.* XVI, 6), puniti per la stessa colpa di sodomia. L'espressione 'ben fare', provveniente direttamente dall'opera del Latini, *Il tesoretto* (vedi versi 175-179), non riguarda, è ovvio, il problema della salvezza; il concetto di essa non ha nemmeno impedito all'ideatore di rendersi colpevole di uno dei più esecrandi peccati. Anzi, dal momento in cui ogni atto prende forma, si compie e si esaurisce in rapporto a questa vita, oltre la quale non vi è che la materia perpetua e il costante influsso delle stelle, ogni genere di godimento si giustifica in se stesso. La ragione del peccato di Brunetto Latini dipende, appunto, dalla sostanza del suo sistema universale. Anch'egli parla del viaggio della vita, della stella che deve aiutare il navigante a non smarrire la direzione e a raggiungere il glorioso porto. Sono tutti elementi che in apparenza contengono significati di ordine universale ma che, in realtà, riguardano soltanto il mondo terreno. Il glorioso porto è solo la fama del "ben fare", in rapporto al giudizio utilitaristico dei posteri e ad una etica nella quale la virtù non include la sorte eterna dell'uomo, perchè l'eternità dello spirito è a priori negata. Può darsi, come dice Brunetto, che la gloria doni al prode uomo una specie di seconda vita e che per la nominanza che rimanga delle sue opere si possa in qualche modo affermare ch'egli sia ancora parte della vita. Tale genere di immortalità non costituisce, però, la mèta del viaggio dantesco; nè sono le stelle a guidare il pellegrino.

Tra la visione immanentistica di Brunetto e quella teologica del poeta il significato morale dell'episodio si rivela in tutta la sua forza: Sodoma era stata punita col fuoco, così pure i sodomiti nell'inferno. Nella lettera a Cangrande della Scala l'autore dichiara che nel viaggio per i regni d'oltre tomba egli ha visto le anime godere e soffrire nella misura dei meriti acquistati sulla terra. Nella distribuzione della giustizia, tanto per gli spiriti del paradiso che per quelli dell'inferno, l'unica realtá ormai non piú contestata è Dio. Se Brunetto non ne fa menzione, ciò non vuol-dire che non ne abbia piena coscienza:

> In somma sappi che tutti fur cherci
> e litterati grandi e di gran fama,
> d'un peccato medesmo al mondo lerci.
>
> (vv. 106-108)

Il poeta, certo, presuppone che il lettore capisca con facilità il rapporto di continuità tra gli atti di questa vita e la condizione nell'eternità. Ogni episodio, infatti, tende a mettere in luce sopratutto il legame concreto tra l'esistenza temporale e quella perenne del personaggio. Consideriamo ancora la figura di Brunetto Latini. La sua etica era rimasta opaca alla luce della rivelazione: la vista gli è adesso acciecata dal fuoco. Aveva posto tutta la sua fiducia negli astri, nella loro luce e nella loro guida: ora cammina senza insegna e senza mèta, per sempre, nell'oscurità totale dell'inferno. Volutamente aveva consumato la sua esistenza nel fuoco di una passione perversa: ora è consumato da un fuoco vero. Avendo creduto soltanto in questa vita, egli scopre ora quella eterna, e la terrena, che gli è stata tolta via, rivive nella sua mente solo come desiderio irraggiungibile, in contrasto con la pena dell'eterno presente in cui non aveva posto fede. D'altra parte, l'esecrando peccato del vecchio maestro era stato commesso contro la natura, rappresenta quindi un atto di violenza contro l'ordine sacro, naturale e fruttifero, delle cose. Ora il mondano personaggio vive, appunto, in una terra sconsacrata, non bagnata da nessuna pioggia benefica, bensì incessantemente bruciata da quella di fuoco. Sodomia è anche sterilità. Liberamente e quindi deliberatamente il Latini aveva infranto la legge naturale: ora è privo di qualsiasi autonomia. Ogni forma di libero arbitrio è stata rimossa da lui ed è lasciato solo con l'inabilità di dimenticare il mondo, *la bella vita,* e con la certezza più assoluta della mancanza di ogni speranza. Negando e violentando il principio di ordine infuso da Dio nella natura, nella quale sapientemente esso si manifesta, la natura stessa viene distrutta, e ciò che rimane è solo la deturpata faccia del male, il diforme viso di Brunetto. Colui che, con atto di orgoglio, pretendeva di insegnare come l'uom s'eterna viene ora dal poeta mostrato al mondo non solo come falso filosofo, ma come un uomo distrutto dal disordine morale, grottescamente ridotto a correr nudo per la landa infernale, raccomandando un suo inutile *Tesoro*.

* * *

Quanto all'atteggiamento di Dante-pellegrino in questo episodio, esso non va certamente identificato con quello del poeta.[4] Il poeta non fa altro che raccontare oggettivamente ciò che, come protagonista aveva visto, detto e fatto nel mondo ultraterreno. La questione della realtà, storica o immaginata, del viaggio non muta minimamente la natura del rapporto. L'autore, nel momento in cui seduto al suo scrittoio si mette a dar forma alla sua narrazione, ha già una precisa visione della realtà nella quale ogni aspetto della trama si doveva definire ed inquadrare. Al livello letterale del racconto la fusione tra protagonista e scrittore avviene al di là del fiume Lete, sulla riva, cioè, dove si trova Beatrice. E sarà proprio lei a comandare, per la prima volta, al pellegrino di far nota la straordinaria vicenda. Prima di tale momento il protagonista agisce secondo il livello di miglioramento intellettuale raggiunto e rappresentato da ogni episodio dell'inferno e del purgatorio (nel paradiso la differenza tra i due Dante è già stata colmata). Non dobbiamo aspettarci che la capacità di discernimento e di valutazione del viandante sia la stessa all'inizio del viaggio e dopo l'incontro con Beatrice.

Nell'episodio di Bruneto Latini, perciò, il protagonista Dante è assai lontano dal comprendere pienamente la complessità del male. Se fosse altrimenti, il viaggio, intrapreso per mezzo della Grazia, e non della ragione, non sarebbe stato necessario. Nel citato terzo canto del *Purgatorio* proprio questo Virgilio mette in rilievo. La

---

[4] La necessità di distinguere tra le azioni e i pensieri di Dante viaggiatore, e quelli del poeta, sistematicamente e con fervore proposta e difesa da Rocco Montano (*Storia della Poesia di Dante*), oggi non incontra più forti opposizioni nemmeno fra i critici di temperamento estetizzante.

ragione, sappiamo, era fallita miseramente di fronte agli ostacoli posti dalle tre fiere. Qui, nell'incontro con "la cara e buona immagine paterna" (v. 83) di Brunetto, il viandante dà tutte le prove di non vedere, e di dire, invece, cose che gli sgorgano dal cuore, con una garrulità che lascia perplessi. Anche per lui, in questa occasione, c'è una possibilità che "nel mondo", tramite un insegnamento mondano, uno possa apprendere "come l'uom s'etterna" (v. 85). Tale specie di universalità e di eternità è, infatti, ciò che costituisce la ricchezza del *Tesoro* di Brunetto. Ma, bisogna ripetere, Dante deve "tener altro viaggio" per un differente bisogno di educazione. *Educare*, si sa, significa guidare fuori da una situazione di periglio e di inferiorità, verso una di maggiore comprensione della realtà e, quindi, verso un miglioramento del giudizio. Il processo educativo a cui Virgilio sottopone il pellegrino è, in realtà, la somma delle azioni, degli episodi, attraverso i quali Dante viene guidato fuori dall'inferno e avviato verso la mèta del pellegrinaggio: l'incontro con Beatrice. Dobbiamo qui far presente che la parola 'pelegrino' non viene mai adoperata nell'*Inferno*, perchè nessuno degli incontri con gli spiriti dannati costituisce una vera mèta. Solo sulla riva del *Purgatorio* il vocabolo acquista significato, perchè solo lì comincia il viaggio verso un punto d'arrivo spirituale.

Il poeta, con un senso di simmetria che stupisce, nella lettera a Cangrande della Scala assegna alla *Divina Commedia* un ufficio uguale a quello tenuto da Virgilio: guidare l'umanità dallo stato di miseria verso lo stato di felicità:

> Finis totius et partis esse posset multiplex, scilicet propinquus et remotus. Sed omissa subtili investigatione, dicendum est breviter quod finis totius et partis est, removere viventes in hac vita de statu miseriae, et perducere ad statum felicitatis.

Tale obiettivo si raggiunge per mezzo della visione prospettica della realtà (che si scopre progressivamente a Dante nel viaggio) tramite cui il genere umano può misurare, spiritualmente, le vere proporzioni delle cose e degli atti umani. Il *Tesoro*, di cui l'anima dannata di Brunetto Latini si vanta, non contiene questo genere di prospettiva. Nel viaggio, poi, di cui parla nel *Tesoretto* il vecchio maestro incontra, in ordine cronologico, la natura, la virtù (certo con significato stoico- immanentistico), l'amore (il solito puto nudo di origine pagano-livresca), l'astronomia. Mai la fede, o qualche suo attributo.

* * *

La figurazione pittorica e la realizzazione stilistica dell'episodio contribuiscono intrinsecamente a delineare la condizione morale del personaggio Brunetto e dei suoi compagni. Gli spiriti, infatti, appaiono fin dall'inizio come creature notturne, come larve incapaci di sostenere la luce. Inoltre, il ritratto che il poeta ci dà del gruppo ha la vigorosità e la violenza terribilmente paurosa che preannunciano la totale rovina del sistema architettonico di Brunetto. Va notato altresi la qualità bassa del linguaggio in tutto l'episodio. Certa critica s'è sforzata di mettere in risalto l'aspetto umano e caldo dell'incontro, gli appelli frequenti ad una famigliarità e nobiltà d'affetti che esistono tra il pellegrino Dante e il vecchio notaio e maestro. Ma ha trascurato di chiedersi perchè l'espressione di questi particolari atteggiamenti non si elevi mai ad una dignità di lingua poetica. Nel nono canto del *Purgatorio* Dante indica con precisione il rapporto che deve esistere tra la materia e lo stile:

> Lettor, tu vedi ben com'io innalzo
> la mia matera, e però con più arte
> non ti maravigliar s'io la rincalzo.

(vv. 70-72)

Se, quindi, il linguaggio dell'episodio di Brunetto Latini rimane sempre ad un livello inferiore di conversazione domestica, ciò è dovuto al fatto che la materia, nella sua sostanza, lo richiedeva. L'*Inferno,* con i suoi personaggi e con le caratteristiche che essi hanno, non viene considerato dall'autore nell'ambito positivo della nuova poesia. Soltanto quella parte della *Commedia,* dove si manifestano i meriti degli uomini e gli attributi della Grazia è dichiarata dal dallo scrittore come materia poetica. Infatti, solo con il primo canto del *Purgatorio* si parla, per la prima volta, del bisogno di una risurrezione della poesia:

> Ma qui la morta poesì resurga,
> o sante muse, perchè vostro sono.

(vv. 7-8)

Si tratta, è ovvio, di una risurrezione che accompagna l'uscita del viandante dal regno dell'errore, la sua rinascita ai valori veri di una arte compatibile con la mèta del viaggio e con il destino del poeta. D'ora in avanti il linguaggio della narrazione assumerà dignità di vita e si vestirà dei colori del sole.

LE SENS DES *TROIS CONTES*

Par René Jasinski
Harvard University

En ces quelques pages [1] nous ne rappellerons pas la genèse de l'œuvre, pourtant éclairante. Nous n'envisagerons les *Trois contes* que dans leur présentation définitive, tels qu'ils s'offrent à nous. Que doivent-ils suggérer?

Une question préalable se pose. Ils se qualifient "contes". Et là-dessus les avis de diverger. Pour les uns, le conte est un récit de moindre ampleur, auquel Flaubert serait venu dans sa jeunesse lorsque son souffle restait court, et auquel il serait revenu quand sa force créatrice déclinait. Pour d'autres, il n'aurait cherché qu'une détente après la dure élaboration de *Madame Bovary,* puis de *Salammbô,* et conterait surtout pour le plaisir de conter. Selon d'autres encore, le conte marquerait comme une prise de distance de l'auteur par rapport à ses personnages, donc un relatif détachement de sa part et une plus libre transposition sur le plan proprement esthétique.

Mais les dimensions du récit importent peu. *Candide* ou *La fée aux miettes,* classés parmi les contes, sont pour le moins aussi développés qu'*Adolphe,* tenu pour un roman ; et les nouvelles, qui tendent maintenant aux raccourcis frappants, ne sauraient passer pour des contes. Surtout, peut-on croire à un fléchissement créateur ou à un moindre engagement de Flaubert lorsqu'il conçoit et entreprend

---

[1] J'ai développé ces interprétations dans deux de mes "séminaires" à Harvard University, en 1958 et 1964. Je les résume ici très brièvement. Je ne peux commenter les déclarations de Flaubert lui-même: allusions révélatrices mais volontiers obliques, plus ou moins adaptées à ses divers correspondants, et qui comportent presque toujours une part voulue d'ironie ou de paradoxe.

Bouvard et Pécuchet, où l'ont voit aujourd'hui, après tant d'incompréhensions et malgré son inachèvement, le vigoureux aboutissement de sa pensée, à plus d'un titre aussi de son art?

Il faut donc reconsidérer le problème en serrant de plus près les caractères distinctifs du conte. Selon nous, deux éléments capitaux le différencient des genres apparemment similaires. D'abord, et ce n'est pas une lapalissade car on l'oublie trop, il est une "histoire racontée" (Littré). C'est dire qu'il fait intervenir d'une façon visible ou sous-entendue la personnalité du conteur. Et il ne s'agit pas tant des données plus ou moins personnelles qui peuvent entrer, comme pour le roman, dans la trame de l' "histoire", mais de l'esprit suivant lequel, présent ou par sa présence implicite, le narrateur oriente son récit. En vertu du même principe le conte s'adresse à des auditeurs, eux aussi présents ou supposés. Une sorte d'entente sinon de complicité doit s'établir avec eux: même savant et "littéraire", il est censé rester un genre oral. Maupassant, qui en possédait à fond la technique et mettait une coquetterie à en diversifier la présentation, introduisait mainte fois un cercle d'auditeurs, et il ressortait assez que par delà l'auditoire mis en scène le narrateur s'adressait au lecteur-auditeur. On peut relater un fait-divers. On peut aussi le raconter. Mais ce n'est pas le "conter": là se mesure la différence. Dès lors, loin de s'éloigner de ses héros, Flaubert se lie plus subtilement à eux, même s'il paraît les peindre davantage par le dehors, même s'il ne retient que ce qui peut s'aménager selon l'optique d'une belle "histoire". En déroulant le fil de leurs aventures, sans avoir besoin de le spécifier, il laisse deviner ses propres impressions, qui commandent celles du lecteur. Son adresse, liée à son art de romancier, est de donner au récit un caractère apparemment objectif: telle est en ce sens, croyons-nous, son originalité. N'oublions pas toutefois que dans les années où il rédigeait ses trois contes, il relisait ceux de Voltaire.

Question de manière: question aussi de matière. Littré donne une définition complémentaire qui exclut toute ambiguïté: "récit d'aventures fait en vue d'amuser". Donc, où l'imagination peut en principe se donner plus de champ et s'évader vers l'irréel. Certes, le roman lui aussi peut inventer à son gré. "L'un et l'autre", poursuit Littré, "sont des narrations mensongères ou regardées comme telles". Mais le conte peut se permettre plus ouvertement de passer les vraisemblances: d'où le foisonnement des "contes bleus", des contes de fées, des contes fantastiques, ou en un autre sens des contes libres ou graveleux. "Quand on dit", ajoute Littré, "c'est un conte ou c'est une fable, on entend que le récit n'est pas vrai. Quand on dit: c'est un roman, on veut dire que les aventures racontées sont extraordinaires; elles peuvent néanmoins être vraies". Ainsi, le propre du conte est d'offrir des fictions qui peuvent s'inspirer de la réalité, qui peuvent accéder aussi à une vérité supérieure, mais qui entendent ressortir plus ou moins à l'irréel.

Dès lors se précise le genre des *Trois contes*. Certes, ils font large part aux réalités proches. On n'a pas manqué de retrouver les éléments pris sur le vif dont se tisse la vie de Félicité dans *Un cœur simple*. Cadre, personnages, souvenirs, impressions, tout a été strictement inventorié. Il n'est pas jusqu'au perroquet Loulou, dont les modèles n'aient été savamment identifiés. On n'a pas manqué non plus de rendre hommage à la documentation serrée d'*Hérodias*, quitte à en juger lassants les "étalages archéologiques". Mais que cette reconstitution se suffise à elle-même, rehaussée par sa propre splendeur et les magies du style, n'a fait aucun doute. "Tranche de vie dans le passé", a-t-on dit: étant entendu qu'à la faveur du recul dans le temps et l'espace la vérité s'élevait à la poésie sans qu'il fût besoin d'interroger le texte plus avant. Mais à bon escient le réalisme, proche ou historique, n'en est pas moins ici un trompe-l'œil.

Ce sont "contes", et non histoires ou récits. Contes merveilleux, puisqu'ils comportent des miracles et transfigurations. Contes hagiographiques, puisqu'ils évoquent dans leurs péripéties les plus signifiantes la vie de trois saints. Mais le triptyque n'est-il pas sujet à caution? Comment n'a-t-on rien induit de l'ordre dans lequel en sont présentés les trois volets? On sait que *Saint Julien*, conçu dès 1846 et amorcé dix ans plus tard, fut achevé en 1875. Vint ensuite *Un cœur simple* en 1876, et l'on peut croire qu'*Hérodias*, conçu en avril 1876 pendant l'élaboration d'*Un cœur simple*, s'ajouta non seulement pour corser un volume dont on pouvait espérer le succès, mais pour parachever une pensée qui s'était affermie, enrichie. D'où l'ordre définitif. De la sainte moderne, en passant par le saint médiéval, on remontait à saint Jean-Baptiste, donc aux origines mêmes du christianisme. Histoire ou légende? Le titre "contes" fournissait de lui-même la réponse. Mais évitons avec Flaubert les jugements simplistes. "J'ai fait dire, selon ma coutume, beaucoup de sottises", écrira-t-il à Mme des Genettes après la publication du livre. Pour n'en pas ajouter de nouvelles, tâchons, s'il se peut, de ressaisir sa pensée.

Tout de suite, le sarcasme saute aux yeux. Il est manifeste dans *Un cœur simple*. Oh! il n'exclut pas un attendrissement dont Flaubert ne cherche pas trop à se défendre. Parce qu'il traverse alors une crise de découragement et presque de détresse. Parce qu'il prolonge les échos de lointaines souffrances. Parce que G. Sand l'incite à se faire moins désolant et à ne pas tant refouler sa bonté profonde. Mais tout en s'efforçant de ne pas la décevoir, il ne peut, lui objecte-t-il, "changer ses yeux"; et G. Sand mourant avant l'achèvement de l'élaboration —un peu comme Mme du Châtelet avant l'achèvement de *Zadig*—, le pessimisme reprend toute sa virulence. D'où l'implacable logique du récit. Un cœur simple. Donc une simplicité qui pourra faire de l'humble servante, au nom prédestiné, une bienheureuse. Heureux en effet les simples d'esprit. Mais cette simplicité n'est pas ingénuité. Elle ne vient pas d'une inexpérience candide qui garderait sa fraîcheur, sa grâce, et n'exclurait pas l'intelligence comme chez l'Agnès de *L'école des femmes*. Il s'agit ici d'inintelligence radicale. Félicité est obtuse. Elle ne comprend rien à rien. Elle a des qualités de cœur: mais elle s'enchaîne aux êtres et aux choses d'instinct, sans même une ébauche de discernement et de réflexion. Voilà pourquoi le royaume des Cieux lui appartiendra. Le principe de sa sainteté est une bêtise congénitale.

Or l'ineptie ne fait que croître à mesure que se déroule cette existence dès le début vide, et qui progressivement, paradoxalement, trouve le moyen de se vider encore. Félicité peut dans sa jeunesse apparaître comme une pauvre fille de la campagne, crédule et sans défense. Elle ébauche une idylle qui tourne court. La douleur amortie, elle accepte son sort, surmontée, sans même assez de lucidité pour avoir à se résigner, dans un esclavage qui annihile chez elle toute pensée; et comme elle garde un instinctif besoin, moins de tendresse que de dévouement presque animal, elle s'attache à la famille Aubain, aux enfants, à son neveu, enfin, lorsque les deuils et l'âge achèvent de l'isoler, à son perroquet, puis au perroquet empaillé, puis à ce perroquet empaillé plein de vers et qui se défait, où elle voit l'image du Saint Esprit. Et c'est lorsqu'elle atteint la limite extrême de l'absurde, que s'opère la transfiguration: "Quand elle exhala son dernier souffle, elle crut voir, dans les cieux entr'ouverts, un perroquet gigantesque planant au-dessus de sa tête". Selon le terme flaubertien, il était difficile de pousser plus loin l' "hénaurmité".

La sainteté de Julien tient à un autre principe non moins probant: la cruauté. Sa vocation s'annonce dès son enfance lorsque sans raison, dans l'église, avec préméditation et toutes circonstances aggravantes, plus encore, avec une sûreté dont il s'ébahit lui-même, il tue une petite souris blanche. Cette cruauté se confirme par l'irrésistible facilité avec laquelle il massacre les oiseaux, par les carnages auxquels il se livre lorsqu'il est initié à la chasse. Après l'affreuse prédiction du cerf, dans la terreur de commettre le parricide auquel il est voué il s'exile au loin: mais pour aller guerroyer et, toujours avec la même infaillible aptitude, faire massacre d'hommes. Victorieux, pacifique, il s'abstient de chasser. Mais de cruelles visions le hantent, la tentation est un jour la plus forte. Or cette fois son adresse reste vaine, les bêtes le narguent, et c'est au retour de cette expédition hallucinée que la prophétie s'accomplit: par un fatal concours de circonstances il tue son père et sa mère. Dès lors il renonce à tout. Dira-t-on qu'il se convertit, dans une ferveur mystique? Non pas. Il se dépouille et se meurtrit suivant la même propension qui le portait à tuer. Sa cruauté se retourne contre lui-même. Flaubert était assez obsédé par Sade pour avoir approfondi ce que les psychologues d'aujourd'hui qualifient de complexe sado-masochiste. Julien se prend en horreur. Il se jette au milieu des pires dangers. Il se fait passeur près d'une rivière où se déchaîne un courant violent. Il vit dans un dénuement complet, en ascète acharné à se faire souffrir, et c'est au cours d'une nuit sinistre entre toutes qu'il accueille un lépreux de cauchemar, le réchauffe de sa chaleur et de son souffle: paroxysme d'horreur dans lequel éclate le miracle.

Ces singulières hagiographies se confirment et se parachèvent par le dernier volet du triptyque, entendons par les vices fondamentaux qui, selon Flaubert, corrompent les sources mêmes de la foi. La sainteté de Jean-Baptiste s'authentifie par la virulence de ses haines. Sur les traditions touchant sa naissance et ses rapports peut-être dès l'adolescence avec Jésus, le silence est complet. De son ascétisme et des purifications qu'il consacrait par le baptême ne subsiste que la hideur. Ses cheveux "se confondent avec les poils de bête" qui couvrent son dos. Son visage surgit de l'ombre "comme une broussaille où étincellent deux charbons". Et il vomit des injures. Ses hurlements s'enflent et roulent avec des "déchirements de tonnerre" que répercute la montagne. "Malheur à vous, Pharisiens et Sadducéens, race de vipères, outres gonflées". Puis à Hérodiade: "Tes sanglots te briseront les dents. L'Éternel exècre la puanteur de tes crimes. Maudite! Maudite! Crève comme une chienne!"

Dira-t-on que sa voix se fait "douce, chantante" pour annoncer la venue du Messie? Mais il ne laisse entrevoir qu'un absurde âge d'or suivant les moins admissibles superstitions: "Ce qui maintenant vaut soixante kiccars ne coûtera pas une obole. Des fontaines de lait jailliront des rochers. On s'endormira dans les pressoirs le ventre plein." Et il reprend sa terrible violence pour dépeindre le triomphe du Maître. Le Sauveur! "Les murs crouleront, les villes brûleront; et le fléau de l'Éternel ne s'arrêtera pas. Il retournera vos membres dans votre sang (...) Il vous déchirera comme une herse neuve; il répandra sur les montagnes tous les morceaux de votre chair!" On ne pouvait mieux souligner la filiation avec les anathèmes des prophètes juifs et les cruautés du Dieu vengeur, donc la tradition sanglante que perpétuera le christianisme.

Cette barbarie trouve-t-elle son aboutissement dans une transfiguration finale? Même pas. La décollation tant de fois idéalisée par la peinture et la statuaire s'effectue dans l'ombre, obscurément. Le bourreau descend dans la fosse et rapporte la tête, qu'il tient par les cheveux. Et pourquoi cette immolation? Glorieux supplice? Non, vengeance de femme, perfide et machiavélique; forfait qui s'ajoute à tant d'autres dans la lignée criminelle des Hérodes; aggravé de luxure et de lâchetés; au milieu des rivalités locales, des âpres et sceptiques diplomaties romaines. Le festin au cours duquel Salomé par sa danse lascive arrache au tétrarque l'ordre de mort assemble une foule hétéroclite, prêtres, soldats, notables des villes grecques, montagnards du Liban. Tous goinfrent et s'échauffent. Les Pharisiens et les Sadducéens se prennent à partie sur leurs croyances en une burlesque chamaille qui rappelle de près le chapitre du *Banquet* dans *Zadig*. Les passions orientales contrastent avec l'indifférence et le dégoût du proconsul Vitellius, dont le fils Aulus, atteint déjà de sa monstrueuse boulimie, accédera bientôt à l'Empire; et le messianisme juif se mêle sous un jour cru aux querelles d'intérêts, aux grossiers préjugés, aux fanatismes les plus intolérants.

"On y causait de Iaokanann [Jean-Baptiste] et des gens de son espèce. Simon de Gittoï lavait les péchés avec du feu. Un certain Jésus... Le pire de tous, s'écria Eliazar. Quel infâme bateleur! (...) —Mensonge! Jésus fait des miracles. —Antilas désirait en voir. Tu aurais dû l'amener!" Oui, éclairante naissance d'une religion. A. France gardera beaucoup plus de modération dans *Le procurateur de Judée*.

Ainsi l'intention militante ne fait aucun doute. Le pieux triptyque entend édifier sur les récits édifiants. Mais pour s'en prendre à la religion, Flaubert prêche-t-il une trop facile incrédulité? On sait en quel sens achevaient de se fixer alors ses idées. Ennemi des religions révélées, il n'en condamnait pas moins un voltairianisme dégénéré, que renouvelait certes l'essor de l'idéalisme positiviste, mais toujours imbu des lumières de la raison. Il avait depuis longtemps renvoyé dos à dos Homais et Bournisien, ennemis jurés et pourtant englobés dans le même discrédit. Cette fois, avec un redoublement de sarcasme, il répudie ce qu'il tient pour une égale imposture, celle des prêtres et celle des savants. Imposture des prêtres, non suivant un anticléricalisme étroit et la haine aveugle de l' "obscurantisme": parce qu'ils se font forts de tout expliquer par d'indéfendables mythologies. Imposture des savants, faux ou vrais, parce qu'à l'opposé ils nient le mystère, parce qu'ils croient l'esprit humain capable de résoudre progressivement les grands problèmes et d'embrasser un insondable univers. Sous l'influence de Spencer, il fait de plus en plus large la part de l'inconnaissable. Fiasco des grandes prétentions humaines, tant religieuses que scientistes: nous sommes bien sur les voies qui mènent, qui ont déjà mené à *Bouvard et Pécuchet*.

Mais la conclusion n'est-elle que négative? De ce qu'il tient pour un immense naufrage subsistent quelques épaves, dérisoires au prix de tant d'illusions perdues, consolantes pourtant et presque inespérées. D'abord, même pour qui n'en attend ni bonheur ni profit, le dévouement et l'oubli de soi donnent une sorte d'apaisement, et, si l'on peut dire, d'obscur bien-être. Ils dispensent de réfléchir plus avant. La chasse plus que la prise, disait Montaigne. L'effort plus que le résultat, dirait Flaubert. Dans un monde où rien n'en vaut la peine, tout se vaut. Reste la peine elle-même, parce qu'elle nous occupe et, si l'on ne se pose pas trop de questions, parce qu'elle nous fait agir et remplit le vide irrémédiable de nos jours. Félicité se sacrifie à la piètre famille Aubain, à son non moins piètre neveu, et pour finir aux pitoyables vestiges d'un passé déjà mort: elle trouve dans le sacrifice même et une absence quasi totale de pensée une manière de sérénité, on n'ose dire bovine. Bouvard et Pécuchet tueront eux aussi le temps en se remettant à copier, comme autrefois. N'est-ce atteindre que par le vide à la paix du cœur et de l'esprit? Oui, pour une part. Cependant Bouvard et Pécuchet n'en feront pas moins le tour des prétentions humaines. Colligeant les bévues et incohérences des prétendus experts, non sans ironie, à l'échelle des hommes de bonne volonté, ils constitueront un formidable sottisier. Dans l'universelle vanité, estimait encore Montaigne, savoir que l'on est soi-même le "scrutateur sans connaissance", le "magistrat sans juridiction" et pour tout dire le "badin de la farce", n'est-ce pas malgré tout un progrès, condition préalable à un avenir peut-être meilleur?

Les saints des *Trois contes* remontent la pente par d'autres voies. Ils poussent le dépouillement jusqu'à l'immolation. Martyre chrétien? En fait l'esprit est autre, bien que l'ambiguïté soit à dessein ménagée. Il fallait sauvegarder le cadre hagiographique en évitant de pénétrer les âmes: les éclairer de l'intérieur suivant une logique impie eût paru blasphématoire et scandaleux. C'est aussi une des raisons pour lesquelles Flaubert adopte la forme du conte, qui lui permet de se tenir au comportement de ses héros sans que leurs sentiments soient spécifiés. Prudence, mais aussi redoublement de dérision, avec le secret plaisir de mystifier les "bien-pensants". Il s'agit donc bien d'une conformité plus superficielle que profonde avec les données de la tradition. Des martyrs proprement chrétiens les saints des *Trois contes* n'ont ni la charité mystique, ni l'ineffable amour de Dieu, ni la certitude exaltée. Rien n'oriente en ce sens le lecteur.

Ils n'en consomment pas moins leur martyre. Si l'oubli de soi est d'abord pacifiant, il a pour couronnement l'ivresse du sacrifice total. On retrouve cet appel de la sainteté dont Flaubert ne cessa jamais d'être obsédé. Ne venait-il pas de publier enfin (1874) dans sa rédaction définitive son *Saint Antoine*, où s'étaient débattues et fixées tant de ses aspirations? Mathô n'achevait-il pas en martyr le supplice qui le faisait expirer aux pieds de Salammbô? A sa façon le malheureux Bovary n'achevait-il pas dans la mort, après les renoncements et une désappropriation de plus en plus complète, son pitoyable calvaire conjugal? Et pourquoi cette hantise de la sainteté sinon parce que *mutatis mutandis* Flaubert n'avait cessé d'y tendre lui-même? Sa passion pour Mme Schlesinger, sans être si candide qu'on l'a cru, n'avait-elle pas été une longue abnégation? Ne s'était-il pas dévoué à sa mère et dépouillé pour sa nièce? Ne s'était-il pas donné à son œuvre par un absolu qui faisait de l'artiste un ascète? Que d'aveux douloureux mais aussi de fières déclarations en ce sens dans la *Correspondance*!

Voilà pourquoi lorsqu'il semble se détacher le plus de ses récits, à travers des transfigurations travestissantes et dépaysantes à souhait il incarne plus que jamais en ses héros ses propres tourments. Lui-même l'avait dit: "Mme Bovary, c'est moi". Par un paradoxe où il ne lui déplaît pas de raffiner sa virtuosité, il est plus encore Félicité. Il revit par elle ses lointains souvenirs, la première crise nerveuse qui l'avait terrassé brutalement sur la route de Honfleur, le vide qui s'était fait peu à peu dans son existence, l'absurdité peut-être de son labeur dans un monde où tout est vain. Il met en elle aussi la constance de ses dévouements, ses ferveurs, les joies qui l'inondaient parfois et qu'il goûtait, sinon comme sa bienheureuse par un obscur transfert de sexualité "avec une sensualité mystique", mais selon sa foi plus forte que tout: sa mystique de l'art.

En Julien il incarne une cruauté qu'il abhorrait, lui si profondément bon, mais dont il subissait l'attrait capiteux, comme Baudelaire ou Gautier, parce qu'elle réagissait contre les fadeurs sentimentales et le conformisme bourgeois; parce que les fureurs sanglantes prêtaient aux évasions dans l'espace et le temps, aux puissants effets d'art, aux rêves éperdus; parce que suivant le courant d'idées qui se réclamait de Sade le mal apparaissait comme un moyen de connaissance et d'accès à une vérité plus haute: vertige dont il avait dû se défendre, de son propre aveu. Mais la non moins cruelle conversion lui permet de transposer ses propres renoncements, sa cellule de Croisset devant le "grand fleuve" aux "flots verdâtres", ses dégoûts devant "l'air bestial des figures, le tapage des métiers, l'indifférence des propos" lorsqu'il se rendait à la ville voisine, et jusque dans le hideux accouplement avec le lépreux l'ineffable transfiguration du réel dans l'art.

Il n'a rien de commun, dira-t-on, avec saint Jean-Baptiste. En raison d'un recul beaucoup plus lointain? de l'objectivité de ses "étalages archéologiques"? Sans doute. Et pourtant! Les flaubertiens n'ont pas manqué de reconnaître en cette savante reconstitution maints souvenirs du voyage en Orient, et à travers la danse de Salomé celle de la petite Kuchouk-Hânem telle que la relatent les *Notes de voyage* et les lettres d'Égypte. Mais ce ne sont là que détails. La logique intime du texte va beaucoup plus loin. En Jean-Baptiste Flaubert pousse à l'extrême son insociabilité grandissante, l' "ours" qu'il était devenu, et jusqu'à l'enlaidissement dont il souffrait, lui qui dans sa jeunesse avait été d'une magnifique beauté : ce n'est pas sans humour noir —liaison par plaisante antinomie, dans l'apparent accord avec la tradition— que sa calvitie et son visage empâté se muent en une face émaciée, hirsute, et ses yeux plus globuleux, qu'il fermait volontiers à demi, en braises flamboyantes. Surtout, par le "gueuloir" de son terrible saint, il maudit les hypocrisies, les rivalités des sectes et des partis, les machiavélismes cyniques, les bassesses mercantiles déjà flétries à travers l'égoïsme des marchands et armateurs carthaginois dans *Salammbô*, son dégoût d'une humanité qu'il jugeait de plus en plus lâche et hideuse. Après tant d'années, il n'a rien répudié des véhémences de sa jeunesse. Il les avait refoulées de son œuvre. A mesure que s'assombrissaient sa vie, sa pensée, il avait héroïquement contenu la montée de ses indignations. Avec les anathèmes du martyr elles éclatent enfin, par la force d'une authenticité qui sous le masque laisse deviner le vrai visage.

Mais si, hors des religions révélées, se peut encore une ascèse, n'est-ce pas toujours une accession à un monde supérieur? Le positivisme lui-même estimait dépassés les stades religieux et métaphysique ; mais n'en venait-il pas à une religion de l'humanité? Renan, tempérant ses premiers enthousiasmes sur l'avenir de la science, ne croyait-il pas encore au divin, qui donne à l'homme son besoin d'infini? Et les doctrines de Spencer n'aboutissaient-elles pas à une "religion de l'inconnaissable", qui, sans nier la légitimité de la science, réservait la part du mystère, affirmait "l'omniprésence de quelque chose qui passe l'intelligence"? Comme eux, Flaubert se défend des explications trop simplifiantes. Les saints de ses *Trois contes* ne sont pas "ce qu'un vain peuple pense". Mais par une dialectique de la thèse, de l'antithèse et de la synthèse qui pourrait aussi faire songer à Hegel, ils ne se réduisent à la mesure ni des imageries pieuses, ni des conformismes de l'incrédulité. Dans un univers aux inconcevables profondeurs il se peut que tressaillent des ombres, que résonnent des appels. Nous ne sommes pas si loin des correspondances baudelairiennes. Déjà se multipliaient les thèmes allégoriques dans *Salammbô*: les dieux et les forces de la nature s'y affrontaient en une lutte qui sous-tendait l'action, la psychologie des personnages, les jeux d'allusions. Il était une symbolique, et presque une mystique de *Salammbô*. De même la troisième *Tentation de saint Antoine* prêtait au Mal, incarné dans l'extraordinaire personnage d'Hilarion, un rôle complexe, et ressaisissait à travers l'accidentel une essence peut-être illusoire, mais plus vraie que l'apparence dans un monde où il se pourrait que tout fût illusion.

Dès lors, l'absurde Félicité n'est-elle pas à sa façon une élue, puisque ses renoncements la sanctifient? et qu'importe si le miracle final n'est qu'une suprême chimère, lorsque l'illusion peut se découvrir la réalité la plus vraie? La prédestination de Julien prolonge de lointaines croyances et transpose le "fatal présent du Ciel" cher aux romantiques; mais les prédictions formulées dès son berceau et que confirme le cerf dans la forêt enchantée, l'implacable rigueur avec laquelle se déroule et se parachève son destin, ne disent-ils pas assez les forces qui tout à la fois le subjuguent et le marquent pour son rôle d'exception? Le paroxysme de l'horreur, comme les religions l'avaient mainte fois suggéré, ne consacre-t-il pas ici la grâce d'un martyre qui les rappelle en les dépassant? Iaokanann enfin peut succomber. Il n'en est pas moins le Précurseur. Non d'une religion d'amour qui s'annonce par la haine et multipliera les impostures: celui d'une Vérité peut-être illusoire elle aussi, mais qui se voudra plus haute. Voilà pourquoi sa révolte contre la turpitude prend tant de farouche grandeur, pourquoi son chef sanglant sera si lourd à porter.

Cette vigoureuse unité de l'œuvre en commandait la manière et le ton. Sarcasme et ferveur s'y associent étroitement. Certes, le dosage varie d'un conte à l'autre, et plus encore: pour chaque épisode, pour chaque scène. Mais cette alliance d'âpre satire et d'émotion profonde s'avère une des originalités maîtresses de l'esthétique flaubertienne. Elle se cherchait dès les œuvres de jeunesse. Elle s'affirme avec éclat dans celles de la maturité. Par son impitoyable dérision des sentimentalités romantiques, *Madame Bovary* constituait un anti-roman: ses inépuisables richesses n'en font pas moins un roman d'une extraordinaire plénitude. Pareillement les *Trois contes* sont d'abord des anti-contes. Ils discréditent ce qu'ils tiennent pour fadeur et faux merveilleux. Un détail cru ou caricatural intervient sans pitié lorsque l'on risquerait de s'attendrir: dissonances voulues, dont il a poussé l'art à l'extrême. C'est ici le jeu des inflexions qui nuancent le geste et la voix du conteur. Mais le récit n'en suit pas moins son cours, captivant, exaltant. "Voilà l'histoire de saint Julien l'Hospitalier, telle à peu près qu'on la trouve, sur un vitrail d'église, dans mon pays". "Telle à peu près" n'allait pas sans sourire. Mais comme il sied aux contes, les trois martyres ne s'en achevaient pas moins dans le merveilleux.

LATIN *POSSUM*

By ALLAN R. KEILER
The University of Michigan

In the current view of transformational grammar [1] there are a number of possible ways of representing the deep structure of sentences in which Latin *possum* occurs. First let us consider two possibilities which reflect traditional syntactic classifications of verbs like *possum*. According to some grammars, *possum* is classed as a modal verb, or modal auxiliary. Thus, e.g., Woodcock: "In English the ideas of duty, obligation, and necessity, are commonly expressed by the verbs 'ought,' 'should,' 'must'; the idea of permission by 'may,' 'might'; and the idea of possibility by 'may,' 'might,' 'can,' and 'could.' Latin also has various 'modal' verbs which, with a prolative infinitive, can express similar ideas...." [2] Taking as an example the sentence

1) Caesar potest Marcum vidēre.

we can make the above description more explicit by representing the deep structure of 1) as

---

[1] The theoretical framework used here is that of N. Chomsky, *Aspects of the Theory of Syntax*, M. I. T. Press, 1965, P. Rosenbaum, *The Grammar of English Predicate Complement Constructions*, M. I. T. Press, 1967, and R. Jacobs and P. Rosenbaum, *English Transformational Grammar*, Blaisdell Publishing Company, 1968. A knowledge of these is assumed throughout the exposition.

[2] E. C. Woodcock, *A New Latin Syntax*, Harvard University Press, 1959, page 92.

2)

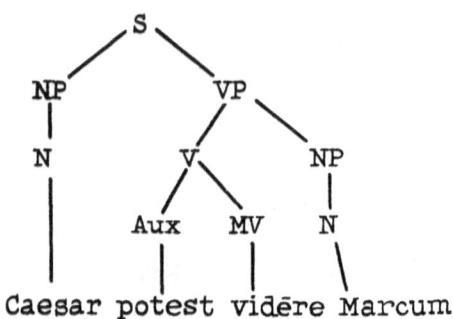

Caesar potest vidēre Marcum

where *vidēre* but not *potest* is the MV, and *possum* is analyzed as one of a class of modals that could be compared directly with the English modals 'may,' 'can,' etc.

On the other hand, traditional grammars have also classified verbs like *possum* as those which may govern complementary infinitives. Hale and Buck explain that "with most of the personal verbs of this class, the Infinitive *completely fills out* the meaning (as in *volō īre*, 'I wish to go'). Hence it is called the complementary infinitive."[3] Now it is hard to characterize this description in terms of deep structure representation, since the looseness of this kind of semantic definition would not rule out *any* infinitive (when not part of the embedded subject NP of a sentence) from being classified as a complementary infinitive, especially when there is no subject accusative. Hale and Buck themselves would classify sentences like

3) volō īre.
4) possum īre.

as similar, i.e., sentences in which the syntactic relation between finite verb and infinitive is the same. But there are obviously important syntactical differences between 3) and 4) which cannot be brought out by such definitions. Sentences like 3), e.g. do occur with subject accusatives: *volō te īre, volō eum īre*. In other words, the subject of the infinitive in 3) may be chosen independently of

---

[3] W. G. Hale and C. D. Buck, *A Latin Grammar*, Mentzer, Bush and Co. 1903, p. 316.

the subject of the finite verb. If similar subjects are chosen, the subject of the infinitive sentence (embedded complement) is normally deleted by Equi-NP deletion. For sentences with *possum*, however, the subject of the finite verb must always be understood as the same as the embedded verb. A reflection of this difference in deep structures is that verbs like *volō* can generally have impersonal passive transformations when the embedded subject is different from the matrix subject:

5) audiō constitūtum esse... in Siciliam mē mittere.

(Cic. *Att.* 7, 7, 4)

possum, however, cannot be thus transformed.

Hale and Buck's definition of *possum* as a verb taking a complementary infinitive is too vague, therefore, and fails to distinguish among a number of classes of verbs with different deep structures, but similar surface structures, as e.g. 3) and 4). Sweet gives a more precise grammatical definition of the complementary infinitive, but one which is perfectly in line with such traditional Latinists as Hale and Buck. He characterizes the infinitive in the environment of verbs like *possum* thus: "The infinitive functions in the sentence like a neuter noun; it has only one form which is nominative and accusative singular." [4] In this way infinitives, along with gerunds, are classified as verbal nouns, and the parallelism here between transitive verbs and verbs like *possum* is clear. "Regular" transitive verbs co-occur with noun complements, generally in the accusative case, while *possum* governs a special kind of noun complement, the infinitive. We are justified, I think, in representing the deep structure of 1) in terms of the complementary infinitive approaches as

---

[4] W. E. Sweet, *Latin: A Structural Approach*, University of Michigan Press, 1957, p. 182.

6)

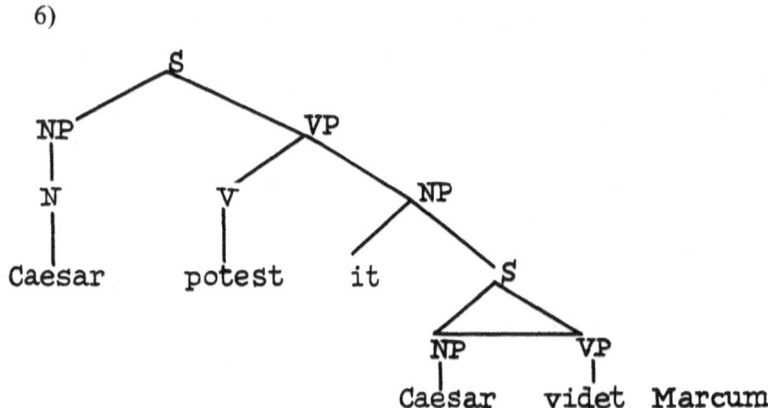

This deep structure representation, accordingly, analyzes the infinitive and its constituents as an S node dominated by NP, and immediately dominated by VP, and makes explicit the noun complement relation inherent in the above traditional definitions.

Now there is limited but straightforward evidence in Latin that both of the above deep structure representations are incorrect for sentences containing *possum*, or at least the normal kind of sentence in which *possum* co-occurs with a surface personal subject and infinitive construction. Consider passive type sentences in which the infinitive is intransitive, e.g.

7) hīs persuadērī nōn poterat. (B. G. 2, 10, 5.)

By analyzing *poterat* as a modal, 7) would have the following deep structure:

8)

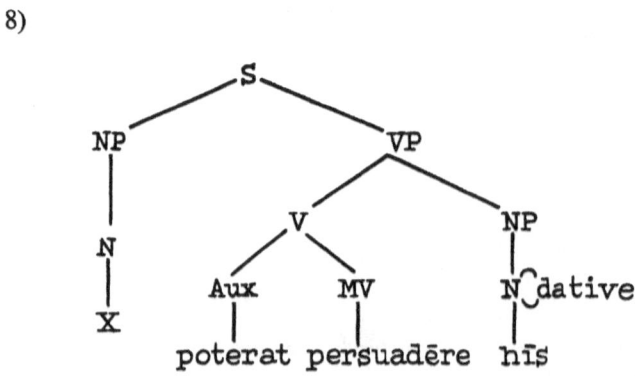

The passive transformation would then affect the underlying form of *persuadēre,* but not *poterat,* and the impersonal nature of 7) (i.e. without a surface subject) would result from the adjunction of the deep structure subject to the VP as agent, which can of course be deleted. If *possum* occurred in deep structures similar to 6), however, the result of passivization on the second cycle would be* *hīs persuadēre (ā Cæsare) poterātur,* which is ungrammatical, or, if passivization applies in each cycle, **hīs persuadērī (ā Cæsare) poterātur,* which is impossible.

It appears, then, on the basis of sentences like 7), that *possum* does not appear in deep structure like 6), but is more compatible with deep structures like 8). This is certainly true regarding the clear-cut surface facts of passivization, but there is a problem with deep structures like 8) with respect to verb-surface subject agreement, i.e. with respect to the impersonal form of sentences like 7). This involves the subject-verb agreement rule for impersonal verbs, or in general for verbs which have only a third person singular form. In English, the counterpart to impersonal agreement is agreement with *it* after extraposition has taken place. In Latin also, generalizible instances of impersonal or *it*-agreement occur when *it* and S originate in the deep structure as an NP.[5] To take one example, the deep structure of

9) Cæsarem pontem facere dictum est.

is

10)

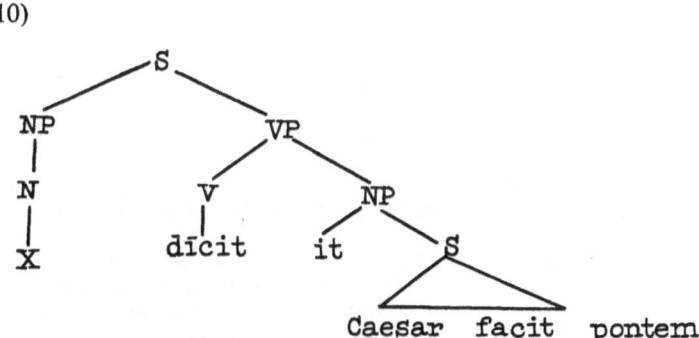

---

[5] I will continue to talk about *it*-replacement in Latin even though *it*-deletion is mandatory in Latin. When it does not occur it is normally a stressed form of the pronoun that is found.

The result of passivization on the second cycle and then extraposition would result in the following derived structure:

11)

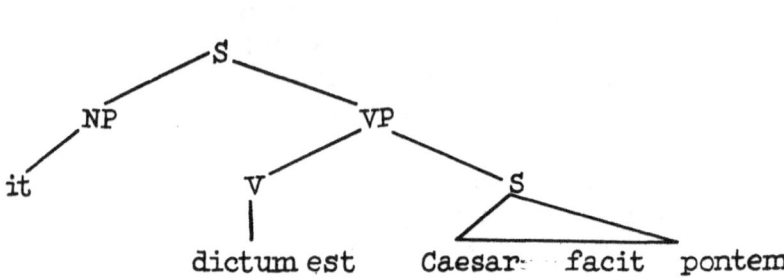

Thus impersonal agreement (*dictum est*) is generalizible as *it*-agreement. The difficulty with deep structures like 8), therefore, is that there is no *it*+S:NP in the deep structure, and the result of passivization does not replace the deep structure subject with a new derived subject for *poterat* to agree with.[6]

There is still a third possibility for representing the deep structure of sentences like *possum* which, like 2) and 6), requires deep structure animate subjects. This type of deep structure, intransitive verbphrase complementation, analyzes the sentential complement as an immediate constituent of V, which together form a VP.[7] 1) would, therefore, have the following deep structure,

---

[6] Cf. Robin Lakoff, *Abstract Syntax and Latin Complementation*, M. I. T. Press, 1968, p. 94.

[7] It may be the case that, as others have suggested, it is not necessary to postulate intransitive verb phrase complementation in addition to deep structures like 6), called transitive verb phrase complementation (see Rosenbaum, 1967, for a discussion of these). This is so because, to take only the problem of passivization, it seems that for object complement verbs with like-subject constraint passivization cannot apply to the matrix sentence. But, if this is correct, it is still ad hoc, since why this is so is not clear. If it turns out to be an incorporable generality, the criticism of deep structures like 6) with respect to passivization may not be necessary.

12)

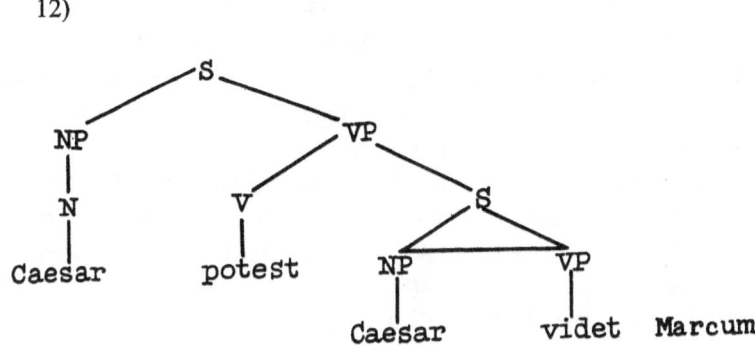

in which *possum* would manifest (just as in 6) the like subject constraint, requiring that the subject of the embedded S be identical to the subject of the matrix sentence. According to this analysis, however, the deep structure of

13) Marcus potest vidērī ā Cæsare.

would then be

14)

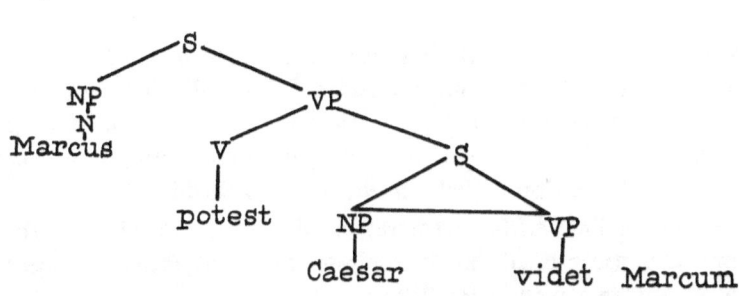

where the like-subject constraint would be fulfilled only after passivization on the first cycle inverts the deep structure NP *Marcum* to the subject position. But now 1) and 13) will turn out to have different deep structures —the deep structure subject of *potest* in 1) is *Cæsar* but in 13) *Marcus*— although they are absolutely *synonymous*. The only difference is clearly that the complement sentence in 13) has undergone passivization. 14) has to be rejected as the proper deep structure representation since it entails different deep structure analyses on perfectly synonymous sentences.[8]

Now although the syntatical evidence for the behavior of sentences in which *possum* occurs is slight, it is possible to represent adequately their deep srtucture so that passivization, *it*-agreement and the synonymy of sentences like 1) and 13) are properly handled. This is possible by insisting that the types of sentences whith *possum* examined here reflect a deep structure analysis in which *possum* requires *subject complementation*, in which case the following represents the deep structure of 1):

15)

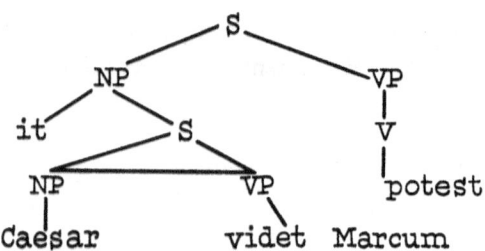

15), like 2), requires no deep structure like-subject constraint. The fact that both matrix S and embedded S have the same subject is the natural consequence of 15). In this case, it is the result of subject promotion by *it*-replacement, so that the surface subject of *potest* will always be the promoted subject of the embedded S.

Sentences like 7), furthermore, in which the embedded verb is intransitive, are properly analyzed in terms of subject complementation. The deep structure for 7) is

---

[8] This criticism, of course, is also applicable to deep structures like 6), and in fact to all deep structure object complementation analyses.

16)

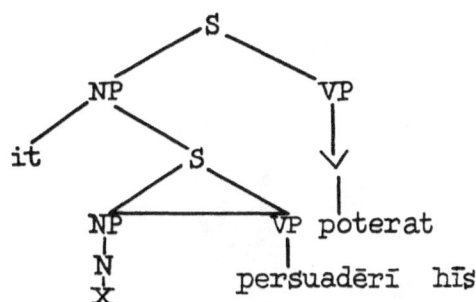

Passivization, when applied in the first cycle, will fail to replace the inverted deep structure subject. *It-replacement,* which can only follow on the next cycle, provides the following derived structure:

17)

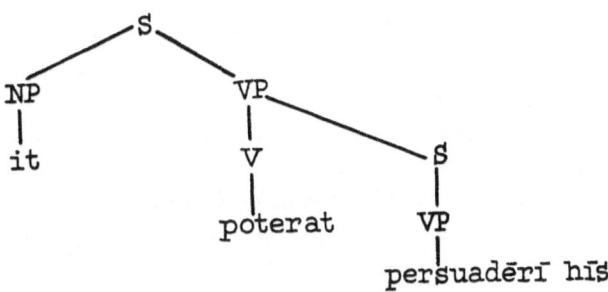

It-agreement, therefore, is responsible for the impersonal verb *poterat* in this example. In addition, synonymous pairs of sentences like 1) and 13) will now have the *same* deep structure:

---

[9] I leave out the negative and interrogative features, since they are not relevant to the argument.

18)

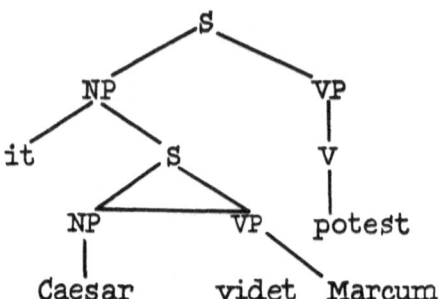

1) is derived by subject promotion (*it*-replacement) without passivization of the embedded S, and 13), with subject promotion of the inverted object of the embedded S, i. e. with subject promotion following passivization of the embedded S. It follows, therefore, that only an analysis of *possum* as requiring subjejct complementation accords with the facts examined here.

There is, finally, additional evidence that *possum* takes deep structure subject complements. This evidence is diachronic in nature. In early Latin writers, especially writers of Latin comedy, Plautus and Terence, *possum* was less restricted in the kinds of surface syntatic environments in which it could appear. Morphologically, *possum* was not yet a coalescence of *potis sum*, i.e. of 3rd declension adjective and *sum*. Consider, therefore, the following sentences:

19) potine ut quiēscās. (Pl. *Men.* 466)
20) potin ut mihi molestus nē sīs. (Pl. *Men.* 627)

Now 19) and 20) can only be analyzed as containing subject complements (with *ut* + subjunctive complementizers), where *potis* (*est*) is analagous to other adjective + copular constructions, e.g. *iustum est, æquum est*, etc.

The deep structure representation for 19), e.g. is then

21)

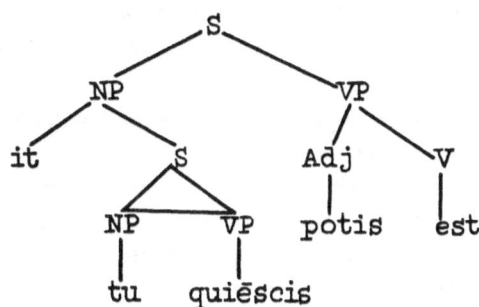

19) is derived from 21) by adding the right form of the complementizer to the subject complement. 19) and 20) are, therefore, examples of impersonal uses of *potis est*, requiring deep structure subject complements. But examples of personal uses of *potis est* are just as frequent in early Latin, as e.g.

22) emere amīcum tibi mē potis es sempeternum. (Pl. *Pers.* 35)

It is hardly likely that personal and impersonal sentence types with *potis est* occurred in entirely different deep structures during the very same period of Latin, the first with some sort of object complement, and only the second with subject complement. One could, in fact, just as easily have said, as the equivalent to 19), the following.

23) potin es quiēscere:

19) and 23) must obviously have the same deep structure, since they are perfectly synonymous. A second point is that, with the morphological coalescence of *potis est* to *potest* between earlier Latin and the Classical Latin period the deep structures of sentences containing these could hardly have shifted so radically, i.e. from subject complementation to object complementation. One must, therefore, conclude again that *possum* in Classical Latin requires deep structure subject complements. What did happen, of course, between earlier Latin and Classical Latin, is that in the later period,

it-replacement became obligatory for *possum*, hence no impersonal types similar to 19) and 20) eventually occur. But this is a change merely in the lexical feature make-up of *possum* as a dictionary entry, rather than in the deep structure representations associated with it.

I have tried to bring together the relevant syntactic facts in order to pin down what the deep structure of sentences with *possum*, with surface structure infinitive, must be represented as in Latin. The class of verbs in Latin with similar deep structure properties is certainly larger, and an extended investigation of them is certainly warranted, in which one must get behind the surface facts of morphological implementation alone to their more abstract syntactic properties.

O.F. IMP. + *ET* / *OU* + IMP.: TWO PROBLEMS

By Diana Teresa Mériz
Rutgers University

The present article seeks to provide a re-examination of the two structures *taisiez vos et me lessiez* and *ostez de ceste place le lion, ou vos vos rendez recreanz*. Each of these structures has received an interpretation which has remained unquestioned for decades. That each interpretation contains a flaw which makes it unacceptable is our contention. In the course of this article we hope to present evidence in support of our argument and to replace each interpretation with one which corresponds more successfully with the facts of the O.F. language as we know them.

Whereas all other conjs.[1] which serve to co-ordinate imps. in O.F. either do or do not make position, *et* and *ou* to all appearances represent the exception, in that they may or may not be followed by atonic pron. obj. Though *ou* has not, to our knowledge, received

---

[1] The following abbreviations are used in the course of this article:
adv.	adverb
conj(s).	conjunction(s)
imp(s).	imperative(s)
Mod. Fr.	Modern French
O. F.	Old French
pers.	person
plur.	plural
pres. indic.	present indicative
pres. subj.	present subjunctive
pron. obj.	pronoun object
pron. subj.	pronoun subject
S	subject
V	verb

mention in this connection, the existence of the two types *taisiez vos et lessiez moi* and *taisiez vos et me lessiez* has been noted and discussed in most syntactic studies which have treated the O.F. imp.

As the examples below indicate, there is no difference in the function and/or meaning of *et* which could explain the two contrasting structures. It is assumed, therefore, that *et* when linking imps. is optionally tonic:

(a) ...ET+*imp.*+*pron. obj.*

> Biax amis Erec, alez i
> au chevalier, *et dites li*
> que il veigne a moi, nel lest mie.
>
> *E+E*, vv. 201-203 [2]

> É ore tuz ces ki a mun seignur querent mal seient si cume est Nabal. Pur çó, si te plaist, receif cest present de ta ancele *é dune le* á ces cumpaignuns ki te síwent.
>
> *QLR*, I, p. 51, 26-27

---

[2] The following abbreviations are used in referring to the O. F. texts cited in this article:

AnNic	*L'évangile de Nicodème* (version anonyme), ed. Paris and Bos (Paris, 1885).
CdeC	*Le chevalier de la charrete* by Chrétien de Troyes, ed. Roques (Paris, 1958).
Cl	*Cligés* by Chrétien de Troyes, ed. Micha (Paris, 1957).
E+E	*Erec et Enide* by Chrétien de Troyes, ed. Roques (Paris, 1955).
FCP	*La fille du comte de Pontieu*, ed. Brunel (Paris, 1926).
GdeV	*La conquête de Constantinople* by Geoffroy de Villehardouin, ed. Faral (Paris, 1938).
LdeO	*Le lai de l'ombre* by Jean Renart, ed. Bédier (Paris, 1913).
LY	*Lyoner Ysopet*, ed. Foerster (Heilbronn, 1882).
MdeR	*Récits d'un ménestrel de Reims*, ed. de Wailly (Paris, 1876).
MH	*La male Honte* by Huon de Cambrai, ed. Långfors (Paris, 1957).
MRA	*La mort le roi Artu*, ed. Frappier (Genève, 1956).
PdeN	*Mémoires* by Philippe de Novare, ed. Kohler (Paris, 1913).
PM	*Poème moral*, ed. Cloetta (Erlangen, 1886).
QFA	*La chanson des quatre fils Aymon*, ed. Castets (Montpellier, 1909).
QLR	*Li quatre livre des reis*, ed. Curtius (Dresden, 1911).
QSG	*La queste del saint graal*, ed. Pauphilet (Paris, 1965).
Yv	*Le chevalier au lion* (*Yvain*) by Chrétien de Troyes, ed. Roques (Paris, 1960).

Galaad, serjant Dieu, verais chevaliers de qui je ai si longuement atendue la venue, embrace moi *et lesse moi* reposer sor ton piz, si que je puisse devier entre tes braz...

QSG, pp. 262-263, 30 and 1-2

Sire, ne faites, mais alés a l'empereour, *et menés nous* ovec vous, et chascun de nous avera un couteau en sa chauce priveement...

PdeN, XXXIII

(b) ...ET + *pron. obj.* + *imp.*

Et li rois li dit: "Car te teis
et me croi, si feras que sages."

CdeC, vv. 5030-5031

Et li quins leur dist: "Segneur, en li retenir n'arons nous mie grant preu, mais menon le en ceste forest et faisons de li nos volentés, puis le remetons a voie *et le lasons* aler."

FCP, I, 140-143

Et quant il ot fete sa proiere, si li dist une voiz: "Oz tu, chevaliers aventureus, va t'en droit au Chastel as Puceles *et en oste* les mauveses costumes qui i sont."

QSG, p. 46, 27-30

...se ge le puis conquerre as armes, lessiez le *et me prenez.*

MRA, sec. 26, 53-54

S'il set bien sa reson ouvrir
Et sa parole descouvrir,
Qu'il ait la chose por bien dite,
Si l'en rendez haute merite
Et li amendez le mesfet.

MH, vv. 157-161

To explain how *et* atonic particle can possess an optional tonicity, appeal is usually made to the influence of a tonic element more or less closely related to it.[3] Among the possible sources of analogy

---

[3] Not all linguists who have studied co-ordinated imps. have appealed to analogy in order to explain the two types under consideration. For

put forward by various scholars, the one most generally accepted is *si* co-ordinating conj., since its meaning is held to be very close to that of *et*.[4] However, the semantic relation of *si* to *et* is that of marked to unmarked: whereas *et* admits of general use to translate temporal concomitance or subsequence or addition, *si* is more restricted in meaning and thus enjoys a more limited use, being employed only if it is wished, as Gérald Antoine states, to mark the pause between two "moments" or "aspects."[5] Consequently, beside examples of *si* there occur examples with similar or identical environments in which *et* is used because it is not wished to mark the pause between "moments" or "aspects." The contrasting pair below illustrates such an instance:

> E ore meyntenant alez
> As disciples *sis lur diez*
> Et as fréres ke il serra
> Avant de vos, come dit a,
> En Galile...
> *AnNic*, vv. 983-987

---

example, Lars Bergh —"Quelques réflexions sur l'inversion après la conjonction 'et' en ancien et en moyen français," in *Mélanges de philologie romane offerts à M. Karl Michaëlsson* (Göteborg, 1952), pp. 50-51— argues that, though *et* is atonic, it can function psychologically as the initial element of the clause, thus permitting pron. obj. to precede imp. Since no atonic element in O. F. (with the exception of atonic pron. obj. in a restricted number of cases) can occupy the initial position under any circumstances, Bergh's explanation is unacceptable.

Ferdinand Brunot —*Histoire de la langue française des origines à 1900* (Paris, 1905), I, 482— solves the problem by stating as a general principle that if an imp. is preceded by another imp., the two linked by a co-ordinating conj., pron. obj. will precede the second imp. It can be said with certainty that such is not necessarily the case.

[4] See Lucien Foulet, *Petite syntaxe de l'ancien français*, 3rd ed. (Paris, 1958), sec. 166. *Si* is by no means the only tonic element proposed to explain the optional tonicity of *et*. For example, K. Sneyders de Vogel —*Syntaxe historique du français*, 2nd ed. (Groningue, 1927), sec. 441— appeals to analogy with such elements as *ne* negative particle, adv., and pron. subj., though what these elements and *et* co-ordinating conj. have in common to warrant such an analogy is not specified. Gérald Antoine —*La coordination en français* (Paris, 1958), I, 620-622— proposes analogy with the particles *car* and *or*, frequently used with imp. in O. F., but fails to establish any point in common between these particles and *et*.

[5] Antoine, II, 989: "...*si*...est en son fond un signal auquel on fait le point de la situation, prise à un 'moment' ou sous un 'aspect' donné: un 'stop' par conséquent, marquant aussi bien du reste un *terminus a quo* —*quo*— ou *ad quem*..."

Biax amis Erec, alez i
au chevalier, *et dites li*
que il veigne a moi, nel lest mie.

E+E, vv. 201-203

The examples of ...ET+*imp.*+*pron. obj.* quoted above also present such unmarked pauses between "moments" or "aspects."

It can be argued that if *si* influenced *et,* then the influence should have been exercised precisely in those environments in which both *et* and *si* could be used. Examples have been presented, however, which belie such an argument and make it difficult to justify the proposed analogy with *si*. In addition, if the analogy with *si* is accepted, then we are faced with a unique phenomenon in the history of the French language: an atonic element, on the analogy of a tonic element in some way similar to it, develops a purely optional tonicity. That such a development is not represented elsewhere in the language is one more reason for not accepting analogy with *si* as a valid explanation.

Underlying the unquestioned interpretation of *taisiez vos et me lessiez* is the assumption that in O.F., as in Mod. Fr., only imp. clauses can be co-ordinated. Once this assumption is made, however, it becomes impossible to explain ...ET+*pron. obj.*+*imp.* except by having recourse to analogy which, as we have seen, does not provide a satisfactory explanation. The question then presents itself of whether the assumption in question is indeed valid for O.F.

If we put aside for the moment the problem posed by co-ordinated imps. and examine the data for other co-ordinated finite verb forms, we find that the following rule applies to all co-ordinated finite verb forms without exception: co-ordinated clauses with identical subjects can be rewritten as co-ordinated verb phrases by deleting all occurrences of the subject beginning with the second clause.[6] This rule can be illustrated by such contrasting pairs as

(1) Li pelerin s'atornerent bien et il s'armerent.
    Li pelerin s'atornerent bien et s'armerent.
(2) Il ne passe la riviere mais il retorne en arriere.
    Il ne passe la riviere mais retorne en arriere.

---

[6] In the first clause the subject may either be explicitated, in which case it remains, or be understood from contextual indications.

(3) Il vient si l'aide il.
    Il vient si l'aide.

Imp. with implicit subject is the equivalent of any other finite verb form with explicitated subject: *va!* is the equivalent of *tu vas*. In addition, the normal word order *imp.+pron. obj.* corresponds to the normal word order *S+pron. obj.+V,* applicable to all other finite verb forms: *atornez vos bien!* and *il s'atornerent bien* are equivalent as to the ordering of their elements.

If *atornez vos bien!* and *il s'atornerent bien* are equivalent structures, so are *atornez vos bien et armez vos!* and *li pelerin s'atornerent bien et il s'armerent* equivalent structures. It then becomes evident that *atornez vos bien et vos armez!* and *li pelerin s'atornerent bien et s'armerent* are also equivalent structures: inverting the position of imp. and pron. obj. of *et armez vos!* is equivalent to deleting the subject of *et il s'armerent*.

The types *taiseiz vos et lessiez moi* and *taisiez vos et me lessiez,* consequently, do not represent a contrast atonic-tonic with regard to *et,* but rather a contrast clause-phrase with regard to the elements co-ordinated. Such as interpretation permits us to consider *et* as atonic while explaining the contrasting structures in a manner consistent with the facts of the O.F. language as we know them. Rather than arbitrarily impose on co-ordinated imps. in O.F. a characteristic which they possess only in Mod. Fr., we can now assign them their proper place in a general rule governing co-ordinated finite verb clauses with identical subjects. The rule would read as follows: in O.F. all co-ordinated clauses containing any finite verb form except imp. and having identical subjects can be rewritten as co-ordinated verb phrases by deleting all occurrences of the subject beginning with the second clause. Co-ordinated imp. clauses consisting of the elements *imp.+pron. obj.* and having identical subjects can be rewritten as co-ordinated imp. phrases by inverting the position of imp. and pron. obj., beginning with the second clause.

It is to be noted that the rule governing co-ordinated imps. is restricted to those cases in which imp. occupies the initial position in the clause. This means, of course, that the co-ordinating conj. is atonic. Such a restriction is necessary, because only in the environment *imp.+pron. obj.* does the contrast clause-phrase apply. In all other cases there is no way of determining whether the co-ordinated elements are clauses or phrases:

> Sache ta spee, si m'oci!
> N'en mentez mie, ne ne fetes fole aramie!
> Lessiez le et tost me prenez!
> Honore mei, e mei reconois a seignor!
> Prenez cest brief e a l'apostoile tost en alez!

The conj. *ou* also permits the ordering. *imp.+pron. obj.*, so that we can expect the clause-phrase contrast to apply also to imps. co-ordinated with this conj. That it does apply is amply illustrated by the contrasting pair below:

> Une grant partie des genz... li distrent: "Sire, chevauchiez devant Phynepople, *ou envoiez y* t'ost... [7]
>
> *GdeV*, II, sec. 399

> "Leus, nostre froumenz est en point de cuiedre; venez i vous, *ou i envoiez.*" —Par foi, dit li leus, je n'i puis aleir ne n'i puis envoier..."
>
> *MdeR*, sec. 407 [8]

There exists in O.F. another structure involving imp. and the co-ordinating conj. *ou* which deserves to be re-examined. This is the type *ostez de ceste place le lion, ou vos vos rendez recreanz.*

---

[7] The forms *grant*, *chevauchiez*, and *envoiez y* are found in MS. B.

[8] We have omitted *mais* from the present discussion, since all the examples of imps. co-ordinated with *mais* available to us (obtained from the examination of seventy-six texts of varying length and provenance from the O. F. period) show the ordering *imp.+pron. obj.* Gust. Rydberg —*Übersicht der geschichtlichen Entwicklung des ə in alt- und neufranzösischer Zeit bis ende des 17. Jahrhunderts* (Upsala, 1897), II, 568-570— and J. Melander —*Étude sur MAGIS et les expressions adversatives dans les langues romanes* (Upsal, 1916), pp. 65-86— both of whom concerned themselves with the question of word order after *mais*, list no example in their exhaustive documentation of the ordering *pron. obj.+imp.* prior to the fourteenth century. However, since the ordering ...MAIS+*pron. obj.+finite verb* (other than imp.) is found during the O. F. period, it can be assumed that ...MAIS +*pron. obj.+imp.* also existed during the same period, and that the clause-phrase contrast, consequently, applied likewise to imps. co-ordinated with *mais*.

This structure was first examined at length by Tobler who, influenced no doubt by the obligatory presence of pron. subj. before the second verb form, analyzed it as *imp.*+ou+*pres. indic.*, and devised the following rule concerning it:

> Quand une phrase alternative, formée de deux propositions liées par *OU*, exprime un ordre, la seconde a en ancien français la forme affirmative [i.e., the declarative word order], et, par suite, son verbe est à l'indicatif; il a pour sujet le pronom personnel, et il est précédé de pronoms atones, s'il y en a pour lui servir de compléments. [9]

Meyer-Lübke analysed the structure in question in the same fashion, and presented the following explanation for the use of the pres. indic.: "...si la première alternative ne se réalise pas, la seconde apparaît à celui qui parle comme une chose tellement certaine qu'il ne recourt plus à la forme de l'ordre..." [10] Subsequent linguists who have treated the structure in question, such as Gamillscheg [11] and Antoine [12] have unquestioningly accepted Tobler's analysis and Meyer-Lübke's explanation.

In the same article, Tobler listed a number of examples of the type *vont il le pas ou il s'en fuient?*, which he considered to be identical to the type *ostez de ceste place le lion, ou vos vos rendez recreanz*, in that the second clause "pouvait... prendre la forme qui est propre à l'affirmation..." [13] In equating these two structures, however, Tobler failed to realize that, whereas it is a simple matter to explain the declarative word order in the type *vont il le pas ou il s'en fuient?*, it is a much more difficult matter to explain it in the type *ostez de ceste place le lion ou vos vos rendez recreanz*.

The type *vont il le pas ou il s'en fuient?* is used whenever it is wished to learn which of two possible interpretations applies to a given situation. The two interpretations stated are presented as the

---

[9] Adolf Tobler, "Construction différente des deux membres d'une phrase alternative d'interrogation," in *Mélanges de grammaire française*, trans. Max Kuttner, 2nd ed. (Paris, 1905), p. 30.

[10] W. Meyer-Lübke, *Grammaire des langues romanes*, trans. Auguste and Georges Doutrepont (Paris, 1900), III, 617.

[11] Ernest Gamillscheg, *Historische französische Syntax* (Tübingen, 1957), page 524.

[12] Antoine, I, 500.

[13] Tobler, p. 30.

only interpretations the speaker considers possible for the given situation, so that if the first interpretation does not apply, the second of necessity does. The declarative word order after *ou* underlines this inevitability of the second interpretation if the first interpretation is rejected.[14]

A similar situation is presented by the type *venez avec moi ou vos morez*: though the listener may choose either to accept or reject the speaker's command, he is informed that his refusal will inevitably be attended by certain consequences, usually dire. The use of the pres. indic. underlines the inevitability of these consequences.

However, if we examine closely the type *ostez de ceste place le lion ou vos vos rendez recreanz*, we find that such is not the case where this type is concerned. Below are three of the examples presented by Tobler, with the context in which they occur:

> Et quant cil le voient, si dïent:
> "Vasax, *ostez de ceste place*
> *vostre lyeon*, qui nos menace,
> *ou vos vos randez recreanz*;
> q'autremant, ce vos acreanz,
> le vos covient an tel leu metre
> que il ne se puisse antremetre
> de vos eidier et de nos nuire;
> seul vos covient o nos deduire,
> que li lyeons vos eideroit
> molt volentiers, se il pooit."
>   *Yv*, vv. 5530-5540

> "Mais se gentelise et pitiez
> Vous prendoit de moi et franchise,
> Ja nus qui d'amors chant ne lise
> Ne vous en tendroit a pior,
> Ainz en feriez au siecle honor,
> Se vous me voliiez amer:
> A une voie d'outremer
> En porriez l'aumosne aatir.
> —Or me fetes de vous partir,
> Sire," fet ele; "c'estroit lait;
> Mes cuers ne me sueffre ne lait
> Acorder en nule maniere;
> Por ce s'est oiseuse proiere,

---

[14] Torsten Franzén, *Étude sur la syntaxe des pronoms personnels sujets en ancien français* (Uppsala, 1939), p. 69.

> Si vos pri que vos en sofrez.
> —Ha! dame," fet il, "mort m'avez.
> Gardez nel dites mès por rien,
> Mès fetes cortoisie et bien:
> *Retenés moi par un joiel,*
> *Ou par çainture ou par anel,*
> *Ou vous recevés un des miens,*
> Et je vous creant qu'il n'ert riens
> Que chevaliers face por dame,
> Se j'en devoie perdre l'ame,
> Si m'aït Diex, que je ne face."
>
> LdeO, vv. 498-521

> Ogiers s'en va fuiant à coite d'esperon;
> Venus est à Dordone, ens se fiert à bandon.
> Broiefort l'emporte oltre de merveilleus randon.
> De l'autre part descent de la rive el sablon.
> Li dus Renaus l'apele par contralioison.
> "Ogiers, ce dist Renaus, estes vos pescheor?
> Se tu as pris anguiles, ou troites ou saumon,
> *Fai m'ent tel compaignie,* com doit faire frans hom; [15]
> *Ou tu passes cele ewe, si vien joster à nos.*
> Fius à putain, traïtres, lechieres, malvais hom,
> Vo foi aves mentie à vo seignor Charlon."
>
> QFA, vv. 7835-7845 [16]

In these examples we are not dealing with a second alternative which will inevitably come to pass if the first alternative is rejected, but with two courses of action, between which the listener is to choose. That this is indeed the case is shown by the word *autremant* in the example from *Yv*: the word refers back to the second course of action, *vos vos randez recreanz,* and serves to introduce a statement of what Yvain will have to do *if he rejects the second course of action.* Yvain, therefore, is clearly not being presented with a "do this or else" type of situation but is, rather, being commanded to choose between two courses of action. It follows, then, that *vos vos randez* is not a pres. indic. but an imp. and that the structure analysed by Tobler as *imp.*+ou+*pres. indic.* should be analysed as *imp.*+ou+*imp.*

---

[15] The semicolon should be replaced by a comma.

[16] The verse numbers in the Castets edition correspond to the following page and verse numbers in the Michelant edition used by Tobler: p. 206, vv. 35-39, and p. 207, vv. 1-7.

The same can be said for the example from *LdeO*. This passage presents, as the context shows, not the lover's ultimatum to his lady but his request for the lady's love: he asks his lady either to give him a token-symbol of her love or to receive one from him. *Vos recevez*, therefore, is not a pres. indic., but a 2nd pers. plur. imp. preceded by pron. subj.

Conclusive evidence in favor of an analysis *imp.*+ou+*imp.* is contained in the passage from *QFA* quoted above. In this passage *tu passes cele ewe* and *vien joster à nos* are clearly co-ordinated by means of the conjuction *si*. Since the only non-imp. form which can be co-ordinated with imp. in O.F. is the 3rd pers. pres. subj., when used as what is traditionally called the "third-person imperative," *tu passes* must of necessity also be an imp. The analysis *imp.*+ou+*imp.* is therefore confirmed.

The underlying structure of *imp*+ou+*pron. subj.*+*imp.* is the more familiar ou+*pron. subj.*+*imp.*+ou+*pron. subj.*+*imp.*:

> Leisse ton duel, si te conforte,
> Car se vive ne la te rant,
> *Ou tu m'oci, ou tu me pant.*
>
> *Cl*, vv. 5828-5830

> *Ou tu vis de ton repouser*
> Et soffre fain, *ou tu travaille*!
>
> *LY*, 2969-2970

As the following example shows, pron. subj. in the first clause can be deleted:

> Ne fai mie a ton pole solonc sa felonie.
> Se tu ci les ocis, Egipte en serat lie:
> *U cest mal lor pardonne, u tu me toz la vie.*
>
> *PM*, strophe 320

Given ou+*imp.*+ou+*pron. subj.*+*imp.*, deletion of the first *ou* will yield *imp.*+ou+*pron. subj.*+*imp.* The reason for this deletion is not certain. Perhaps the resulting lack of symmetry made for a heightened dramatic effect? In that case *imp.*+ou+*pron. subj.*+*imp.* would have been used as a more intensive variant of ou +(*pron. subj.*+) *imp.*+ou+*pron. subj.*+*imp.* There seems, however, to be no way to prove this one way or the other.

NARCISSE ET PYGMALION DANS *LE ROMAN DE LA ROSE*

Par Daniel Poirion

L'Institut Français de Naples

Parmi les différents types de langage qui se suivent, se mêlent et se superposent dans le *Roman de la Rose,* les récits mythologiques jouent un rôle plus important qu'il ne semble au premier abord. Ces récits n'appartiennent, en effet, ni au discours didactique, ni à l'aventure imaginaire, ni même à la personnification allégorique. Se présentant comme des *exemples* savants, ils semblent ne jouer qu'un rôle ornemental. Toutefois, si l'on cherche à préciser cette fonction proprement esthétique, on s'aperçoit qu'il existe une subtile correspondance entre l'exemple choisi et le tempérament, le style de l'auteur. Si Guillaume de Lorris a choisi Narcisse, et Jean de Meun Pygmalion, à tel ou tel moment de l'aventure allégorique, c'est sans doute que ces personnages leur ressemblent. Mais au niveau même de l'interprétation didactique on s'aperçoit, en dégageant les différentes significations symboliques auxquelles se prêtent ces vieux mythes, que nos auteurs leur ont assigné une place et un rôle bien déterminés dans leur programme d'initiation ou d'enseignement amoureux: Narcisse est là pour prévenir l'amoureux d'un certain danger, Pygmalion pour lui montrer un certain savoir-faire. Enfin, au-delà de l'intention allégorique qui reprend et utilise son symbolisme, le mythe semble garder le sens d'un certain mystère, et le choix qu'en a fait l'auteur renvoie, en dernière analyse, à une certaine façon de considérer l'existence, une attitude fondamentale devant le monde, qui est du ressort métaphysique et religieux.

Il conviendrait d'étudier ainsi toutes les allusions mythologiques du *Roman de la Rose.* Mais la seule comparaison des deux légendes de Narcisse et de Pygmalion peut déjà nous aider à comprendre la différence entre les deux parties de l'œuvre, les 4028 premiers vers, composés par Guillaume vers 1230, et les 17750 rajoutés par Jean de Meun quarante années plus tard. Car les mythes sont comme les chevilles de toute la charpente allégorique: ils en traversent tous les niveaux pour en assurer la cohérence, à certaines articulations du récit.

L'épisode de Narcisse a souvent retenu l'attention des critiques.[1] Il intervient comme une allusion indirecte au moment où le narrateur lui-même s'approche de la Fontaine d'Amour. C'est une inscription commémorative qui incite l'auteur à en parler:

> si ot desus la pierre escrites
> el bort amont letres petites,
> qui disoient, ilec desus
> estoit morz li biau Narcisus.
>
> (éd. Lecoy, 1433-36)

L'histoire de Narcisse n'aura pas d'incidence directe sur la quête de la rose; mais c'est dans la fontaine, ainsi rattachée à la tradition mythologique, que le narrateur va apercevoir, aussitôt après, le bouton de rose dont il devient amoureux.

Le récit ne semble pas fait d'après Ovide, ni d'après le *Lai de Narcisse*. L'auteur résume la tradition. Il parle de la "haute dame" Echo, dédaignée par Narcisse, de sa souffrance et de sa malédiction. Narcisse arrive près de la fontaine, assoiffé, découvre sa propre image et en devient amoureux. Ne pouvant "....avoir confort/en nule fin ne en nul sen" (1498-99), il meurt rapidement, et c'est justice, car il a laissé mourir Echo. L'auteur ne décrit ni les tourments d'Echo, ni ceux de Narcisse. Il ne reprend pas les développements ingénieux d'Ovide sur l'impossible amour. Son récit de 140 vers est bien plus bref que celui des *Métamorphoses*.[2] Guillaume abrège, se montrant, par cette concision même, fidèle à l'esthétique du lyrisme courtois.

---

[1] Voir E. Köhler, "Narcisse, la fontaine d'amour et Guillaume de Lorris", dans *L'Humanisme médiéval dans les littératures romanes du XIIe au XIVe siècle*, Paris Klincksieck, 1964, p. 147-166.

[2] *Métamorphoses*, III, v. 339-511, éd. Lafaye, Paris, Les Belles Lettres, 1928, 2 vol.

Cependant quelques images retiennent l'attention. L'eau évoque la fraîcheur, la fragilité et la grâce, toutes qualités que la description du verger a déjà mises en valeur. La vanité de l'image, "ombre" comme on disait alors, par son évanescence nous prépare à l'évocation d'une beauté insaisissable, d'une demoiselle inaccessible. Le thème du miroir, qui va être plus longuement repris pour expliquer le mécanisme de l'amour, est ainsi amené d'une manière habile. Le passage est donc en harmonie avec le contexte stylistique.

Mais cette harmonie n'exclut pas une sympathie plus subtile de l'auteur pour la légende et pour le personnage. Il y a un certain Narcissisme de Guillaume qui peut expliquer la complaisance avec laquelle il décrit la beauté du jeune homme, alors que la beauté féminine sera analysée abstraitement ou symboliquement. N'oublions pas que le récit de la quête amoureuse est fait à la première personne, et que l'auteur s'identifie avec le jeune damoiseau. Narcisse n'est pas un simple épouvantail, c'est le signe d'une tentation.

L'*exemple* de Pygmalion, déjà mentionné par Jean de Meun au vers 13058 (13088, éd. Langlois) comme le thème d'une chanson souvent chantée par la Vieille, intervient à la fin du roman (Langlois 20815-21214), quand Vénus va envoyer sa flèche enflammée pour embraser le corps de la femme aimée. Un blason du corps féminin est alors esquissé dans une perspective étrange : moitié statue, moitié femme, cette "image" que vise d'en bas Vénus est comparée à celle de Pygmalion. C'est donc un jeu de l'hyperbole, un artifice de rhétorique qui amène le récit mythologique. La même formule hyperbolique le terminera pour enchaîner avec l'aventure allégorique de l'amoureux disciple, aventure poussée jusqu'à son dénouement sexuel. Cette apparente digression suit d'assez près la description de la Fontaine de Vie, tandis que l'épisode de Narcisse précédait la description de la Fontaine d'Amour.

Cette fois nous n'avons plus abrègement, mais amplification : 400 vers, contre 50 chez Ovide.[3] Jean de Meun ajoute des détails, il fait preuve d'une imagination riche, précise et concrète. L'introduction du style direct donne plus de spontanéité à l'analyse :

> "Las! que faz je"? dist il, "dor gié?
> Mainte image ai fait e forgié
> Qu'en ne savait prisier leur pris,

---

[3] *Métamorphoses*, X, v. 244-297.

> N'onc d'eus amer ne fui seurpris.
> Or sui par cete mal bailliz...."
>
> (Langlois, 20843-47)

Avec le discours, les artifices de la rhétorique, comme la délibération, viennent nourrir et construire la pensée. Ainsi Pygmalion se compare à Narcisse, pour se juger moins fou:

> N'ama jadis ou bois ramé,
> A la fontaine clere et pure,
> Narcisus sa propre figure,
> Quant cuida sa seif estanchier?
>
> (Langlois, 20876-79)

Mais l'originalité de l'auteur apparaît surtout dans les scènes d'adoration décrites avec une audace assez grande. Pygmalion habille et déshabille la statue, il lui met des bijoux, la couvre de pierreries comme une idole du Xe siècle. Il chausse ses petits pieds avec des souliers ajourés. Il la couronne de fleurs, célèbre son mariage avec elle, lui chante des chansonnettes en s'accompagnant de tous les instruments connus. Il la met dans son lit, la prend dans ses bras, lui donne des baisers.

Enfin l'auteur, qui a laissé parler son imagination, suit plus fidèlement Ovide pour raconter la fête de Vénus à laquelle Pygmalion adresse sa prière. Mais le dénouement ne manque pas non plus d'aimable fantaisie quand, de retour chez lui, le sculpteur trouve réalisé le miracle espéré: sa statue est de chair, elle a de blonds cheveux ondulés, du sang bat dans ses veines, elle parle pour lui dire qu'elle ne lui refusera rien. "Tant ont joë qu'ele est enceinte/ De Paphus...", et entraîné par son élan l'ateur se met à raconter les amours incestueuses de Paphus et Mirra, dont naquit Adonis. Mais il s'aperçoit qu'il s'est dangereusement éloigné de son sujet:

> Mais c'est trop loing de ma matire,
> Pour c'est bien dreiz qu'arriers m'en tire;
> Bien orreiz que ce senefie
> Ainz que cete euvre seit fenie.
>
> (21211-14)

Tout cet épisode traduit un goût prononcé pour la mythologie amoureuse. Jean de Meun en accentue encore la chaude sensualité. Il semble plus près de l'*Ars Amatoria* que des *Métamorphoses*. Mais il va au-delà du libertinage, soucieux de montrer la fécondité de cette étonnante union. Souci qui trouve sa juste expression dans ce style abondant, ces énumérations inépuisables, ces périodes lourdes, pétries comme de la glaise, où nous reconnaissons bien notre auteur, mais aussi, un peu, Pygmalion. Car son récit n'est plus une aquarelle légère comme celui de Guillaume de Lorris. C'est une sculpture massive, intégrée à une architecture grandiose. Si donc la mythologie représente un autre registre de l'image que l'épopée allégorique et sa croisade quasi burlesque et pornographique, le ton et le style du narrateur donnent à l'épisode de Pygmalion une résonance singulière, en harmonie avec le projet d'enseignement amoureux.

L'allégorie à proprement parler, la conquête d'une rose défendue par des personnifications comme Danger, Malebouche et Honte, est un schéma directeur qui organise, autour d'un symbole central (la rose) un texte hétérogène. Les personnages mythologiques sont d'une autre nature que les personnifications : le dieu Amour, Vénus ont toute l'épaisseur d'une longue tradition légendaire. Cependant la pensée médiévale sait faire une exégèse de ces exemples mythologiques. Et si les docteurs de l'église se sont montrés peu soucieux d'éclairer les lecteurs sur la signification réelle des mythes païens, rien n'empêche l'homme du treizième siècle d'en utiliser le symbolisme.

Dans le cas de Narcisse, on est d'abord déconcerté par la morale que Guillaume de Lorris croit devoir tirer de l'épisode :

> Dams, cest essample aprenez,
> qui vers vos amis mesprenez ;
> car se vos les lessiez morir,
> Dex le vos savra bien merir.
>
> (Lecoy, 1505-1508)

Ce contre-sens délibéré nous aide malgré tout à retrouver la valeur morale du récit : car l'auteur a voulu souligner la culpabilité de Narcisse. Et si son châtiment peut servir d'exemple à toutes celles qui seraient tentées de dédaigner leurs amis, il constitue aussi un avertissement, une mise en garde à tous les amoureux : l'amour a ses lois, qu'il ne faut pas transgresser sous peine de mort. Avant de nous dire ce qu'il faut faire, on nous montre ce qu'il ne faut pas faire. L'enseignement négatif précède ainsi l'enseignement positif.

Mais la cohérence de la leçon apparaît à un niveau plus profond de signification. Car en somme il s'agit d'illustrer le piège de l'amour. Ce piège est représenté par l'eau, où précisément le narrateur va voir l'image du buisson de roses, avec le reflet de toute la nature qui l'entoure. Comme Narcisse le jeune homme sera attiré par le miroitement de la beauté. Ainsi l'amour prend les jeunes gens au piège, comme des oiseaux:

> car Cupido, li filz Venus,
> sema d'Amors ici la graine
> qui toute acuevre la fontaine,
> et fist ses laz environ tendre
> et ses engins i mist por prendre
> demoiseilles et demoisiaus,
> qu'Amors si ne velt autre oisiaus.[4]

L'image du mirage est doublée par une autre, celle de la soif. L'amour est cette folle passion qui s'empare de l'homme assoiffé de désir. Tristan meurt d'avoir bu le philtre: Narcisse meurt de soif auprès de la fontaine.

Le mythe de Narcisse rejoint donc celui d'Erôs. En est-il l'ennemi (Antérôs) comme dans certaines traditions? Narcisse est plutôt l'envers, voire l'inversion du désir amoureux. Et son histoire n'est pas sans rapport avec l'érotisme courtois. L'amour raffiné des troubadours et de certains trouvères est fondé sur le désir masculin. Il cultive le désir, il est culte du désir. L'*autre*, la femme, idole inaccessible ou non, semble privée de chaleur et de chair. Elle est l'image de la beauté pure mais froide, froide comme l'eau. Elle n'a pas plus de personnalité et de présence qu'Echo. Elle est le reflet du désir masculin qui, en quelque sorte, s'enferme en lui-même dans la mesure où il n'est pas attentif à la personne féminine, à ses qualités particulières, à ses défauts mêmes dont un amour authentique saurait tirer aliment. Guillaume de Lorris semble ainsi vouloir nous faire prendre conscience du narcissisme qui caractérise le lyrisme courtois. La chanson d'amour n'établit pas un véritable dialogue avec l'aimée. Elle n'obtient pour toute réponse que l'écho de ses propres paroles, elle n'offre à l'amoureux que ce qu'il a pu

---

[4] V. 1586-1592. F. Lecoy rétablit ici le texte d'un manuscrit, tandis que Langlois prenait le mot *graine* au sens de "teinture". S'il y a jeu de mots sur la graine d'amour, c'est entre le sens de *germe* et le sens d'*appât*.

y mettre lui-même. Narcisse nous suggère qu'aimer l'amour, aimer le désir, c'est s'aimer soi-même. L'art d'aimer risque d'aboutir, là, à une impasse.

C'est ce qu'a compris Jean de Meun. On peut dire qu'il a eu pour perpétuel souci, tout au long de son art d'aimer, de dénoncer les formes d'amour non conformes à la nature. Il est, sur ce point, fidèle à l'enseignement d'Alain de Lille. Mais son originalité apparaît surtout, Gunn l'a bien montré, dans l'attention qu'il porte à la psychologie féminine. Il le fait, il est vrai, à partir d'un savoir frelaté, celui que transmettent les œuvres satiriques et un peu libertines. Mais l'intention est claire. Le rôle de Vénus, déesse de l'amour féminin, devient plus important que celui de Cupido, dieu de l'amour-désir masculin. Nous assistons à une réhabilitation de la sensualité féminine. Seule Vénus peut assurer à l'amour sa fin naturelle, la procréation. Elle intervient pour émouvoir la statue féminine, la jeune fille chaste ou la Belle Dame Sans Mercy, femme frigide. C'est le brandon de Vénus qui "réchauffe", qui "embrase" la femme.

De ce point de vue l'épisode de Pygmalion illustre parfaitement l'allégorie amoureuse du *Roman de la Rose*, tel que Jean de Meun l'a compris. Car c'est Vénus qui transforme la statue en jeune femme. Mais le mythe, élaboré par notre auteur, apporte un enseignement plus utile et plus précis. Car le miracle, la métamorphose viennent récompenser Pygmalion d'avoir tout tenté pour fléchir, "amollir" l'idole. Par ses cadeaux, ses parures, ses paroles, ses caresses il a mérité l'amour de la belle. Allons plus loin, Pygmalion, le sculpteur, l'homme qui travaille avec ses mains, illustre une véritable leçon d'éducation sexuelle. Nous voilà sortis de l'adoration respectueuse dont on semblait faire une loi de l'amour courtois. A l'amour-contemplation succède l'amour-action. Après Narcisse, l'homme du regard, Pygmalion, l'homme de la main.

Mais s'agit-il d'une succession logique, ou d'une opposition? En d'autres termes, Jean de Meun n'a-t-il fait que reprendre le projet de Guillaume de Lorris où il l'avait laissé, comme le suggérait Gunn?[5] En fait nous assistons à un changement très important dans l'attitude médiévale à l'égard de la femme. La substitution d'Aphrodite à Eros ne fait qu'exprimer cette promotion de la femme qui est en train de se réaliser et aboutira vraiment, au début du XVe siècle,

---

[5] *The Mirror of Love*, Texas tech. Press, Lubbock, 1952, p. 285-290.

le siècle de Jeanne d'Arc et d'Anès Sorel, à une authentique reconnaissance de sa personnalité. Car l'idole courtoise, nous l'avons déjà suggéré, n'est qu'un phantasme de la rêverie masculine. Jean de Meun, lui, parle explicitement du plaisir féminin, qui doit accompagner le plaisir masculin. Evidemment, avec lui, la statue ne reste pas sur son piédestal. Il est douteux que Guillaume ait voulu l'en faire descendre; c'est pourquoi il laisse l'amoureux en larmes devant la forteresse imprenable. En tout cas Jean de Meun ne manque pas une occasion de souligner la différence de sa propre philosophie. La Fontaine de Vie est une réplique à la Fontaine d'Amour, et l'épisode comporte même une critique précise et prolongée des termes dont s'était servi Guillaume. Cette opposition est confirmée par l'usage que nos deux auteurs font de la mythologie.

En effet la mythologie antique, dans les deux cas, est étroitement associée au mythe du Paradis. Paradis carré, chez Guillaume de Lorris, paradis circulaire, chez Jean de Meun, selon une rectification pleine de sens, la dialectique du carré et du cercle étant un des éléments fondamentaux de la symbolique médiévale. Or la Fontaine de Narcisse, confondue par Guillaume avec la Fontaine d'Amour, est un symbole de la connaissance plutôt qu'un symbole de vie.[6] On se rappelle que, chez Ovide, Narcisse risque d'emblée la mort s'il se connaît:

>   ...De quo consultus, an esset
> Tempora maturæ uisurus longa senectæ,
> Fatidicus uates: "Si se non nouerit" inquit.[7]

La fontaine de Guillaume révèle en effet la vérité. La nature y apparaît dans son ordre essentiel ("a orne", v. 1550). Son miroir révèle l'*être* de la nature qui s'y mire en une sorte de narcissisme cosmique, comme dirait Bachelard: "...tot l'estre dou vergier encuse / a celui qui en l'eve muse" (v. 1559-60). Le miroir purifie, idéalise. Le monde des images apparaît comme plus vrai parce qu'il est plus pur que la matière. On passe ainsi de l'apparence à l'essence, selon une métaphysique assez élémentaire.

Mais c'est pour avoir vu le bouton de rose dans ce miroir, et non directement, que le narrateur en devient amoureux. C'est la connais-

---

[6] Voir E. Köhler, art. cité, discussion p. 165-166.
[7] *Métamorphoses*, III, v. 346-348.

sance qui fonde l'amour. Or il s'agit d'une connaissance magique. Le mécanisme de cette magie est expliqué par référence au cristal de l'eau qui est comme le tain du miroir.[8] L'amour est donc donné tout d'un coup, en une sorte d'éblouissement par la vérité. Dans ces conditions l'art d'aimer n'implique pas vraiment une éducation, mais une initiation. L'amour reste un pouvoir magique auquel il faut se préparer: c'est ce que nous fait voir Guillaume dont l'allégorie comporte tout un rituel d'initiation. Près de la fontaine c'est un mystère qui se célèbre, une révélation religieuse qui se fait, où la mort de Narcisse a son rôle, avec le pin, arbre éternel, l'eau sacrée, la souffrance, enfin, que le dieu chasseur va infliger au myste.

Cette atmosphère magique n'est-elle que littérature? On découvre ici une résurgence de l'orphisme auquel était associé, chez Ovide, le mythe de Narcisse. Le prestige de la magie était assez grand, au Moyen Age, pourqu'il ne soit pas absurde de supposer que certains poètes lyriques, souvent si soucieux de conserver la secret du *trobar clus*, aient mis ce qui nous semble une rhétorique au service du mystère. Iy n'est d'ailleurs pas exclu que ce mystère se soit parfois réduit à l'homosexualité. Chez Ovide Narcisse dédaigne, il est vrai, les garçons comme les filles. Mais il est désiré par les uns comme par les autres: "Multi illum juuenes, multæ cupiere puellæ". Et n'oublions pas qu'il s'agit d'une histoire orphique. Orphée, Jean de Meun nous le rappelle, s'était fait le chantre de l'homosexualité.[9] Et c'est un fait que le continuateur de Guillaume considère avec une égale méfiance l'orphisme et le narcissisme.[10] La substitution de Bel Accueil à la rose, dans les protestations amoureuses qui terminent l'œuvre de Guillaume, nous laisse sur une équivoque troublante.

---

[8] Le texte est un peu incertain. L'allusion à deux cristaux (v. 1534) est un raffinement inutile, dû peut-être à l'image des deux yeux de Narcisse, ou plus simplement à la présence de deux ruisselets (v. 1530).

[9] Voir le début du livre X des *Métamorphoses*:

........omnemque refugerat Orpheus
Femineam Venerem, seu quod male cesserat ille,
Siue fidem dederat; multas tamen ardor habebat
Iungere se uati; multæ doluere repulsæ.
Ille etiam Thracum populis fuit auctor amorem
In teneros transferre mares......(v. 79-83).

[10] V. 19651 et suiv. inspirés par Alain de Lille: "Solus homo...sub delirantis Orphei lyra delirat (*De Planctu Nature*, col. 449 C, cité par Langlois, V, 100); et v. 20409-424.

Mais ce que Jean de Meun reprochera à Guillaume, c'est d'avoir fait de la Fontaine d'Amour une Fontaine de Mort:

> L'en li devrait faire la moe
> Quant il cele fontaine loe.
> C'est la fontaine perilleuse,
> Tant amere e tant venimeuse
> Qu'el tua le bel Narcisus
> Quant il se mirait iqui sus.
> Il meïsmes n'a pas vergoigne
> Dou requenoistre, ainz le tesmoigne;
> E sa cruauté pas ne cele
> Quant perilleus mirail l'apele,
> E dit que quant il s'i mira
> Maintes feiz puis en soupira....
>
> (Langlois, 20407-418)

Guillaume semble bien avoir été lui-même victime de cette sombre magie. Il est mort avant d'avoir pu finir son récit, ou plutôt, c'est sa propre expérience qu'il a racontée, et il n'a pu éviter le destin de Narcisse dont l'image le hantait. Nous ne voyons plus dans ce roman que jeu littéraire. Mais qui sait si le mythe n'était pas évoqué justement parce qu'il était, pour l'auteur, la vérité de son existence? En tout cas il semble révélateur d'une mentalité qui ne s'est pas affranchie encore des charmes de la magie.

Jean de Meun s'oppose nettement à cette magie. Il cite, dans un longs passage, les propriétés apparemment merveilleuses des miroirs, mais nous dit que les savants peuvent en expliquer les causes (Langlois, 18044-18286). En face de Guillaume, il fait figure d'homme de science. En tout cas il a confiance en la technique, en l'art des hommes. Ainsi son art d'aimer se présente comme un traité technique. Il ne s'agit plus d'une initiation au mystère, mais bien d'une éducation. Au lieu d'une révélation, le disciple bénéficie d'un enseignement progressif, critique, dialectique. On le met à l'école de la nature, une nature désacralisée. Le caractère positif de cette éducation sexuelle lui donne une apparence très moderne.

Mais il s'agit d'une apparence, et il nous faut bien prendre garde de ne pas prêter à notre auteur du XIIIe siècle un rationalisme, voire un scientisme anachroniques. Car alors on s'expliquerait mal l'enthousiasme dionysiaque, le mysticisme assez confus que révèlent les longs développements sur la nature, sa beauté, sa fécondité. On ne verrait surtout pas comment concilier l'objectivité scientifique avec cette métaphysique de la plénitude qui amène notre auteur à prêcher un évangile de la fécondité, ressemblant fort, parfois, à un hymne en faveur de la fornication. L'appareil scientifique n'est-il là que pour masquer une œuvre pornographique?

En fait nous risquons d'être induits en erreur par nos catégories modernes. La pensée de Jean de Meun s'élabore précisément dans un univers mythique où les concepts fondamentaux de *science*, de *nature* et *d'histoire* ne sont pas encore dégagés d'un certain halo religieux. Il y a d'abord ce mythe du Paradis où il place sa Fontaine de Vie, avec l'olivier, arbre de fécondité, qu'il substitue au pin de Guillaume de Lorris (on retrouve ici la dualité mythique de l'arbre de vie et de l'arbre de connaissance, dualité conservée par la *Genèse*). Mais en relation avec le Paradis, c'est le mythe des origines qui retient l'attention dans son œuvre, avec de nombreux passages consacrés à l'Age d'or, à la chute dans le Temps ou Age de fer, au Déluge dont il cherches les traditions à la fois païennes et chrétiennes.

Un mythe comme celui de Pygmalion n'est donc pas un ornement isolé. Il intervient pour donner un élément de réponse à une interrogation métaphysique et non pas seulement technique. De ce point de vue Pygmalion n'est pas le symbole de l'artisan moderne, nouveau Prométhée d'une civilisation fondée sur la science. Pygmalion c'est plutôt l'alchimiste, l'homme qui, avec l'aide de Vénus, réalise une difficile transmutation. Nous sommes à une étape entre la pensée magique et la pensée scientifique: les structures semi-scientifiques de l'alchimie assurent la transition. Au reste, le pansexualisme de Jean de Meun, cette interprétation de toutes les manifestations physiques et cosmiques à partir des deux principes masculins et féminins, sont bien caractéristiques de la pensée des alchimistes telle qu'elle dérive du *Timée*. Et le mythe de Pygmalion, décrivant les rapports de l'homme et de la femme, nous ramène au schéma fondamental: c'est l'élément mâle, force créatrice, qui donne forme à l'élément féminin. Jean de Meun croyait donc vraiment à l'alchimie:

> Nepourquant, c'est chose notable,
> Alkimie est art veritable:
> Qui sagement en ouverrait
> Granz merveilles i trouverrait.
>
> (Langlois, 16083-86)

On ne saurait demander un aveu plus net à quelqu'un qui, au demeurant, ne prétend nullement connaître tous les secrets du Grand Art.

Nous voulions d'abord montrer que les exemples mythologiques ne doivent pas être considérés comme de simples ornements dans le *Roman de la Rose*. Ils nous aident à comprendre la pensée allégorique, qui n'est pas aussi rationnelle, intellectuelle que nous le croyons. Bien sûr il faut distinguer entre l'utilisation littéraire et la pratique religieuse des mythes, et il serait imprudent de prêter à nos auteurs, sur la foi de leur œuvre, une affiliation à quelques sociétés secrètes, bien que le XIIIe siècle ait connu de telles choses, comme nous l'apprendrons par les persécutions inaugurées à la fin du siècle. Mais la pensée a des hardiesses, ou des paresses, dont l'histoire ne coïncide pas exactement avec celle des moeurs et des pratiques. De ce point de vue la littérature est souvent à prendre au sérieux, car elle laisse s'exprimer des idées qui ne sont pas en accord avec l'idéologie officielle. Les structures mythiques nous aident à comprendre, non seulement les intentions de Guillaume de Lorris et Jean de Meun, mais aussi le climat affectif et intellectuel dans lequel se sont épanouies les œuvres dont le *Roman de la Rose* cherche à dégager la philosophie. La poésie lyrique, dont nous ne retenons que la rhétorique, retrouve ainsi le postulat magique sans lequel elle se dessèche, et la poésie savante, qui ne nous semble jamais assez savante, se juge dans sa vraie perspective, celle de l'alchimie.

Enfin cette confrontation des mythes, à laquelle nous invite la lecture des deux parties du *Roman,* nous éclaire sur l'évolution de la civilisation au XIIIe siècle. Comme de nos jours, l'art d'aimer est remis en question quand la civilisation en crise cherche un nouvel art de vivre. La critique de l'ordre établi prend ainsi l'aspect d'une utopie érotique. Autour du mythe d'Erôs une révolution cherche à se définir. L'Erôs courtois, qui avait été révolutionnaire et antisocial, est désormais confondu avec l'idéologie régnante. Aux yeux d'une humanité qui se transforme l'amour courtois associe, d'une manière injustifiée, Erôs à Thanatos. Jean de Meun veut montrer comment échapper à ce destin de mort, et c'est pourquoi il fait intervenir Vénus, personnage latin d'Aphrodite, symbole de fécondité, de féminité et de vie. Il propose ainsi à son lecteur l'utopie d'un triomphe sur le vide et la mort. Pour nous, aujourd'hui, que menacent toutes les conséquences d'une effarante surpopulation, son message n'est ni plus faux ni plus vrai que celui de Guillaume de Lorris. Il répondait au besoin d'expansion humaine du XIIIe siècle (expansion réussie, il apparaît, puisqu'au XIVe siècle la population européenne aura doublé par rapport au Xe siècle). Au milieu du XXe siècle le mythe d'Erôs est plus que jamais triomphant, et nous ne manquons pas d'arts d'aimer dont les uns enseignent le libertinage, d'autres la fabrication des enfants. Mais pour ne pas se laisser égarer par les mauvais prophètes les jeunes gens feraient bien de relire le *Roman de la Rose*: ils y apprendraient, non certes l'art d'aimer qu'ils pensent si bien savoir, mais la permanence des mythes et la relativité des utopies.

LOVE AND THE OTHER WORLD IN MARIE DE FRANCE'S *ELIDUC*

By HOWARD S. ROBERTSON
Glendon College, York University

The *Lais* of Marie de France treat the subject of love from a number of standpoints. Successful or not, pure or physical, symbolic or real, adulterous or innocent, love is the mainspring of Marie's psychology and the unifying factor of her variety. In such complexity, the divers facets of Marie's art may be revealed by an appeal to the patterns intertwined in the tales. Our purpose here is to explore an extraordinary occurrence of one such pattern: the relationship between love and that "other world" which Marie compares to normal society in *Yonec, Guigemar* and *Lanval*. After isolating the distinctive features of this pattern, we shall apply them to *Eliduc*, a *lai* which takes place in the world of human beings and reality. Our thesis is that love in *Eliduc* is treated as it is in the Other World *lais* except that *Eliduc* goes beyond them to take love to its logical conclusion in the highest expression of *caritas* — the love of God.

Yonec, Guigemar and *Lanval,* all clearly involved in the confrontation of the real world with the Other World, each possesses certain features which, while found individually in the other *lais,* are as a group distinctive of the Other World *lai.* (1) The Other World is the source of an ideal and reciprocated love which arises naturally between two mutually attractive people despite their social obligations; unsuccessful in *Yonec,* it is successful in the other two for a variety of reasons unimportant here. (2) A physical barrier exists between the two worlds and a journey or passage of some sort is demanded: in *Yonec,* the journey through the *hoge*; in *Guigemar,* the sea and the voyages aboard the mysterious vessel; in *Lanval*, the stream and the dreamlike transition to the Other World. (3) The *merveilleux* occurs in each; *Yonec* offers the mysterious castle and the *hoge*; *Guigemar* the fabulous and magical ship guided by a mysterious power and the appearance of the antlered and prophetic doe; *Lanval* the exotic *pays féerique*, the omniscient *dame fée*, and the eventual disappearance of the hero. (4) The separation motif is tragic in *Yonec* where the lovers are never to be united; in *Guigemar*, the lovers are reunited by their fidelity symbolized in the knot and the girdle; Lanval and his lady suffer a separation which is only repaired by his decision to ride to Avalon with her. (5) The lovers in these *lais*, like most of Marie's lovers, are pure and upright: Yonec is approved as he takes the sacrament, Guigemar's sole imperfection is his failure to love, Lanval is exceptionally upright and pure if a little too straightforward with the queen. The real point here is that the type of love engendered in these tales — true, heartfelt, natural — subordinates the real consideration of adultery. (6) The human lover in each of these *lais* is driven to action by an intolerable situation in his own life: the lady of *Yonec* is the victim of a traditional *vieil jalous*; Guigemar is made to feel in his wound the need for love in his life; Lanval is the lonely and disregarded stranger.

The main problem posed by these three *lais* is the inevitable mingling of reality and the Other World when the lovers reach for happiness with each other. Yonec invades the real world and is killed by it; Guigemar is challenged to invade the Other World (perhaps is called by it) and comes near disaster, while his lady runs similar risks entering the mysterious ship and launching out into the world of love, the two of them being saved only by their fidelity; Lanval living in the real world while enjoying the fruits of the Other World, is human enough to speak of the latter against his promise and, having courted disaster, finds happiness in the Other World. A major aspect of the differing solutions offered by each *lai* to their common problem is the extent to which each of the two worlds is clearly demarcated and separated from the other. *Yonec* provides the clearest example of separation between the two; we and the characters know when the Other World is entered, the *chevalier fée* invades the real world, the lady knows where she is when she finds him dying; Yonec suffers the penalty of encountering brutal reality. In *Lanval,* one would suspect a dream were it not for the physical evidence of the knight's new wealth; once Lanval invokes the Other World as a defense in the real, the consequent entrapment can only be resolved by the actual physical appearance of his lady from the Other World; the complication is more subtle if less physical, the solution is the reverse. *Guigemar* offers the greatest degree of complexity wherein the world of the knight and that of the lady appear equally real and brutal; each of the couple appears to enter the Other World by embarking on the mysterious ship in search of true love. This may be viewed as the clue to the highest significance of the Other World motif. Pure, disinterested, heartfelt love is consistently a value in the *lais* of Marie de France. So rare a possession is it in the real world, that in these three *lais* it is more clearly the property of the Other World. Bringing such love into contact with the real world, however, risks its destruction as in *Yonec.* Flight to the Other World preserves love for Lanval; only the greatest fidelity saves the love of Guigemar and his lady.

It is arresting to notice at work in *Eliduc* the motifs (with perhaps one exception) distinctive of the Other World *lai*. Let us review them in order. (1) A foreign land is the source of a natural and reciprocal love; (2) Eliduc crosses the barrier of the sea, an experience which proves a real barrier to happiness on the return journey; (4) death threatens to make permanent the separation already experienced once; (5) Eliduc is a man of honour and adherence to duty, even avoiding adultery in a Christian world of reality; the young lady is similarly honourable as she reacts violently to the news of Eliduc's married state; (6) an intolerable situation in his own land motivates Eliduc's venture abroad. The third motif — the *merveilleux* — is missing, but perhaps not entirely. In this setting of reality, folklore replaces the exotic supernatural of the Other World *lais*; the function of the cure of the weasel and of the storm at sea or Jonah motif is in a structural sense similar to the conventional *merveilleux*.[1] Even as *Eliduc* shares the structure of the Other World *lais*, so its problem is theirs: the insecurity of true love in the real world. The solution

---

[1] Naturally, other folkloric elements exist in *Eliduc,* but their enumeration is incidental to the present analysis. See Mary H. Ferguson, "Folklore in the *Lais* of Marie de France," *R. R.* LVII (1966), 3-24.

offered to this problem and the account given by the poem of pure, disinterested human love constitute the distinctive features of *Eliduc*. With the preceding as background, we may attempt an analysis of this Other World *lai* in real world dress.

The main problem of *Eliduc* is the familiar one of the dangerous mingling of two worlds of reality and love in order to find happiness. [2] Tied by more durable bonds of duty to the real world, to his *seigneur* and to his wife, and by bonds of love to the young lady, Eliduc attempts to bring his love into the world of his real obligations and meets disaster. The solution offered is unique in the *Lais*: the wife's love manifests itself as *caritas* towards one's fellow and leaves the way open for the lovers' legitimate happiness — directly contrary to the *vieil jalous* situation in *Yonec* and *Guigemar*. Love thus liberated by love evolves into the highest form of *caritas* — the love of God.

The poem presents a symmetrical structure of seven divisions, the fourth and central one containing the material of crisis. On a lesser scale, the Other World *lais* trace a course from ignorance or deprivation of true love to a realization of its nature and even possession of it regardless of the consequences. In the first three divisions Eliduc finds both love and success in the Other World; in the fourth and central division, the uneasy balance between love and duty accentuates the inevitability of his having to choose; in the last three divisions, Eliduc's attempt to unite conflicting allegiances precipitates a calamity only cured by *caritas*.

(1) vv. 1-88. [3] The impact of this first division centres squarely on the upright moral character of Eliduc. The ideally capable vassal and knight (6, 8, 32-40), falsely and successfully accused by jealous opponents and banished without opportunity for self defence, takes his fate philosophically (55-65), neither reviling his seigneur nor becoming a rebel. Responsible attention to duty in the preparation for his wife's security (71-74) and in his assurances of faith-

---

[2] Leo Spitzer's view of the problem ("Marie de France: Dichterin von Problem-Märchen," ZRP L [1930], 31-32) examines the *amor-crestienté* struggle which we view as one aspect of Eliduc's moral nature. F. Schnürr ("Komposition und Symbol in den *Lais* der Marie de France," ZRP L [1930] 556-82) rejects the problem hypothesis, seeing the poem as a female-centred view of love.

[3] All line references are to A. Ewert, ed., *Marie de France: Lais* (Blackwell's, Oxford: 1952).

fulness to her (83-84), supported by his explicit statement in v. 70, indicates that he views his absence as a finite vacation and that his choice is not to go either adventuring or philandering. Eliduc's preference for home and duty is rendered impossible of fulfillment by his intolerable situation.

(2) vv. 88-270. The function of this second section is to demonstrate Eliduc's natural responsibility in new and freer circumstances. He cannot overlook the war around him (104-105) and his sympathies naturally go to the underdog (107-110). Eliduc's polite offer (116 117), his generosity and modest style (138-144) and his willingness to act (153) culminate in a display of generalship (165-204) not common to the knights of medieval romance in whom personal bravery against even foolhardy odds is frequently regarded positively. Once the king's moment of doubt has passed (227-232), Eliduc receives the reward of responsible service — the protectorship of the land. This episode further reinforces Eliduc's probity in establishing success abroad in juxtaposition to injustice at home; the comparison in no way obscures his view of duty to his original *seigneur*.

(3) vv. 271-549. The virtues of Eliduc rehearsed in the opening lines of the third section reach the ear of the maiden (271-274) and cause her to fall in love with the hero (304-306). Experiencing desperation at the thought that he may not reciprocate (348-350, 398-400), she sends him presents (352-81). Like many heroines of Marie de France, she realizes the power of this love to run counter to "social necessity" (387-394), yet blind passion does not drive her to excesses; she is willing to campaign a little (449-457). Eliduc's reaction is slow, even unwilling. At first only "murnes et trespensez" (314), he clings to the faithfulness promised to his wife (322-326). His reported lack of reaction confirms his state of mind (422-433), later frankly described as "dolur" (458-459). The conflict of love and duty is precisely resumed in vv. 460-476. Electing a course which hopefully will pacify desire and satisfy duty while preserving honour, Eliduc attempts to balance the conflicting demands in a fashion which one may condemn as casuistic or understand as human. The key limitation, in Eliduc's view, is found in vv. 473-474:

> Mes ja ne li querra amur
> Ke li aturt a deshonur.

The outstanding feature of this relationship with the maiden —typical of its "otherworldliness"— is its ideal nature; the combination of frank (513-517) but unhurried and trusting maiden (532-536) and approving father (493-496) provides Eliduc with a situation almost devoid of compromise. Stating frankly that he must return at the call of duty (528-30), he adds a "by your leave" which the maiden's confidence freely grants. Despite the moral positions available concerning the degree of fidelity exhibited by Eliduc, the poem, consonant with the moral framework provided by the *Lais*, accepts the situation as harmonious with Eliduc's high character. Although the *Lais* elsewhere condone adultery when true love is at stake, Eliduc stops short of that expedient. This is the period of bliss before the crisis. Duty and love are held in balance as Eliduc's oath keeps him at the foreign court for a year; this is no facile excuse, however — once duty calls, he will leave.

(4) vv. 550-704. In this section, the full extent of the crisis is felt: the occasion is the conflict between the need for Eliduc's services at home (552-570) and the depth and purity of his love for the maiden (572-580). In the very central passage of the poem, Eliduc enunciates his problem:

> 'Allas!' fet il, 'mal ai erré!
> Trop ai en cest païs esté!
> Mar vi unkes ceste cuntrée!
> Une meschine i ai amée,
> Guilliadun, la fille al rei,
> Mut durement e ele mei.
> Quant si de li m'estuet partir,
> Un de nus deus estuet murir
> U ambedeus, estre ceo peot.
> E nepurquant aler m'esteot;
> Mis sires m'ad par bref mandé
> E par serement conjuré
> E ma femme de l'autre part.
> Or me covient que jeo me gart!
> Jeo ne puis mie remaneir,
> Ainz m'en irai par estuveir.
> S'a m'amie esteie espusez,
> Nel suffereit crestïentez.
>
> (585-602)

The above passage of eighteen lines states the problem in a curious division: twelve lines for home, wife and duty; six for the maiden and her love. Eliduc is no Tristan.[4] The central line of the poem strikes an ominous note of prophecy: "Un de nus deus estuet murir" (592). During the maiden's swoon, itself a foreshadowing of death, Eliduc is at last free to speak his mind in a moment of great emotion, conscious of the disaster which his secret may precipitate, but growing more helpless under the power of love:

> Mes jeo ferai vostre pleisir,
> Que ke me deive avenir.
> (677-678)

The essence of the love between Eliduc and the maiden is perfect trust; for this reason she grants him leave to a specific time:

> Cele ot de lui grant amur;
> Terme li dune e nume jur
> De venir e pur li mener.
> (697-699)

The function of Eliduc's falsity in concealing his marriage is clear in its contrast with the king's generous kindness and the maiden's unselfish love: his deceit violates the essential atmosphere of trust which the poem has established. While any attempt to unite his two worlds would bring disaster, it is for this specific violation that he will suffer. His relief will come through a manifestation of higher love and the trust which it engenders. In his attempt to balance the demands of the two worlds, Eliduc has set up a tension which definite action alone can resolve but which can only end in misfortune. Since act he must, Eliduc seeks out each alternative in turn.

(5) vv. 705-952. Having crossed the sea in pursuit of his duty, Eliduc is unhappy, separated from his love. His wife's reaction is ironic (718-725) in view of his real trouble, but it stirs him to try his second alternative. Although he seizes on duty to the foreign

---

[4] S. Hofer's parallel of the two tales ("Zur Beurteilung der *Lais* de Marie de France," *ZRP* LXVI [1950], 418) is convincing for the physical detail but he vitiates any possible comparison of meaning by dismissing the ending of *Eliduc* as "nichts anderes als die Konzession der Dichterin an die religiösen Anschauungen ihrer Zeit." Other studies are similarly restricted to external detail: see G. Schoepperle, *Tristran and Isolt* (Frankfurt and London: 1913), vol. 1, pp. 161 ff., and R. N. Illingworth, "La Chronologie des *Lais* de Marie de France," *Romania* LXXXVII (1966), 433-75.

king as an excuse to leave, Eliduc's actions from this point on are dictated by his passion. Increasingly, he acts out of emotion and desperation, not out of logic or reason, thus rejoining the main body of Marie's lovers:

> Tels est la mesure de amer
> Que nul n'i deit reisun garder.
> *(Equitan,* vv. 19-20)

Eliduc's precautions in taking the maiden away (749-814) under cover of night and aided by trusted men, while understandable in his own world, seem needless in view of the friendly and generous attitude of the foreign king. Eliduc attempts to operate in a sphere of total unreality, trying to preserve his love in an isolation in which they may live without external references. But contact with reality is inevitable, and brutal in the form of the sailor's accusation (831-840) which both breaks the isolation and reveals the extent of Eliduc's trespass into the other world. She has loved him ideally and with complete trust; he, more human (or perhaps more entangled and therefore more real), has concealed his marriage, lying in preference to losing her.

The result is fitting. Even as Eliduc sought isolation for his love, now he is similarly punished. After losing his head and killing the sailor (his first dishonourable act), he then renounces worldly life entirely:

> 'Bele,' fet il, 'ja Deu ne place
> Que jamés puisse armes porter
> Ne al secle vivre ne durer!
> (938-940)

> Le jur que jeo vus enfuirai
> Ordre de moigne recevrai.
> (947-948)

But love is also gone, being now only a subject of lament for him. His decision to found an abbey and church to have prayers said for her and to become a monk that 'his grief may resound daily upon her tomb' (949-950) is less an act of piety than of regret, less a positive movement than a negative substitution. The prophecy of vv. 592-593 has in a sense come true. While Eliduc's grief and renunciation are real and almost a penance, once love in a higher form intervenes, their negative aspect is completely reversed.

(6) vv. 953-1144. The wife's motivation to *caritas,* to love of one's fellow, is expressed in vv. 1027-1028:

> 'Tan par pité, tant par amur,
> Jamés n'avrai joie nul jur.'

From concern for the happiness of her husband, the wife passes to a first dramatic reaction to her rival — a reaction not explored, explained or motivated explicitly by the narrator. It is pure unselfishness, an effusion of *caritas* toward the couple, motivated by a desire for and confirmed by the sight (1120) of their happiness. The wife echoes (1128-1130) the reservation early felt by Eliduc about the impropriety of bigamy. She takes the veil and the lovers are allowed to enter upon their idyllic period.

(7) vv. 1145-1184. Properly speaking, this idyllic period is disposed of in two lines:

> Ensemble vesquirent meint jur,
> Mut ot entre eus parfit' amur.
>
> (1149-1150)

The brevity is functional, permitting a logical statement of their happiness without losing the thread of the development of their love into *caritas* of the highest order. The survival of true human love in a real world of duty and social responsibility (i. e., the survival of the ideal in a real setting) is made possible only by an act of purest charity. The application of one facilitates the other.[5] But both are of course viewed as subordinate to the love of God. The negative aspects of Eliduc's renunciation of the world and penitential service of God are reversed by the wife's *caritas.* Restored to love and to a functional worldly life, the couple turn to God's service, eventually renouncing human love and worldly position in order to serve Him directly (1163-1166).

---

[5] "... loving his neighbour as himself, a man turns the whole current of his love both for himself and his neighbour into the channel of the love of God, which suffers no stream to be drawn off from itself by whose diversion its own volume would be diminished." Saint Augustine, *De doctrina christiana,* I, 21 (22). Translation in *A Select Library of the Nicene and Post-Nicene Fathers of the Christian Church,* ed. by Philip Schall (New York: 1899).

The nature of true human love throughout the *Lais* of Marie de France is such that it overrides the social strictures set upon it (eg., arranged unsuitable marriages, social injunctions against adultery and pre-marital relations). Pure and disinterested love, arising naturally between two mutually attractive people, is an ideal state whose source Marie de France may fittingly state as the Other World. *Caritas*, whose source is God and therefore "otherwordly," is similarly presented as superior to human love, encompassing the latter only as a reflection of itself. *Eliduc* alone among the *Lais* carries love to this conclusion — a fitting theme for the final *lai* in ms H.[6]

---

[6] We make no claim on the chronology of composition. Note Illingworth's view (*op. cit.*) that *Yonec, Guigemar, Lanval* and *Eliduc* were all written around the same time.

TWO TRANSLATIONS FROM RAIMBAUT DE VAQUEIRAS

By Nathaniel B. Smith

Dawn-Song

Guard our fun,   guard of the castle strong,
When that one   for whom I greatly long
Is with me   till the dawning,
Till the sun   does us great wrong:
        A new song
    Is robbed by dawn, dawn, yes the dawning.

Guard, friend mine,   stand watch and sing thy chaunt;
My joy's fine,   for I've what I most want.
A bad sign,   though, is dawning
And the pain   of day's long taunt
        Me doth haunt
    Still more than dawn, dawn, yes the dawning.

Watch thou out,   my friend guard, and give ear,
For that lout,   my lady's overseer,
Joy would flout   as does dawning
While about   love we talk here
        And in fear
    Holds us the dawn, dawn, yes the dawning.

Dame, farewell!   No longer dare I stay;
I know well   I now must take my way.
Like to hell   is the dawning,
Fast and fell   it comes today
        And away
    Drives joy — the dawn, dawn, yes the dawning.

Plaint on a Crusader

O mighty waves who come upon the sea,
You whom the ranging wind blows far and free,
Tell tidings of my distant friend to me,
How fares he now, when his return may be.
      Alas! O God of lovers,
My joy for pain now sickens, now recovers.

Hark, gentle breeze who blow from far away,
From where my friend must sleep and dwell and stay,
Of his sweet breath bring me a drink this day:
For this I open wide my mouth and pray.
      Alas! O God of lovers,
My joy for pain now sickens, now recovers.

The loves of foreign lands will soon pass by
And e'er their smile and sport turn to a sigh....
I never thought my dearest friend would lie
To one who gave him so much love as I.
      Alas! O God of lovers,
My joy for pain now sickens, now recovers.

CHRISTINE DE PIZAN'S TREATISE ON THE ART OF MEDIEVAL WARFARE

By CHARITY C. WILLARD
West Point, New York

Recent years have witnessed a renewed interest in the writings of Christine de Pizan, France's first "professional" woman of letters. One effect of this interest has been a small, but growing, group of manuscripts containing her writings which has found its way to the United States. There are now seven, one of which, a late fifteenth century copy of the *Fais d'armes et de chevalerie*, belongs to Harvard's Houghton Library. Although the artistic value of these manuscripts varies considerably, and only one or two of them could possibly date from Christine's lifetime, nevertheless each offers a certain interest as it reflects the intellectual situation which produced it and the audience for which it was intended.

The Harvard MS. is thus described in the Houghton Library Catalogue:

> MS. 168: Le Livre des fais d'armes et de chevalerie...
> ms. on paper [France, late 15th c.] 254 fol. (505 p.)
> Red Morocco binding (Chambolle-Duru)
> Formerly owned by Comte Pierre Louis Roederer and his son-in-law, Baron Gaspard Gourjoud, who inscribed it.

An examination of the manuscript itself provides the additional information that the folios (273 × 200 mm) are written in long lines and that the dialect indicates transcription in Northern France. There are no illustrations, but chapter titles are rubricated. The name of the first owner was apparently Guillaume de Nast.

Christine de Pizan's authorship is nowhere mentioned in the text, although the preamble explaining why the book was written appears, as it does in only a few copies. However, the text is well enough known to be easily identified, for there are fifteen other known manuscripts, along with an edition published by Antoine Vérard (Paris, 1488) and another by Philippe LeNoir (Paris, 1527). Even better known is the translation prepared by William Caxton and published by his London press in 1489.

One reason this Caxton version is better known than its French original is that it exists in a modern edition,[1] whereas the French text has not been re-printed since the sixteenth century. At least twenty copies of the Caxton imprint are still in existence, five of them in the United States.[2]

The editor of the Caxton text calls attention to two groups of French manuscripts: Group A, which acknowledges Christine's authorship, and Group B (to which Houghton 168, unknown to Byles, must be added) which does not mention any author and in some cases replaces Christine's references to herself in the text with masculine pronouns.[3] The manuscript tradition presents some other peculiarities which cannot be examined in any detail here, except to suggest that they may represent, at least in some cases, an effort to keep the text abreast with the times. Thus they would indicate that the treatise was considered to have practical value. The manuscripts of Jean de Meung's translation of the Vegetius *De Re Militari* present a similar kind of divergence, although this may not indicate anything more significant than the fact that military men are not necessarily interested in problems of textual accuracy.[4] One variation between the two earliest manuscripts of the *Fais d'armes*

---

[1] Ed. by A. T. P. Byles, (London, 1932; re-issued with corrections, 1937).

[2] Byles mentions copies in the Huntington Library, San Marino, California; Columbia University; the Pierpont Morgan Library, New York; the Rosenbach Company, New York, the Grenville Kane Library, New York.

[3] Group A: British Museum, Royal 15 E vi, 19 B xviii and Harley 4605; Brussels, Bibl. Roy. MSS. 9009-11 and 10476; Paris, B. N. f. fr. 603, 1183 and 1241. The fragment listed as Collection Duchesne 65 is a seventeenth century copy and thus of slight interest here. Group B: Oxford, Bodleian 824; Brussels, Bibl. Roy. MS. 10205; Paris, B. N. f. fr. 585, 1242, 1243, 23997.

[4] *L'Art de Chevalerie; trad. du De Rei Militari de Végèce*, ed. U. Robert pour la Société des Anciens Textes, (Paris, 1897), pp. xvii-xix.

should be mentioned, however. Brussels, Bibl. Royale MS. 10476 has been used to date the composition because of a reference to the Battle of Liège, in which John the Fearless, Duke of Burgundy, scored a great victory on September 23, 1408.[5] Curiously enough, this passage has been omitted in Paris, B. N. f. fr. 603, a detail which gives rise to the suspicion that it might have been prepared for some Armagnac sympathizer during the Duke's banishment from the French capital between 1413 and 1418.[6] It is also interesting that the Caxton translation conforms in general to Group A, whereas the Vérard and Philippe LeNoir editions are related to Group B.

Those who have previously studied Christine de Pizan's writings have differed in their opinions of the value of the *Fais d'armes et de chevalerie,* in certain cases judging it to be little more than a translation of Vegetius with some additions from Honoré Bouvet's *Arbre des batailles.*[7] A better understanding of her methods of composition and her references to contemporary problems makes it evident that something more a translation was intended. Suzanne Solente has characterized it more accurately as a "manuel d'éducation, ouvrage de stratégie, et code du droit pour la société guerrière du Moyen Age."[8]

---

[5] Brussels MS. 10476, fol. 36v°. This manuscript comes from the original library of the Dukes of Burgundy, which contained copies of most of Christine's writings. See G. Doutrepont, *La Littérature française à la cour des ducs de Bourgogne,* (Paris, 1909), pp. 292-93; 478.

[6] Both Brussels MS. 10476 and B. N. f. fr. 603 are attributed by M. Meiss, (*French Painting in the Time of Jean de Berry,* London and New York, 1967, Vol. I, p. 356) to the workshop of an illustrator he names the Cité des Dames Master. However, the miniatures of f. fr. 603 do not fit properly into the spaces left for them, a curious detail which suggests that the manuscript was not illustrated under normal circumstances. For the varied and vindictive nature of the Armagnac attacks on their enemies after 1413, see R. Vaughan, *John the Fearless,* (London, 1966), pp. 193 ff.

[7] M.-J. Pinet, *Christine de Pisan; étude biographique et littéraire,* (Paris, 1927), p. 358 dismisses it as a translation saying, "*Le Livre des Fais d'armes et de chevalerie* n'est qu'une réédition, une adaptation d'auteurs latins appréciés au temps de Christine, traduits en français par d'autres auparavant et utilisés déjà par elle". E. Nyss, however, in his *Christine de Pisan et ses principales oeuvres,* (La Haye et Paris, 1914), gives particular attention to the text as being one of Christine's most interesting compositions. For Bouvet vs. Bonet, see G. Ouy, "Honoré Bouvet (appelé à tort Bonet), prieur de Selonnet", *Romania,* LXXX (1959), 225-259.

[8] Article on Christine in the *Dictionnaire des lettres françaises: le Moyen Age,* (Paris, 1964), p. 186, where she also confirms the date 1410 for the composition of the *Fais d'armes.*

The question still remains why Christine, a middle-aged woman of sedentary habits and literary orientation, should have undertaken to write a treatise on warfare. The preface, in which she tried to explain her intent, suggests that she was aware of the awkwardness of her position, for she says:

> Ainsi qu'à propos j'ay assemblé les matieres et cuilliés en plusieurs livres pour produire à mon intencion ou present volume, mais comme il affiere ceste matiere estre plus executée par fait, diligence et sens, que par soubtilleté de paroles polies, et aussi consideré que les exerçans et expers en la dicte art de chevalerie ne sont communement clers ne intruis en science de langaige, je n'entens de traictier ne mais tout au plus plain et entendible langaige que je pourray à celle fin que la doctrine donné par plusieurs aucteurs qu'à l'aide de Dieu propose en ce present livre d'eclairier puist estre à tous clere et entendible.[9]

This much is evident, then: Christine was undertaking a work of popularization, with the intention of making material collected from literary sources intelligible to men of action, that is to say, military men who might need the information for practical purposes. However, having made her reputation not only as a courtly poet, but also as the author of the *Epître d'Othéa,* a high-flown mythological treatise dedicated to the formation of the perfect knight, she could not resist mentioning these exploits, which she undoubtedly considered more ot her credit than the one upon which she was about to embark. She therefore decided to take refuge behind the figure of Minerva who, according to mythology, had invented the art of forging metal armor, likewise a rather unladylike pursuit:

> Et pour ce que c'est chose non accoustumnée et hors usage à femme, qui communement ne se sieust entremectre ne mes de guenouilles , filaces et chose de mainage, je supplie humblement audit tres hault office et noble estat de chevalerie que en contemplacion de la saige dame Minerve, née du pays de Grece, que les anciens pour sa grant savoir repputerent deesse, laquelle trouva selon ce que dient les anciens escripts, si que autrefois ai dit, et que meismement le recite le pouete Bocace en son *Livre des dames cleres,* et

---

[9] Brussels MS. 10476, fol. 1v°.

semblablement le recitent autres plusieurs, l'art et maniere de faire le harnois de fer et d'acier, qu'ilz ne vueillent avoir à mal se moy, femme, me suis chargée de traictier de si faicte matiere, ains vueillent ensuivre l'enseignement de Seneque qui die, mais que les paroles soient bonnes et pour ce et à propos, en maniere pouetique me plaist adrecier tel oroison à la susdicte dame..." [10]

Obviously Christine had cited Minerva before, not only in her *Cité des Dames*, where Boccaccio's *De Claris Mulieribus* was one of her principal sources, but even earlier in the *Epître d'Othéa* and also in the *Fais et Bonnes meurs du sage roy Charles V*. [11]

Her evocation of the remarkably popular *Epître d'Othéa* [12] suggests the possibility that someone familiar with Christine's earlier work might have asked her to undertake what really amounts to a modernization of Vegetius. If she lacked experience in warfare, she had in any case given ample evidence of a particular interest in educating the young through popularizations of the best known classics. There is, for instance, her own statement that she had written the *Livre du Corps de policie*, based largely on Valerius Maximus, for the Dauphin of France, Louis of Guyenne. [13] She would later dedicate to him her *Livre de la Paix* (1413), a treatise on good

---

[10] Brussels MS. 10476, fol. 4r°.

[11] For Christine's indebtedness to Boccaccio see J. Jeanroy, "Boccace et Christine de Pisan: le *De Claris mulieribus* comme principale source du *Livre de la Cité des Dames*", *Romania*, XLVIII (1922), 93 - 105.

For the *Epître d'Othéa*, B. N. f. fr. 606, fol. 8v°: "Glose: Minerve fu une dame de moult grant savoir et trouva l'art de faire armeures, car devant ne s'armoient point les gens fors de cuir boulu. Et pour la grant science qui fu en ceste dame, l'appellerent deesse". In the *Livre des Fais et bonnes meurs du sage roy Charles V*, she invoked Minerva, saying: "Et quant ad ce que femme suis ose parler d'armes, il est escript que es anciens aages, comme autrefois ay dit, une sage femme de Grece nommée Minerve trouva l'art et science de faire armeures de fer et d'acier, et tous les harnois que on seult porter en bataille, fu par lui premierement trouvé..." (ed. S. Solente, Paris, 1936, Vol. I, p. 192).

[12] For an analysis of the *Epître d'Othéa*, see R. Tuve, *Allegorical Imagery*, (Princeton U., 1966), pp. 33-55; for some idea of its popularity, G. Mombello, *La Tradizione manoscritto dell' "Epistre Othea" di Christine de Pizan: Prolegomeni all'edizione del testo*, (Torino, 1967).

[13] *Le Livre du Corps de Policie*, éd. critique par R. H. Lucas (Genève et Paris, 1967), pp. xii - xiii.

government.[14] It has also been suggested with considerable justice that Philip the Bold might have commissioned Christine to write the *Fais et bonnes meurs du sage roy Charles V* at least partly with the idea of putting before the eyes of the young prince the example of his grandfather's successful reign as well as of his intellectual interests.[15]

The dauphin's education was also a matter of interest to several of Christine's contemporaries and it would appear that an effort was made to provide for him an essentially humanistic education. His tutor and confessor, Jean d'Arsonval, not only seems to have had a taste for classical letters, but was certainly in contact with leading humanists of the first Parisian group. A certain Odo Pictavis was commissioned to prepare for Louis a commentary on the *Ecloga Theodoli,* a treatise on classical mythology.[16] In 1410 the young prince, born January 22, 1397 and thus thirteen years old, would have been deemed to be of a suitable age to begin military training. Even if Christine had a wider audience in view, she could scarcely have overlooked the needs of the dauphin at that particular moment.

Another question which obviously must be considered is what person at the royal court might have been taking a sufficiently great interest in the Duke of Guyenne to have commissioned the *Fais d'armes,* or at least to have suggested that such a treatise would find favor. In 1410 only one answer seems logical: John the Fearless. On December 28, 1409 he had become the official governor of Louis, who was already his son-in-law.[17] The act marked the Duke of Bur-

---

[14] *Le Livre de la Paix,* ed. C. C. Willard, (The Hague, 1958). Here Christine mentions having also dedicated to the dauphin an *Avision du Cocq,* unknown today. See M. K. Sneyders de Vogel, "Une œuvre inconnue de Christine de Pisan", *Mélanges de philologie romane et de littérature médiévale offerts à E. Hoepffner,* (Paris, 1949), p. 360.

[15] Introduction, Solente ed., p. xxviii.

[16] For Jean d'Arsonval, see H. Martin, *Le Térence des Ducs,* (Paris, 1907), Introduction; for Odo Pictavis, B. N. Quinn in *Speculum,* XXXVIII (1963), 480. See also A. Thomas, *Jean de Gerson et l'éducation des dauphins de France,* (Paris, 1930).

[17] Archives du Nord B 1600, fol. 102; R. Vaughan, *John the Fearless,* p. 81 and Note; also the comment of E. de Monstrelet, (*Chronique,* ed. L. Douët d'Arcq, Paris, 1857 - 62, II, 59): (1409) "Mais avant qu'ilz se partissent, par le consentement du Roy et de la Royne, ledit duc d'Acquitaine

gundy's triumph over his political rivals, the Armagnacs. For two years, ever since his involvement in the murder of his cousin, Louis of Orleans, he had been striving to achieve this end, and he lost no time in surrounding the dauphin with his own faithful servants, notably Jean de Nieles, governor of Arras, and Guillaume de Vienne, member of a family long associated with Burgundian affairs. It is difficult to determine the extent to which Jean d'Arsonval was under the Burgundian duke's influence, but at the very least he was a native of Burgundy and John the Fearless does not seem to have opposed his pedagogical ideas. [18]

As the dauphin was also given authority to represent his father during his "absences" at the end of 1409, John the Fearless became the ruler of Paris in all but name. [19] Other members of the royal family, above all the Orleans princes and their friends, immediately united in what is known as the "League of Gien". Formed by April 1410, its first move was to raise an army for the purpose of attacking the Duke of Burgundy in the fall, although their motive was expressed publicly as "rescuing the king and dauphin for the purpose of *restoring* them to power." [20] There followed a period of crisis when both sides had mustered troops around Paris, a situation temporarily resolved on November 2 by the Treaty of Bicêtre, signed in the Duke of Berry's château in the outskirts of Paris. From September 1409 until November 1410 John the Fearless was usually in Paris, strengthening the defenses of his Hôtel d'Artois as well as his popularity among the Parisians. Many of his supporters were artisans, although he was friendly with the University as well. Among the most prominent Burgundian partisans, however, was the Guild of Butchers.

(Louis de Guyenne) fut baillé à garder et endoctriner au duc de Bourgogne, lequel ne désiroit autre chose et à ce avoit moult labouré..."

[18] Jean d'Arsonval founded a mass for the repose of Louis de Guyenne's soul in the church of Arsonval (diocese of Langres), Arch. Nat. KK 48, fol. 123 and L. Pannier, "Les joyaux du duc de Guyenne, recherches sur les goûts artistiques et la vie privée du dauphin Louis, fils de Charles VI", *Revue archéologique*, XXVI (1873), 215n. His place of origin and his appointment, in 1413, as Bishop of Chalons-sur-Saône strongly suggest Burgundian sympathies.

[19] Ordonnance of December 31, 1409, *Ords. des rois de France de la troisième race*, (ed. D. F. Secousse, 21 vol., Paris, 1723-1849), XII, 229-31, cited by Vaughan, p. 81.

[20] Vaughan, p. 82.

It was in these circumstances that on August 23, 1410, Christine addressed to the Duke of Berry her "Epistre sur les maux de la guerre civile." [21] It gives every indication of being Burgundian propaganda, as was indeed the case of all letters written to the Duke of Berry at that time, according to Juvenal des Ursins. [22] The same circumstances presumably surrounded the composition of the *Fais d'armes et de chevalerie*. What is certain is that Christine received a gift from the Royal Treasury, registered on May 13, 1411. The terms of the gift are sufficiently vague to allow for the possibility that she was being rewarded for the letter. Could it also have been a gratification for the *Fais d'armes*? [23]

There are, of course, a number of reasons for believing that the Duke of Burgundy might have wanted to provide some instruction in the art of warfare for his royal charge. In 1410, by order of the king, the *capitainerie* of Creil had already been set aside to encourage the prince to engage in physical exercise, to which he does not seem to have been addicted by nature. [24] At the time it was well known

---

[21] B. N. f. fr. 24874, published by R. Thomassy in *Essai sur les écrits politiques de Christine de Pisan*, (Paris, 1838), pp. 141-149.

[22] Monstrelet (II, 77) for July 1410: "Il est vérité qu'en ces propres jours, le duc de Berry, pour ce qu'il n'avoit plus si grand audience et gouvernement autour du Roy et du duc d'Acquitaine qu'il avoit acoustumé, print tres grant desplaisance, et s'en retourna en son pays, non content de ceulx qui avoit le gouvernement, et par especial de son neveu et filleul le duc de Bourgogne. Et tantost apres, s'en alla à Angers où furent assembléz avecques lui les ducs d'Orléans et de Bourbon et tous les grans seigneurs de ceste aliance...." Juvenal des Ursins (Michaud et Poujoulat, *Mémoires pour servir à l'histoire de France*, Paris, 1836, pp. 454-55): "Et pour ce que le duc de Bourgogne estoit a Paris et avoit en ses mains le Dauphin, toutes les lettres qui s'escrivoient a mon seigneur de Berry et autres seigneurs se faisoient au nom du roy ou dudit monseigneur le Dauphin".

[23] "A demoiselle Christine de Pisan, veufve de feu maistre Estienne Castel, jadis clerc, notaire et secrétaire du Roy, pour considération de bons et agreables services que feu maistre Thomas de Boulogne, en son vivant conseiller et astrologue du feu roy Charles, que Dieu pardoint, et que le dit seigneur et aussi pere d'elle avoit faits et pour certaines autres causes et considerations, deux cent livres, par lettres du Roi, du 13 mai 1411". Bibl. Nat. coll. Dupuy, Vol. 755, fol 97v°, and Denys Godefroy, *Histoire de Charles VI*, (Paris, 1653), pp. 790-91, cited by S. Solente, Intro. to ed. of *Fais et bonnes meurs de Charles V*, pp. xxii-xxiii and Pinet, p. 145.

[24] See L. Douët d'Arcq, *Choix de pièces inédites relatives au règne de Charles VI*, (Paris, 1863), I, p. 325. In both the *Livre des fais et bonnes meurs de Charles V* and the *Fais d'armes* Christine speaks of the value of exercise for children, in citing the example of Romans. See S. Solente, *Fais et bonnes meurs*, I, p. 207 and note.

that the Duke of Burgundy's enemies were arming to attack Paris.[25] Furthermore, John the Fearless was one of the few French princes who can be said to have had any genuine military talent or sense of strategy. It was his victory over the citizens of Liège at the Battle of Othée which had been the bulwark of his triumphal return to Paris in the fall of 1409, a feat which is mentioned in certain manuscripts of the *Fais d'armes*.[26] Not without significance is the fact that John the Fearless had gained his military skill at painful cost. As official head of a spectacular expedition to Hungary in 1396 which met ignominious defeat at the Battle of Nicopolis, the twenty-four year old prince must inevitably have been shocked at the shortcomings demonstrated by the French cavalry in the face of Bajazet's strategy. Furthermore, he had been forced to witness the execution of dozens of his companions-at-armis by the ruthless Turks and had escaped death himself only because he could be more profitably held for a high ransom.[27] During several months of Turkish captivity, he had been given an ample opportunity to meditate on this devastating experience. It is curious that so little attention

---

[25] Juvenal des Ursins, pp. 454-455: (1410) "Les seigneurs dont dessus est fait mention, estans à Gien, partirent dudit lieu, et s'en allerent chacun en son pays. Et sceut-on bien que c'estoit pour assembler gens de guerre... Le duc de Bourgogne, voyant et sachant que l'armee se faisoit contre luy, se pourveut et manda gens de guerre, et en mit dedans la ville de Paris assez competemment..."

[26] The Battle of Liège is mentioned in B. N. f. fr. 1183, fol. 57v° and f. fr. 23997, fol. 47v° in addition to Brussels MS. 10476 and the MSS. on which the Caxton translation is based.

[27] For details of the ill-fated expedition to Nicopolis, see J. Delaville le Roux, *La France en Orient au XIVe siècle*, 2 vol. (Paris, 1886); A. S. Atiya, *The Crusade of Nicopolis*, (London, 1934) and *The Crusade in the Later Middle Ages*, (London, 1938); B. A. Pocquet du Haut Jussé, "Le retour de Nicopolis et la rançon de Jean sans Peur", *Annales de Bourgogne*, IX (1937), 296-302, and R. Vaughan, *Philip the Bold*, (London, 1962).

A more contemporary account of the disaster is to be found in the anonymous *Livre des faits de Jean Bouciquaut*, publ. by J. A. C. Buchon in his ed. of *Les Chroniques de Froissart*, (Paris, 1838), which makes this comment on the reaction of John of Nevers to the execution of his companions (p. 597):

"Si pouvez savoir, vous qui ce oyez, si grand douleur avoit au cœur, luy qui est un tres bon et benin seigneur, et si grand mal luy faisoit d'ainsi veoir martirer ses bons et loyaulx compaignons, et ses gens, qui tant luy avoient esté feaulx, et qui si preux par excellence estoient. Certes, je croy que tant luy en douloit le cœur que il voulsist à celle mort estre de leur compaignie".

has been paid to the influence of this episode of his youth in attempting to account for the sombre personality he developed later. Two details should serve to emphasize the importance of these memories in his later action. In the first place, he had a special devotion to Saint Leonard, patron of prisoners, who is especially commemorated in one of his prayer books; also there is a striking resemblance in the strategy he employed at Liège and Bajazet's tactics at Nicopolis. It should be noted, furthermore, that Jacques de Heilly, a veteran of Nicopolis, was one of his commanders at Liège.[28]

Another reason for assuming that John of Burgundy would have had a particular interest in the dauphin's military training, practical as well as theoretical, is that the prince actually accompanied him on at least two military expeditions: a well-organized attack on the Armagnac encampments in Saint Cloud and Saint Denis in November 1411, and the siege of Bourges in June 1412.[29] By 1412, Louis of Guyenne was showing signs of turning into a very helpful ally. Subsequent history might have been quite different had it not been for the excesses of the Cabochien uprising in the late spring of 1413.[30]

The abortive Parisian effort at government reform inspired the other treatise which Christine dedicated to Louis of Guyenne, the *Livre de la Paix*. Along with a vivid description of the popular uprising, which has lost little of its credibility today, Christine saw fit to admonish the dauphin to play a decisive role in the destinies of his country. Interestingly enough, his effort to do that very thing appears to have been instrumental in bringing about the fall of the Burgundian domination and, for better or worse, the return of the Armagnac faction to power in Paris. From the late summer of 1413 until his premature death in November 1415 Louis of Guyenne gave evidence of trying to live up to the role history had

---

[28] L. Mirot has indeed called attention to the significance of this devotion to Saint Leonard in "Jean sans Peur, de 1398 à 1405", *Annuaire-Bulletin de la Société de l'Histoire de France*, (1958), 187 and "Le Livre d'Heures de Jean sans Peur", *Bibliothèque de l'École des Chartes*, CX (1940), 225n.

[29] The Siege of Bourges is another operation where the presence of Jacques de Heilly is to be noted. Vaughan, *John the Fearless*, pp. 93-96.

[30] *John the Fearless*, p. 100; A. Coville, *Les Cabochiens et l'Ordonnance de 1413*, (Paris, 1888) and *L'Ordonnance cabochienne*, (Paris, 1891).

thrust upon him, and which Christine, among other moderate Parisians, had implored him to assume. Unfortunately for John the Fearless, his ambition to form a "perfect prince" seems to have turned against him.

A final question concerning the *Livre des fais d'armes* must be raised: the reason for the choice of the text used as its basis. Vegetius had been known in French translation since the end of the thirteenth century, for Jean de Meung had translated the text in 1284. Soon afterwards his version had been put into rhyme by Jean Priorat of Besançon. In both cases the Latin text was modified somewhat to make it understandable to medieval minds. Two further translations were added in the course of the fourteenth century: Jean de Vignay's during the first part and an anonymous version dated 1380. It can scarcely be concluded, then, that a fifth text was needed to make Vegetius known to Christine's contemporaries. It has been demonstrated, furthermore, that Christine made use of Jean de Vignay's translation, although she also cited some passages that she quite evidently knew through Henri de Gauchi's translation of Gilles de Rome's *De Regimine Principum,* which she used extensively in composing both the *Fais et bonnes meurs de Charles V* and the *Livre de la Paix*. In these same treatises she speaks of a number of such translations she had used as sources in describing the Royal Library founded by Charles V in a tower of the Louvre. [31]

Thus it seems necessary to look elsewhere for Christine's true source of inspiration for her treatise on warfare. Recent investigations of the intellectual climate in Paris during the early years of the fifteenth century suggest the possibility that she may have been inspired by an idea expressed by Petrarch, that fountainhead of early humanism. [32] Certainly Christine was in touch with the Parisian milieu where he was most admired, made up in large part by secretaries

---

[31] For Christine's knowledge of Vegetius, see P. Meyer, "Les anciens traducteurs français de Végèce", *Romania,* XXV (1896), 401-423. She speaks of the library of Charles V in the *Fais et bonnes meurs,* Solente ed. II, pp. 42-46, and in the *Livre de la Paix,* Willard ed., p. 142. See also *La Librairie de Charles V,* catalogue of an exposition organized by the Bibliothèque Nationale, Paris, 1968.

[32] Franco Simone, *Il Rinascimento Francese,* (Torino, 1961) and *Miscellanea di Studi e Ricerche sul Quattrocento Francese,* a cura di Franco Simone, (Torino, 1967).

of the Royal Chancellery, some of whom had been former colleagues of her husband, Etienne du Castel.[33]

Petrarch had, of course, visited Paris in 1361, as head of the embassy sent by the Duke of Milan to congratulate King John on his return from captivity in England. Thus he had the opportunity to form friendships with such French admirers as Pierre Bersuire and Philippe de Vitry and to discuss with them subjects of mutual interest. He later recalled his impressions of the trip in two letters addressed to Bersuire. The Prior of Saint-Eloi did not live long enough to receive them, but they subsequently appeared in Petrarch's collected correspondence. The second letter, in particular, expresses dismay at the low estate into which France and his native Italy had fallen —France devastated by war with the English and many Italian cities deprived of their liberty. To him the reason was certain: Roman warriors had given way to a lesser, undisciplined breed of men. The need to revive Roman virtues and to provide new inspiration by the example of Roman military and civic heroes was implicit. Such an idea had already been mentioned by Christine in the *Livre des fais et bonnes meurs de Charles V*; it is developed in both the *Corps de policie* and the *Livre des fais d'armes*.[34]

If the connection between Christine and Petrarch seems rather tenuous, one has only to recall that although Pierre Bersuire could not receive Petrarch's letters himself, his nephew headed the Priory of Saint-Eloi until 1406. The occasion of the embassy was not forgotten either. Christine speaks of the French king's fate in the *Fais d'armes* with the following comment:

> Si appert par les grans conquestes que les anciens firent jadis, que les gens ne sont si vaillans comme ilz souloient, et de ce à quoi il tient rent la raison le prealigué Vegece, qui dit que la longue paix a rendu les hommes qui paravant par longs et continuelz travaux se souloient exciter aux armes non chalans d'icelle occupacion. Si se sont mis

---

[33] See especially the contribution of G. Ouy to the above *Miscellanea*, "Un jeune humaniste parisien vers 1395", pp. 357-393, with its estimate of the importance of the Royal Chancellery in the formation of the first group of Parisian humanists, p. 363, note 12.

[34] C. Samaran, "Pierre Bersuire, prieur de Saint-Éloi de Paris", *Hist. litt. de la France*, XXX (Paris, 1952, 297-98); *Epistolæ Familiares*, XII, 13 and 14 in F. Petrarca, *Le Familiari*, ed. critica per cura di V. Rossi, (Firenze, 1942), IV, 136-152.

au delit et repos et aux convoitises de pecune, dont les nobles anciens, qui ne prisoient fors honneur d'armes, ne faisoient conte." [35]

Manuscript collections of Petrarch's letters circulated soon after his death and B. N. f. lat. 8568, for instance, gives evidence of having been copied by a French hand, even if dated Padua 1388. [36] Furthermore, the last miniature of the Duke of Burgundy's celebrated copy of Boccaccio's *De Casibus Viris illustris* (Arsenal MS. 5193) shows his grandfather being borne away to captivity. [37]

The Harvard copy of the *Livre des fais d'armes*, signed by the Baron Gaspar Gourjoud (Napoleon's aide-de-camp, General Gourjoud) shows that this fifteenth century art of warfare was still capable of attracting a military man's interest in the early nineteenth century, but a modern edition of the French text is still lacking. My husband, Colonel Sumner Willard, of the United States Military Academy, and I are therefore undertaking to prepare such an edition, thus carrying on a collaboration which began some years ago in Professor Solano's courses at Harvard.

---

[35] Brussels MS. 10476, fol. 12v°-13r°.
[36] Rossi ed. of *Le Familiari*, I, Introduction.
[37] H. Martin, *Le Boccace de Jean sans Peur*, (Bruxelles, 1911).

ELYAS AS A "WILD MAN" IN *LI ESTOIRE DEL CHEVALIER AU CISNE*

By JOAN B. WILLIAMSON
U. C. Santa Barbara, 1968

In his book *Wild Men in the Middle Ages*, Richard Bernheimer has discussed the wild man motif in medieval culture.[1] There were, in fact, two kinds of wild man known to the Middle Ages. The one was the animal-like man of the woods, who had enormous strength, of which his hairiness, like Samson's, was a sign. He could be without the power of speech and could be insane, hence, to the medieval mind, ignorant of God. The other kind of wild man had an incorruptible quality. He resembled the wild man just described, but the similarity was only external. Where the first was ignorant, this second kind of forest fool was innocent. Because he was reared far away from society, the purity of the simpleton's early life in the forest enabled him to outshine all others in knightly valor and deeds if he eventually became a knight. Such men, Bernheimer says: "...are the innocents of the Pure Life, whose early ignorance and lack of social grace give them an inner strength."[2] The dual meaning of the name given to the Wild Man in Romance languages emphasizes the two types: Italian *salvatico*, Spanish *salvaje* and French *sauvage* are all derived from *salvaticus*, a late Latin form due to vocalic assimilation in Latin *silvaticus* (from *silva*, a forest). These words signify both a turbulent,

---

[1] Richard Bernheimer, *Wild Men in the Middle Ages*, Cambridge: Harvard University Press, 1952.
[2] Bernheimer, p. 18.

fierce or unreasoned state of mind or behavior, and also a state of isolation in the woods, far away from other men.[3]

The author of the first part of the epic cycle on the First Crusade, as it appears in a thirteenth-century manuscript of the Paris Bibliothèque Nationale, fonds français 795, and which I have entitled *Li Estoire del Chevalier au Cisne*, has exploited his audience's awareness of the existence of these two types of wild men to heighten the dramatic impact of his hero's first appearance in society.[4] On this occasion, Elyas, the *chevalier au cisne* and the central figure in this story, is depicted as a wild man. Incorporating characteristics of both kinds, he seems to be the insane man, but is, in reality, the innocent. The audience has already been informed that he is the latter, but the king and the townspeople in the story have to deduce this for themselves from Elyas' comportment.

The poem up to this apearance had narrated the fairy-tale metamorphoses of children into swans. Queen Beatris had given multiple birth to six boys and one girl, each with a silver chain around the neck. Her mother-in-law, Matabrune, then ordered the children killed; convinced her son, Beatris' husband, that his wife had given birth to seven puppies; and so was able to have Beatris imprisoned. The children, however, were not killed, but were abandoned in the forest, where they were found by a pious hermit. This hermit, with the help of a white doe who provided the children with milk during their infancy, cared for them in the forest for more than twelve years. Then, one day, when the hermit and one boy were elsewhere in the forest, a serf, sent by Matabrune, came to the hermit's dwelling and stole the silver chains from around the necks of the children he found there. Deprived of their chains, the children turned into swans and flew away. At this point in the story, Beatris is about to be burned at the stake. The one child remaining in the forest, who is to become the *chevalier au cisne* and who will be called Elyas, assumes his role as her defender. An angel appears to the hermit with instructions for this boy to take the name of Elyas and to go and defend his

---

[3] W. von Wartburg, *Französisches Etymologisches Wörterbuch*, Basel: R. G. Zbinden & Co., no. 82, 1962, pp. 616-621.

[4] J. M. Brockman, *The Old French Estoire del Chevalier au Cisne: Edition and Commentary* (unpublished Ph. D. dissertation, Harvard University, 1966).

mother in judiciary combat. The boy obeys; and it is on this occasion that he first appears in society.

In MS. B. N. f. fr. 795 we learn very little about the life of the children in the forest, or about the personality or destiny of the hero, before the intervention of the angel. Such scant information as is given, however, indicates that life in the hermitage was simple and even primitive. It was the life of the forest innocent. The hermit who cares for the children has a dwelling in the forest where the food is simple. While the children are babies, there is the doe's milk to drink, and later, there are roots and leaves:

> Rachinetes manguent et feuilles de pumier,　　v. 329
> Ne sevent que vins est ne nus autres daintiés.[5]

At this time, in contrast to a later description of the hero, all the children are depicted as being handsome:

> Onques ne vi si biaus puis l'eure que fui nes.　　v. 365

The conversation between the hermit and the angel and that between the hermit and the hero reveal much more about the hero himself. Here, the hero is clearly presented to the audience as an innocent of the pure life. God has sent the angel to inform the hermit that this youth is noble:

> Que tu as .i. enfant de mout grant signourie.　　v. 493

and:

> Ch'est .i. hons de grant sens et de grant signorie;　　v. 495

This noble youth is to have a very special destiny: He is to sire the mother of the crusading hero, Godefroy of Bouillon, and his two

---

[5] The verse numbers which follow this and the other quotations made from the poem in this paper refer to the verses in my edition of the text, as yet unpublished, details of which are given in the preceding note. Célestin Hippeau published a text which contains a variant of this story in *La Chanson du Chevalier au Cygne et de Godefroi de Bouillon*, 2 vols., Paris: Aubry, 1874-77. For reference, the material which corresponds to the subject matter of this paper is to be found on pp. 13-54 of vol. 1 of Hippeau's edition; in vv. 292-1430, according to his numbering.

brothers. But his more immediate destiny is to defend his own mother in armed combat:

> Estuet demain sa mere deffendre au branc molu,   v. 529
> A la lance et as armes et au diestrier grenu.

The hermit's reply reveals that the youth knows nothing of the accoutrement of knighthood. The next morning, when this boy is told by the hermit what he is to do, his questions about these orders are more than naïve, they are those of a simpleton. On learning he is to defend his mother, he asks what a mother is:

> Sire, fait il, qu'est mere, ne s'on le mangera?   v. 567
> Samble il oisiel u [b]ieste?

And when told he must mount a horse, he queries the nature of this beast:

> Ceus bieste est çou cevaus? dist l'enfes errament,   v. 584
> Sanle il ne cien ne cat? Va il isnielement?

The audience thus knows that this youth is a forest fool, but also that he is noble and is destined for greatness.

As the hermit accompanies the youth through the forest towards the city, the author gives his first portrait of the hero. His aspect and wearing apparel are those of a forest dweller and contain no hint of incipient greatness. He was dressed in a short tunic of leaves and had never had a haircut in all his life:

> De robe n'en ot il fors itant seulement   v. 606
> .I. cote de fueiles, courte ne mie grant;
> Caperon i avoit atakiet ensement;
> Sollers ot de pisson, non pas de cordewant;
> N'ot cemise ne braies ne autre garniment;
> Ceviaus n'ot onques res en jour de son vivant.

The next *laisse* takes up his description again, this time insisting on his physical appearance. The idea is introduced here that he is animal-like. He was as hairy as a bear, had long nails and bristly hair, and held a club in his two hands:

> De robe n'ot il plus que vous dire m'oés.   v. 617
> Velus estoit com ours et com leus effraés,
> Les ongles grans et longes et les ceviaus mellés,
> La tieste hurepee, n'ert pas sovent lavés;
> Et tenoit .i. baston qui devant ert quarrés.

These lines suggest, for the first time in the story, that his semblance is that of the wild man of the woods who is devoid of reason. The author then underlines this interpretation of his aspect. Seen from a distance, he seems mad:

> Qui de lonc le voit bien sanle foursenés.   v. 622

When he depicts the hero approaching the city alone, the author re-iterates this interpretation:

> Viers la citet en va tous seus et esgarés,   v. 633
> Ne sanble mie sages, ains sanle foursenés.

The emphasis is on his semblance. The verb used by the author in both instances, and also in following remarks, is *sanler*, to seem. The implication is not that he is, only that he appears to be, to make plausible to the audience the townspeople's reaction to him when he enters the town. We may, I think, deduce from these two portrayals, given just before the hero enters town, that the composer of the poem wished his audience to assume that the townspeople regarded this hairy youth dressed in leaves as mad. Once in town, Elyas is bewildered by the noise and terrified at the sight of the king on his horse whom he encounters there. The author repeats his comment here. Clad in leaves, he appeared to be mad and wild:

> Viestus estoit de fueiles, desous plus n'i avoit.   v. 687
> Home sot et sauvages mierveiles bien sanloit.

The audience has already been shown, mainly from the conversations of the hermit with the angel and of the youth with the hermit, that the hero is, initially, a simpleton. The king and the townspeople now perceive this too, but they think he is also mad. His rustic attire, his *baston* clutched firmly in both hands and his naïve questions all reveal his simplicity. Of the horse, the essential companion of a knight, he asks what it is, and whether it can see:

> Cou qu'est sour coi tu siés, mout le voit fort et roit;   v. 693
> Il a boines oreilles, mais jou ne sai s'il voit."

And, seeing the animal with the bit in its mouth, he wonders if it is eating iron. Later he shows his ignorance of the correct terminology for knightly paraphernalia. He reduces these things to simple, everday objects, devoid of their symbolical meaning, thus showing how foreign to him is the world of knighthood. To him, a coat of mail is a *reube de fer* (v. 1113); a helmet is a *pot* (v. 1129); the mail is a *petit cravechon* (v. 1138); and swords are *coutiaus* (v. 1156). He deserves the king's polite litotes:

> Bien voi n'a pas estet en vile longement.   v. 699

(I see clearly that you have not been long in town).

If the people in the city feel that Elyas is even less than a simpleton, it is perhaps because his animal-like aspect leads them to identify him as an insane man of the woods. Perceval was also a medieval forest fool, dressed in rustic attire and ignorant of knights. He was also to distinguish himself in the world of chivalry. However, he was not described with this quality of hairiness. He was considered a fool by people in the tale which recounts his exploits, but he was never held to be an insane wild man. The tale of Elyas, then, has this added dimension. W. Müller has seen in the *chevalier au cisne* the incarnation of a nature myth, and in his leafy dress a symbol of the re-awakening of the earth after winter.[6] Although this is the possible origin of the figure, the origin was not what was of interest to the composer of the poem. More relevant is Jeanne Lods' remark that the leafy dress serves to accentuate Elyas' savage aspect.[7] The author of this story has so described Elyas' physical appearance as to strongly suggest that of the insane wild man. Perhaps the dominant factor in his physical appearance, as the author gives it in vv. 617-621, and certainly as it must have struck the townspeople, was his excessive hairiness. He was as hairy as a bear; his hair was matted and stood out on his head like bristles.

---

[6] W. Müller, "Die Sage vom Schwanritter," *Germania*, I (1858), 418-440.

[7] Jeanne Lods, "L'utilisation des thèmes mythiques dans trois versions écrites de la légende des enfants-cygnes," *Mélanges offerts à René Crozet*, Poitiers: Société d'Études Médiévales, 1966, p. 814.

It is probably this excessive hirsuteness of Elyas' which labels him most directly as an insane wild man of the woods, for hairiness is one of the attributes of this type of wild man.[8]

Traditionally associated with the wild man, then, and with great physical strength, hairiness can also be an attribute of an ugly person. Twelfth century writers considered that a great amount of hair on any part of the body where one would not expect to find it was most unsightly.[9] By the twelfth century, the description of excessive hair on the body of a person had already become a stereotype in the portraiture of an ugly person; and ugly persons were not usually heroes.[10]

Elyas features another trait frequently found in descriptions of ugly persons; that of hair standing perpendicular to the scalp. Alice Colby notes that the opinion was held in the Middle Ages that a man's hair might be homely because of its refusal to lie flat; and she cites examples of such references which imply ugliness.[11] The graphic description in this poem of Elyas' matted hair standing on end, *la tieste hurepee* (his head bristly), is in keeping with these other citations. So, in this thirteenth-century manuscript, this portrayal of ugliness reinforces the author's strategy of giving Elyas the aura of an insane wild man, a man who had none of the attributes of a hero.

As such, he would not be given credence. Although the concept of the wild man may, as previously indicated, have had its origin in an incarnation of a nature myth, men did not necessarily attribute to every wild man his original significance, nor did they necessarily hold him in any respect. An example of this attitude of disregard for the wild man is to be found in the French prose rendering of the *Historia de Prelijs*, as it occurs in a manuscript of the British Museum, numbered Royal, 15. E. VI, folio 18.[12] Containing a narration

---

[8] Bernheimer, p. 46.

[9] Alice M. Colby, *The Portrait in Twelfth-Century French Literature*, Geneva: Droz, 1965, p. 76 and p. 78.

[10] Colby, p. 76, note 2, discusses the presence of excessive hair in descriptions of ugly persons.

[11] Colby, p. 74.

[12] This manuscript of the middle of the fifteenth century contains the translated composition on Alexander the Great known as the *Historia de Prelijs* or the *Historia Alexandri magni regis macedonie de Prelijs*, which is an abridged Latin version of Pseudo-Callisthenes.

of the marvels of India encountered by Alexander the Great, folio 18 describes how Alexander came across a wild man, whom he captured. This personage is described as a wild man, large in stature and as a swine:

> Si vint ung homme sauvaige, de grant corssaige et velu comme ung porc.

When captured, the wild man neither showed fear nor attempted to flee. He just stood quietly to one side. Alexander decided to test his sanity, which he did by handing over a naked maiden to the wild man to see what he would do with her. The wild man did nothing; whereupon Alexander ordered his men to take the girl away. At this the wild man began to howl and bellow like a wild beast, and it was only with great difficulty that the soldiers were able to remove the girl. This made Alexander conclude that the wild man was without the power of reasoning, and consequently he ordered that he be burned:

> Quant Alixandre le vit, si se commença moult a merveiller de la figure; et pour ce qu'il luy sembloit home sans entendement, si le fist lier et ardre.

This is the type of wild man whom Elyas seems to be. He has, however, as the audience knows, only the outward semblance of the insane wild man; and it is gradually borne in upon the townspeople that this is so. The king, perhaps because he is ready to clutch at any straw which hints of assistance, is the first to accept that this youth might not be crazy. The monarch wonders at Elyas' naïve questions, at his dress and at his appearance, which is so different from that of ordinary men:

> Li rois s'esmierveilla quant il oï l'enfant   v. 697
> Si fierement viestu et si diviers samblant.

When the hero offers to defend Beatris in judiciary combat, the king ponders the question of his semblance and his possible sanity:

> Tu me sambles bien fos a tes fais, a tes dis.   v. 728
> Seulement de parler ies tu formen hardis.

The youth repeats his offer, saying that he will have God's help. The king is still doubtful and not fully convinced, but, because of Elyas' statement that he will have God's help, he dares not object as he is a religious man:

> Li rois s'esmierveilla de çou que il ot dire,   v. 758
> Mais tant croit Diu et aimme, ne l'ose contredire.

Judiciary combat to decide of Beatris' innocence or guilt does not at all please Matabrune, who hastens to suppress in the king's mind the notion that this youth is not insane. Juggling with her words, in a play upon the expressions of 'not being wise' and 'being mad', she tells the king that in trusting in a fool he is as foolish as the one in whom he puts his faith:

> Or pert, çou dist la viele, que fos a fol s'afie.   v. 768
> Vous avés fol trouvet; n'iestes pas sages, Sire.

To which the king replies, with equal verbal dexterity, that she is not at all wise, and that the youth seems wild:

> Mere, çou dist li rois, vous n'iestes mie sage.   v. 771
> Ves ici .i. enfant qui bien sanle sauvage.

The implication behind the king's speech here is that it is the queen who is foolish, if she cannot penetrate beyond an outward appearance of folly to see the true reality beyond it. This play on words and the use of the verb *senler* emphasizes the duality in Elyas' appearance; and suggests a paradox: the fool is less mad than the supposedly normal people who call him insane.

Elyas' sanity, as shown by his remarks, belies his outward appearance; and the crowd recognises this on hearing them. Expressing the paradox again, that those who judge a man to be a fool from his appearance alone are themselves fools, the author has the crowd urge the king to allow Elyas to fight:

> Que teus hons se combate, fos est qui çou ne croit.   v. 787

The crowd has seen through his outward aspect and exclaims to the king that if the youth were properly clad he would look like a gentleman:

> S'il estoit bien viestus, gentius hons sanleroit.　　v. 788

The crowd is right. Baptised and arrayed in his finery, he is, in fact, very handsome:

> Quant il fu baptisiés et viestus de ses dras,　　v. 958
> Ne fu plus biaus vallés tres le tans Caÿphas.

Thus ends the section of this poem involving the wild man theme.

And thus we have seen how the wild man theme was used to set Elyas apart from the everyday newcomer to town and so lend distinction to the hero. We have also seen how use of this theme enriched the poem by creating a tension in the mind of the audience. This tension arises from the audience knowing that Elyas is the one kind of wild man, while watching the protagonists in the story think that he is the other at the outset, but gradually realize that he is not. As a consequence, there is an increase in literary interest in *Li Estoire del Chevalier au Cisne* due to the opposition of these two kinds of wild men. It is possible that this motif of the apparently insane wild man belonged to the repertory of story-tellers: Bernheimer maintains that stories of wild men who became knights had considerable success in the Middle Ages.[13] The fact that it might not be an original idea does not, however, detract from the success with which this motif, by exploiting the hero's ambiguous aspect, is developed in the poem.

---

[13] Bernheimer, p. 46.

TABULA GRATULATORIA

William Alfred
Louise S. Apfelbaum
Norman Araujo
Thomas G. Bergin
Jean-Pierre Boon
Peter Boyd-Bowman
Joseph M. Carrière
Normand R. Cartier
Frank M. Chambers
Louis L. Chinatti
Alan J. Clayton
Gianrenzo P. Clivio
Raymond J. Cormier
Carla Cremonesi
Larry S. Crist
F. Francis D'Addario
Ruth J. Dean
Eugene Di Girolamo
Klaus Faiss
Willa Folch-Pi
Marcel Françon
Joseph G. Fucilla
Geno R. Gemmato
Anthony A. Giarraputo
Herbert H. Golden
Ernest Grey
Peter R. Grillo
Edward Harvey
Helmut A. Hatzfeld
Steven Hess
Urban Tigner Holmes
Nicolae Iliescu
René Jasinski
L. W. Johnson
Pierre Jonin
Marcia Kaufman
Allan R. Keiler

Edgar Knowlton, Jr.
Philip Koch
William N. Locke
Raimundo Lida
Gail K. Meadows
Diana T. Mériz
Judith S. Merrill
James S. Noblitt
Paul R. Olson
Anthony L. Pellegrini
Robert L. Politzer
Daniel Poirion
Guy Raynaud De Lage
Howard S. Robertson
Edward P. Shaw
Nathaniel B. Smith
H. M. Smyser
Maria F. Tymoczko
Alan S. Trueblood
John A. Van Eerde
Antonio Viscardi
James B. Wadsworth
Charity Cannon Willard
Col. Sumner Willard
Joan B. Williamson
Harry A. Wolfson

LIBRARIES

Boston University Libraries
Bapst Library, Boston College
Brown University Library
Cornell University Libraries
Memorial Library, University of
    Notre Dame
University of Pennsylvania Libraries
University of Texas Library

www.ingramcontent.com/pod-product-compliance
Lightning Source LLC
Chambersburg PA
CBHW022021220426
43663CB00007B/1160